The Fifth Revelation

by Kelly Elstrott

"This is a fascinating commentary, easy to read with beautiful black and white reproductions of well-known paintings."
—Mountain Luminary

"Kelly's careful notations and references elevate this fine book to a high level of exciting and enlightening reading."   —Concepts

"If <u>The Urantia Book</u> is a treasure chest of spirituality (and it is), then <u>The Fifth Revelation</u> is the roadmap!"
— Metaphysical Reviews

Mighty Messenger Press

New Orleans

Mighty Messenger Press

Post Office Box 23398, New Orleans, LA 70183

Publisher's Catalog-in-Publication Data

(Provided by Quality Books, Inc.)

Elstrott, Kelly.
  The Fifth Revelation : A collection of key passages from *The Urantia Book* /Kelly Elstrott – 1st ed.
   p. cm.
   Includes index.
   ISBN: 0-9654301-7-0
  1. Urantia book—Quotations. 2. Urantia book—Introductions.
  I. Title.
BP605.U75E57 1998   299

QBI98-771

Dedicated to Catherine
for all the patience

Do everything in love.

1Corinthians 16:14 (NIV)

"This world is only a bridge;
you may pass over it,
but you should not think to build a dwelling place on it."

(*The Urantia Book* Pg. 1735)

Contents

Appendix

Introduction

The morning haze is burning off. Warmed by its heat, the earth silently whirls about the sun. Dreams, those sharp flashing images of sleep, are busily sorting out the previous day's events. We cast out one thought, file another here, put together a new idea there. A shrill alarm peals through the veil of peace, and groggily we awaken to the reality of a new day—getting the kids ready for school, working, shopping, cooking, cleaning, helping with homework, and juggling the bills.

Caught up in everyday life, we rarely reflect on the long view—that is, the eternal nature of our lives. Do we take time to greet each new day as another treasure, an empty canvas waiting to be filled with a spectrum of thoughts, emotions, and dreams? No. Eternity is nothing more than a notion kept in a nice, neat compartment called religion. We rarely slow down long enough to ponder life after death. Most of us only come close to considering our mortality in the midst of a difficult life crisis.

Beginning with the disillusionment of the Crusades and continuing through the merciless Inquisition with its heaps of guilt, suppression of knowledge, and archaic laws, religion has acquired a bad name. Today we associate it with TV preachers trying to fill their coffers or mystical gurus brainwashing gullible youths and turning them into flower-selling zombies. Increasing numbers of us relate to religion as a bureaucratic organization more concerned with self-perpetuation than with eternal values.

As society has become disillusioned by the commercialization of religion, science and technology have unexpectedly stepped in the breach and brought us a new vision of infinity and of the magnitude of God's creation. Telescopes unfold technicolor pictures of the hundreds of millions of galaxies that surround us. One can but stand in awe at the sight of the infinite panorama of these star systems.

Five hundred million years ago, primitive life appeared on our young planet, yet only in the past 3,000 years has humanity sustained a civilization. Our culture is so young. Imagine planets with civilizations as old as our planet. What could their inhabitants have accomplished in a billion years of existence? What have they learned about the universe that surrounds us?

2

Due to the growing complexity of society, modern man is confronted with the task of making more adjustments in this generation than have been made in the last 2,000 years. A hundred years ago we would have scoffed in disbelief at the idea that pictures and sounds could be transmitted by invisible waves across millions of miles. Projecting 1,000 years into the future, imagine the wonders and forces humanity will discover.

It is common in this modern era to envision things we cannot see. We readily accept the existence of microscopic bacteria and invisible radio waves. Pushing our vision even further, we may wonder, what have we yet to learn about God's spiritual creatures—those beings we are unable to see due to the limited chromatic band of human eyesight, beings we are unable to communicate with due to our primitive spiritual depth?

As we grow up, we become able to handle more advanced concepts. Similarly, as civilization matures, the image of the universe progresses and expands. It was first believed that human beings were alone in the universe, living on a flat world, and that the sun and stars revolved around God's only inhabited creation. Finally, much to the dismay of the church, early astronomers dispelled that notion. Now we know not only that we revolve around the sun but that our sun revolves around the Milky Way galaxy, and that the millions of galaxies in the universe revolve around a dark mass whose weight exceeds that of all the stars. This awareness prompts us to wonder: Could that mass of stars be Paradise?

Anthropologists have uncovered fossils revealing the long history of life. These discoveries prompt another question: Are we simply the products of a long-ago biochemical accident, a lonely freak in an endless, cold universe, here on this hostile world for just a short season? Astronomers have detected planets surrounding other nearby stars. How many more inhabited planets are out there? Is there a grand plan to this vast creation?

Our religious concepts have been evolving since the dawn of civilization. In ancient times, humanity feared a volcanic pagan god known as Yahweh. Over the past 3,000 years, the belief in God has matured from fear to faith in a Father whom we describe as love. Now we are ready for an even broader concept: a loving Father who develops life on countless planets. Life, in this sense, is defined as the infinite potential to progress by striving to do God's will. Indeed, life will appear ever more spiritual and less material as, we work toward the center to embrace the Creator.

When we reach the Father, our life is just beginning. We humans are destined to play an integral part in developing the grand universe. The future is not revealed, but we have been assured that our eternity will be far from blissful, or boring. Rather, we can look forward to a challenging eternal life and ever-increasing responsibility.

Enjoy the story of man and the universe as it unfolds in these pages. Here you will learn:

- How the sun broke free from a nebula, and how a later tidal-gravity explosion created the solar system of planets.
- How life, meticulously planned for earth, was planted in the ocean, and how the same salt-solution habitat still circulates through our bodies, submersing every living cell in the "briny deep."
- How primitive humanity evolved to a point of making free-will decisions, leading to rudimentary concepts of God and of an immortal soul.
- How to understand and master the fickle emotions that race through our animal minds.
- Why families are important, and why our earliest years of life affect our personalities for all eternity.
- How humanities sacred books originated, including the truth about prophets who were routinely killed for trying to broaden popular notions of God, yet later glorified in holy scriptures.
- How Jesus lived before he began teaching—how he shouldered the burden of raising a large family after his father's untimely death, experiencing the same swing of emotions and everyday challenges we humans encounter and how he became cognizant of his divinity and laid plans for the revelation of God the Father.
- The nature of God and how the cleansing effect of regular, unstructured prayer can bring strength through peace of mind.
- How the heavenly rebellion into which the earth was dragged 200,000 years ago temporarily isolated humanity from the rest of the universe, providing us with special opportunities for insight.

The passages compiled in this volume were excerpted from *The Urantia Book*, a 2,097 page work first published in 1955. Chapter titles, page and paragraph numbers are included at the end of the selections to help you locate them in the original text of *The Urantia Book*.

The philosophy of living set forth in *The Urantia Book* seamlessly unites together leading-edge scientific discoveries with uplifting spiritual truths. For me, it is a constant reminder of how rich and wonderful life is when I follow the guidance of inner spirit. It beckons me to develop a personal

4

living experience of God and to cultivate an ever-new awareness that the kingdom of God is in fact within each of us. Whereas science can point to the mechanics of life and religion can teach us rules of the road, we each have to choose the best paths to take.

The Fifth Revelation was selected as the title of this work because it contains passages from *The Urantia Book,* which is claimed to be the fifth revelation of God to the peoples of earth.

My discovery of *The Urantia Book* has not caused me to abandon the religion of my parents. If anything, it has taught me the importance of raising my children in a tradition that stresses faith and love as the focal points of life. Since my little ones may not comprehend the rituals on the altar, I bring them to church with a stack of library books to keep them at peace. They know church is important to me, and that is a start.

The type of religious institution you and I attend is not as significant as the attitude we bring with us. Instead of dwelling on differences between faiths we can begin to explore their similarities. Yes, trade and communications have brought the world materially closer. Science has drawn us intellectually closer. For there to be a lasting peace, however, we now need to become spiritually closer.

When you awaken tomorrow, lie still for a few moments and feel the earth turn beneath you. Absorb the immensity of the creation you live in. Consider that the sun rises every morning to salute you just as it does the most powerful and prosperous human beings on earth. Look upon the fresh day as a new piece of art—a chance to learn from your experiences and build a foundation for your eternal future.

Preface

How I Found *The Urantia Book.*

Thirty years ago I was living in a college dorm. It was a Saturday morning, and since the cafeteria was closed, I accepted my brother's invitation to come to his house for a breakfast of apple pancakes. A big blue book belonging to his girlfriend, Patty, was on the coffee table

Patty—artist and truth seeker, painter of grand alien landscapes and mosaics of organic wonderlands—told me to take the book home, and I did. For months I jumped about the blue book. I found it helped me piece together myths and ancient history. I was now prepared to handle any test my Comparative Religions professor could dream up. How I wished I could have used it as a source note in my papers!

I was captivated by the sweeping story of man's attempts to build a civilization: the heavenly rebellion of 200,000 years ago, in which powerful angels, deluded by the ego sick teachings of Lucifer, were pitted against lowly humans as they desperately clung to their belief in one God; Adam and Eve's disillusionment 35,000 years ago, when faced with primitive warring tribes; the steady hand of the Melchizedek, in his 2000 BC attempt to bring earth back to the fold; the succession of prophets pushing the envelope out further to evolve the concept of God from wrathful to forgiving to loving and eternal. I was equally mystified by the picture it conveyed of millions of galaxies, and the countless children of God who lived on the whirling planets of the evolving universes of space.

I remember the day it dawned on me that this book was truth. Patty was painting and I was reading "The Resurrection of Lazarus" to her. The windows were open to a cool, bright afternoon, and the smell of honey and red zinger tea filled the room. Suddenly, in midsentence, I felt a warmth sweep over me. *This is what really happened two thousand years ago*, I told myself.

Soon afterward, the blue book transformed from a historical documentary to a spiritual touchstone, and I began to call it by its name: *The Urantia Book.* By then I had discovered material on the Thought Adjuster, which I reread numerous times, savoring the idea that we each have a piece of God within us. But along with my sudden liberation from years of Catholic guilt came a realization that it was my responsibility alone to discern the Father's will.

One night weeks later, just past midnight, I was lying peacefully in the huge open field used for band practice. The only sound to be heard was the distant whump-whump of an industrial-size air-conditioning fan. Flat on my back, with my arms stretched out, I was looking up for shooting stars when I began to imagine that I could feel the earth turning swiftly beneath me and that I was holding on for dear life. To my ears, the sound of that far-off machine was actually the big engine underground thumping away to keep the earth in motion. I felt like I was on a planet hurtling headlong through space, participating in an eternal adventure. I realized I was really a part of it now. Never again would I be alone. My spirit was with me, and we were traveling through time and the universe together. I had arrived.

~ I ~
Prehistoric Era

1. Formation of Earth

The story of the evolution of life as told in The Urantia Book *is a grand and sweeping epic. Rising from the ooze on the bottom of the ocean, life culminated in proud, courageous beings standing ready to defend their families from wild beasts and the relentless approach of the glaciers. Life is a true testament the power and might of the Creator. As you read these passages, note the relentless struggle for perfection displayed by all forms of life and the infinite patience the Creator has for his people.*

Approximately 6 billion years ago our sun burst free from the Andronover nebula It was a comparatively isolated blazing orb, having gathered to itself most of the nearby circulating matter in space. Then 4.5 billion years ago a dark giant of space, with tremendous gravitational pull, closely approached our sun and drew streams of gaseous material from it out into space. When this matter cooled and condensed, a solar system of planets was formed.

It would be just as easy for the Universal Father to make all mortals perfect beings, to impart perfection by his divine word. But that would deprive them of the wonderful experience of the adventure and training associated with the long and gradual inward climb, an experience to be had only by those who are so fortunate as to begin at the very bottom of living existence.   Evolution of the Local Universe 361:6*
*The Urantia Book excerpt; Chapter title, Page number:Paragraph number

The enormous nebula now began gradually to assume the spiral form and to become clearly visible to the astronomers of even distant universes. This is the natural history of most nebulae; before they begin to throw off suns and start upon the work of universe building, these secondary space nebulae are usually observed as spiral phenomena.

The near-by star students of that faraway era, as they observed this metamorphosis of the Andronover nebula, saw exactly what twentieth-century astronomers see when they turn their telescopes spaceward and view the present-age spiral nebulae of adjacent outer space.

And this is what happened in Andronover ages upon ages ago. The energy wheel grew and grew until it attained its maximum of expansion,

Galaxy M100 (1993) Hubble Space Telescope

and then, when contraction set in, it whirled on faster and faster until, eventually, the critical centrifugal stage was reached and the great breakup began.

500,000,000,000 years ago the first Andronover sun was born. This blazing streak broke away from the mother gravity grasp and tore out into space on an independent adventure in the cosmos of creation. Its orbit was determined by its path of escape. Such young suns quickly become spherical and start out on their long and eventful careers as the stars of space. The Origin of Urantia 653:1,2,5,6

It was scarcely a million years subsequent to this epoch that Michael of Nebadon, a Creator Son of Paradise, selected this disintegrating nebula as the site of his adventure in universe building. Almost immediately the architectural worlds of Salvington and the one hundred constellation headquarters groups of planets were begun. It required almost one million years to complete these clusters of specially created worlds. The local system headquarters planets were constructed over a period extending from that time to about five billion years ago. The Origin of Urantia 654:1

6,000,000,000 years ago marks the end of the terminal breakup and the birth of your sun, the fifty-sixth from the last of the Andronover second solar family. This final eruption of the nebular nucleus gave birth to 136,702 suns, most of them solitary orbs. The total number of suns and sun systems having origin in the Andronover nebula was 1,013,628. The number of the solar system sun is 1,013,572.

And now the great Andronover nebula is no more, but it lives on in the many suns and their planetary families which originated in this mother cloud of space. The final nuclear remnant of this magnificent nebula still burns with a reddish glow and continues to give forth moderate light and heat to its remnant planetary family of one hundred and sixty-five worlds, which now revolve about this venerable mother of two mighty generations of the monarchs of light.

Thus was the stage of local space set for the unique origin of Monmatia, that being the name of your sun's planetary family, the solar system to which your world belongs. Less than one per cent of the planetary systems of Orvonton have had a similar origin.

4,500,000,000 years ago the enormous Angona system began its approach to the neighborhood of this solitary sun. The center of this great system was a dark giant of space, solid, highly charged, and possessing tremendous gravity pull. The Origin of Urantia 655:4,5,8,9

The visiting system did not come quite close enough to actually steal any of the sun's substance, but it did swing sufficiently close to draw off into the intervening space all of the material comprising the present-day solar system.

The five inner and five outer planets soon formed in miniature from the cooling and condensing nucleuses in the less massive and tapering ends of the gigantic gravity bulge which Angona had succeeded in detaching from the sun, while Saturn and Jupiter were formed from the more massive and bulging central portions. The powerful gravity pull of\Jupiter and Saturn early captured most of the material stolen from Angona as the retrograde motion of certain of their satellites bears witness.   The Origin of Urantia 656:4,5

The planets do not swing around the sun in the equatorial plane of their solar mother, which they would do if they had been thrown off by solar revolution. Rather, they travel in the plane of the Angona solar extrusion, which existed at a considerable angle to the plane of the sun's equator.

The Origin of Urantia 657:1

1,000,000,000 years ago is the date of the actual beginning of Urantia history. The planet had attained approximately its present size. And about this time it was placed upon the physical registries of Nebadon and given its name, Urantia.

The atmosphere, together with incessant moisture precipitation, facilitated the cooling of the earth's crust. Volcanic action early equalized internal-heat pressure and crustal contraction; and as volcanoes rapidly decreased, earthquakes made their appearance as this epoch of crustal cooling and adjustment progressed.

The real geologic history of Urantia begins with the cooling of the earth's crust sufficiently to cause the formation of the first ocean. Water-vapor condensation on the cooling surface of the earth, once begun, continued until it was virtually complete. By the end of this period the ocean was world-wide, covering the entire planet to an average depth of over one mile.

At the opening of this faraway era, Urantia should be envisaged as a water-bound planet. Later on, deeper and hence denser lava flows came out upon the bottom of the present Pacific Ocean, and this part of the water - covered surface became considerably depressed. The first continental land mass emerged from the world ocean in compensatory adjustment of the equilibrium of the gradually thickening earth's crust.

The Origin of Urantia 660:3-6

900,000,000 years ago witnessed the arrival on Urantia of the first Satania scouting party sent out from Jerusem to examine the planet and make a report on its adaptation for a life-experiment station. This commission consisted of twenty-four members, embracing Life Carriers, Lanonandek Sons, Melchizedeks, seraphim, and other orders of celestial life having to do with the early days of planetary organization and administration.   The Origin of Urantia 661:1

750,000,000 years ago the first breaks in the continental land mass began as the great north-and-south cracking, which later admitted the ocean waters and prepared the way for the westward drift of the continents of North and South America, including Greenland. The long east-and-west cleavage separated Africa from Europe and severed the land masses of Australia, the Pacific Islands, and Antarctica from the Asiatic continent.
                    The Origin of Urantia 663:1

2. Life Begins on Earth

When earth became stable and ripe for the development of life, members of Life Carriers Corps were dispatched from our local system capital, Jerusem, to survey the planet and determine the life forms most suitable to inhabit it. They conducted more than a half a million experiments before settling on an optimum pattern of life. Like modern-day scientists on earth, Life Carriers could manipulate life but they could not impart it into a lifeless form. Only the spirit of God could provide the initial spark of life and endowment of mind.

About 5 hundred million years ago, when planet earth (Urantia) contained just one continent, the Life Carriers planted life in three locations in the shallows of the ocean. Foreseeing the later breakup of the continent, they made sure each piece of the landmass would carry life along with it.

Although the evolution of the animal kingdom can be traced to plant life, no "missing links" exist between the two. Life did not evolve only in small increments, new orders of life appear 'suddenly.' One million years ago, the Life Carriers were finally rewarded for their efforts when the first human beings appeared among the stock of progressing primates.

600,000,000 years ago the commission of Life Carriers sent out from Jerusem arrived on Urantia and began the study of physical conditions preparatory to launching life on world number 606 of the Satania system.

The Satania Life Carriers had projected a sodium chloride pattern of life; therefore no steps could be taken toward planting it until the ocean waters had become sufficiently briny. The Urantia type of protoplasm can function only in a suitable salt solution. All ancestral life—vegetable and

The Titans Goblet; Thomas Cole (1833),
© Metropolitan Museum of Art

animal—evolved in a salt-solution habitat. And even the more highly organized land animals could not continue to live did not this same essential salt solution circulate throughout their bodies in the blood stream which freely bathes, literally submerses, every tiny living cell in this "briny deep."

Your primitive ancestors freely circulated about in the salty ocean; today, this same oceanlike salty solution freely circulates about in your bodies, bathing each individual cell with a chemical liquid in all essentials comparable to the salt water which stimulated the first protoplasmic reactions of the first living cells to function on the planet.

Life Establishment on Urantia 664:2,4,5

That we are called Life Carriers should not confuse you. We can and do carry life to the planets, but we brought no life to Urantia. Urantia life is unique, original with the planet. This sphere is a life-modification world; all life appearing hereon was formulated by us right here on the planet; and there is no other world in all Satania, even in all Nebadon, that has a life existence just like that of Urantia.

550,000,000 years ago the Life Carrier corps returned to Urantia. In co-operation with spiritual powers and superphysical forces we organized and initiated the original life patterns of this world and planted them in the hospitable waters of the realm. All planetary life (aside from extraplanetary personalities) down to the days of Caligastia, the Planetary Prince, had its origin in our three original, identical, and simultaneous marine-life implantations. These three life implantations have been designated as: the *central* or Eurasian-African, the *eastern* or Australasian, and the *western*, embracing Greenland and the Americas.

Life Establishment on Urantia 667:5,6

We had planted the primitive form of marine life in the sheltered tropic bays of the central seas of the east-west cleavage of the breaking-up continental land mass. Our purpose in making three marine-life implantations was to insure that each great land mass would carry this life with it, in its warm-water seas, as the land subsequently separated. We foresaw that in the later era of the emergence of land life large oceans of water would separate these drifting continental land masses.

Life Establishment on Urantia 668:2

Many features of human life afford abundant evidence that the phenomenon of mortal existence was intelligently planned, that organic evolution is not a mere cosmic accident. When a living cell is injured, it possesses the ability to elaborate certain chemical substances which are empowered so to stimulate and activate the neighboring normal cells that they immediately begin the secretion of certain substances which facilitate healing processes in the wound; and at the same time these normal and uninjured cells begin to proliferate—they actually start to work creating new cells to replace any fellow cells which may have been destroyed by the accident.

This chemical action and reaction concerned in wound healing and cell reproduction represents the choice of the Life Carriers of a formula embracing over one hundred thousand phases and features of possible chemical reactions and biologic repercussions. More than half a million specific experiments were made by the Life Carriers in their laboratories before they finally settled upon this formula for the Urantia life experiment.

When Urantia scientists know more of these healing chemicals, they will become more efficient in the treatment of injuries, and indirectly they will know more about controlling certain serious diseases.

Since life was established on Urantia, the Life Carriers have improved this healing technique as it has been introduced on another Satania world, in that it affords more pain relief and exercises better control over the proliferation capacity of the associated normal cells.   Overcontrol of Evolution 735:2-5

450,000,000 years ago the *transition from vegetable to animal life* occurred. This metamorphosis took place in the shallow waters of the sheltered tropic bays and lagoons of the extensive shore lines of the separating continents. And this development, all of which was inherent in the original life patterns, came about gradually. There were many transitional stages between the early primitive vegetable forms of life and the later well-defined animal organisms. Even today the transition slime molds persist, and they can hardly be classified either as plants or as animals.

Although the evolution of vegetable life can be traced into animal life, and though there have been found graduated series of plants and animals which progressively lead up from the most simple to the most complex and advanced organisms, you will not be able to find such connecting links between the great divisions of the animal kingdom nor between the highest of the prehuman animal types and the dawn men of the human races. These so-called "missing links" will forever remain missing, for the simple reason that they never existed.

From era to era radically new species of animal life arise. They do not evolve as the result of the gradual accumulation of small variations; they appear as full-fledged and new orders of life, and they appear *suddenly.*

The *sudden* appearance of new species and diversified orders of living organisms is wholly biologic, strictly natural. There is nothing supernatural connected with these genetic mutations.

Life Establishment on Urantia 669:2-5

Life was sparse throughout these early times and only slowly made its way over the face of the earth.   Life Establishment on Urantia   670:4

All of this story is graphically told within the fossil pages of the vast "stone book" of world record. And the pages of this gigantic biogeologic record unfailingly tell the truth if you but acquire skill in their interpretation. Many of these ancient sea beds are now elevated high upon land, and their deposits of age upon age tell the story of the life struggles of those early days. It is literally true, as your poet has said, "The dust we tread upon was once alive."   Life Establishment on Urantia 671:5,6

We reckon the history of Urantia as beginning about one billion years ago and extending through five major eras:

1. *The prelife era* extends over the initial four hundred and fifty million years, from about the time the planet attained its present size to the time of life establishment.   Your students have designated this period as the *Archeozoic.*

2. *The life-dawn era* extends over the next one hundred and fifty million years. This epoch intervenes between the preceding prelife or cataclysmic age and the following period of more highly developed marine life. This era is known to your researchers as the *Proterozoic.*

3. *The marine-life era* covers the next two hundred and fifty million years and is best known to you as the *Paleozoic.*

4. *The early land-life era* extends over the next one hundred million years and is known as the *Mesozoic.*

5. *The mammalian era* occupies the last fifty million years. This recent-times era is known as the *Cenozoic.*

The Marine-Life Era on Urantia 672:1-6

180,000,000 years ago. This age was one of great life impoverishment. Thousands of marine species perished, and life was hardly yet established on land. This was a time of biologic tribulation, the age when life nearly vanished from the face of the earth and from the depths of the oceans. Toward the close of the long marine-life era there were more than one hundred thousand species of living things on earth. At the close of this period of transition less than five hundred had survived.

The peculiarities of this new period were not due so much to the cooling of the earth's crust or to the long absence of volcanic action as to an unusual combination of commonplace and pre-existing influences—restrictions of the seas and increasing elevation of enormous land masses. The mild marine climate of former times was disappearing, and the harsher continental type of weather was fast developing.

The Marine-Life Era 682:8,9

160,000,000 years ago The vast oceanic nursery of life on Urantia has served its purpose. During the long ages when the land was unsuited to support life, before the atmosphere contained sufficient oxygen to sustain the higher land animals, the sea mothered and nurtured the early life of the realm. Now the biologic importance of the sea progressively diminishes as the second stage of evolution begins to unfold on the land.

The Marine-Life Era 684:2

60,000,000 years ago, though the land reptiles were on the decline, the dinosaurs continued as monarchs of the land, the lead now being taken by the more agile and active types of the smaller leaping kangaroo varieties of the carnivorous dinosaurs.   Early Land-Life Era 691:1

Early in this period and in North America the placental type of mammals *suddenly* appeared, and they constituted the most important evolutionary development up to this time. Previous orders of nonplacental mammals had existed, but this new type sprang directly and *suddenly* from the pre-existent reptilian ancestor whose descendants had persisted on down through the times of dinosaur decline. The father of the placental mammals was a small, highly active, carnivorous, springing type of dinosaur.   The Mammalian Era on Urantia 693:5

45,000,000 years ago the continental backbones were elevated in association with a very general sinking of the coast lines. Mammalian life was evolving rapidly. A small reptilian, egg-laying type of mammal flourished, and the ancestors of the later kangaroos roamed Australia. Soon there were small horses, fleet-footed rhinoceroses, tapirs with proboscises, primitive pigs, squirrels, lemurs, opossums, and several tribes of monkeylike animals. They were all small, primitive, and best suited to living among the forests of the mountain regions. A large ostrichlike land bird developed to a height of ten feet and laid an egg nine by thirteen inches. These were the ancestors of the later gigantic passenger birds that were so highly intelligent, and that onetime transported human beings through the air.   The Mammalian Era 694:1

The Creation of Man; Michelangelo (1511) Sistine Chapel, Vatican

35,000,000 years ago marks the beginning of the age of placental-mammalian world domination.

On land this was pre-eminently the age of mammalian renovation and expansion. Of the earlier and more primitive mammals, over one hundred species were extinct before this period ended. Even the mammals of large size and small brain soon perished. Brains and agility had replaced armor and size in the progress of animal survival. And with the dinosaur family on the decline, the mammals slowly assumed domination of the earth, speedily and completely destroying the remainder of their reptilian ancestors.

The Mammalian Era on Urantia 695:1,3

The great event of this glacial period was the evolution of primitive man. Slightly to the west of India, on land now under water and among the offspring of Asiatic migrants of the older North American lemur types, the dawn mammals *suddenly* appeared. These small animals walked mostly on their hind legs, and they possessed large brains in proportion to their size and in comparison with the brains of other animals. In the seventieth generation of this order of life a new and higher group of animals *suddenly* differentiated. These new mid-mammals—almost twice the size and height of their ancestors and possessing proportionately increased brain power— had only well established themselves when the Primates, the third vital mutation, *suddenly* appeared. (At this same time, a retrograde development within the mid-mammal stock gave origin to the simian ancestry; and from that day to this the human branch has gone forward by progressive evolution, while the simian tribes have remained stationary or have actually retrogressed.)

1,000,000 years ago Urantia was registered as an *inhabited* world. A mutation within the stock of the progressing Primates *suddenly* produced two primitive human beings, the actual ancestors of mankind.

The Mammalian Era on Urantia 700:2,3

3. The First Human Beings

One million years ago, the earth became registered as an inhabited world when a mutation in the stock of the progressing primates, on the West Coast of the Mesopotamian peninsula, produced two primitive human beings named Andon and Fonta. Their ability to produce the first moral, intelligent, free will decisions set them apart from their ancestors.

For 150,000 years, the descendents of Andon and Fonta grew in number, but fierce tribal battles broke out, decimating the population. The next race to step on the stage of life was the Neanderthals, appearing in northern India about 850,000 years ago. They dominated the world for half a million years.

The evolutionary planets of the universe all evolve races of multiple colors. On most planets inhabited by evolutionary beings, the six races appear one by one. On earth, however, they emerged simultaneously and from one family about a half a million years ago.

We are all one family. Everyone on earth has the same ancestral parents.

You can hardly realize by what narrow margins your prehuman ancestors missed extinction from time to time. Had the ancestral frog of all humanity jumped two inches less on a certain occasion, the whole course of evolution would have been markedly changed. The immediate lemurlike mother of the dawn-mammal species escaped death no less than five times by mere hairbreadth margins before she gave birth to the father of the new and higher mammalian order. But the closest call of all was when lightning struck the tree in which the prospective mother of the Primates twins was sleeping. Both of these mid-mammal parents were severely shocked and badly burned; three of their seven children were killed by this bolt from the skies.   Dawn Races of Early Man 705:8

And now, after almost nine hundred generations of development, covering about twenty-one thousand years from the origin of the dawn mammals, the Primates *suddenly* gave birth to two remarkable creatures, the first true human beings.

Thus it was that the dawn mammals, springing from the North American lemur type, gave origin to the mid-mammals, and these mid-mammals in turn produced the superior Primates, who became the immediate ancestors of the primitive human race. The Primates tribes were the last vital link in the evolution of man, but in less than five thousand years not a single individual of these extraordinary tribes was left.

From the year A.D. 1934 back to the birth of the first two human beings is just 993,419 years.

These two remarkable creatures were true human beings. They possessed perfect human thumbs, as had many of their ancestors, while they had just as perfect feet as the present-day human races. They were walkers and runners, not climbers; the grasping function of the big toe was absent, completely absent.   Dawn Races of Early Man 707:5-8

These first two humans—the twins—were a great trial to their Primates parents. They were so curious and adventurous that they nearly lost their lives on numerous occasions before they were eight years old. As it was, they were rather well scarred up by the time they were twelve.

Very early they learned to engage in verbal communication; by the age of ten they had worked out an improved sign and word language of almost half a hundred ideas and had greatly improved and expanded the crude communicative technique of their ancestors. But try as hard as they might, they were able to teach only a few of their new signs and symbols to their parents.

When about nine years of age, they journeyed off down the river one bright day and held a momentous conference. Every celestial intelligence stationed on Urantia, including myself, was present as an observer of the transactions of this noontide tryst. On this eventful day they arrived at an understanding to live with and for each other, and this was the first of a series of such agreements which finally culminated in the decision to flee from their inferior animal associates and to journey northward, little knowing that they were thus to found the human race.

While we were all greatly concerned with what these two little savages were planning, we were powerless to control the working of their minds; we did not—could not—arbitrarily influence their decisions. But within the permissible limits of planetary function, we, the Life Carriers, together with our associates, all conspired to lead the human twins northward and far from their hairy and partially tree-dwelling people. And so, by reason of their own intelligent choice, the twins did migrate, and because of our supervision they migrated northward to a secluded   region where they escaped the possibility of biologic degradation through admixture with their inferior relatives of the Primates tribes.

Dawn Races of Early Man 708:4-7

It was an eventful day on Urantia when our small group gathered about the planetary pole of space communication and received the first message from Salvington over the newly established mind circuit of the planet. And this first message, dictated by the chief of the archangel corps, said:

"To the Life Carriers on Urantia—Greetings! We transmit assurance of great pleasure on Salvington, Edentia, and Jerusem in honor of the registration on the headquarters of Nebadon of the signal of the existence on

Seri Candelaria; Photograph by William Dinwiddie (1894);
© AZUSA Publishing Englewood Colorado

Urantia of mind of will dignity. The purposeful decision of the twins to flee northward and segregate their offspring from their inferior ancestors has been noted. This is the first decision of mind—the human type of mind—on Urantia and automatically establishes the circuit of communication over which this initial message of acknowledgment is transmitting."

Next over this new circuit came the greetings of the Most Highs of Edentia, containing instructions for the resident Life Carriers forbidding us to interfere with the pattern of life we had established. We were directed not to intervene in the affairs of human progress. It should not be inferred that Life Carriers ever arbitrarily and mechanically interfere with the natural outworking of the planetary evolutionary plans, for we do not. But up to this time we had been permitted to manipulate the environment and shield the life plasm in a special manner, and it was this extraordinary, but wholly natural, supervision that was to be discontinued.

Dawn Races of Early Man 710:1-3

But the autumn sun was getting lower in the sky, and as they journeyed northward, the nights grew cooler and cooler. Already they had been forced to make use of animal skins for warmth. Before they had been away from home one moon, Andon signified to his mate that he thought he could make fire with the flint. They tried for two months to utilize the flint spark for kindling a fire but only met with failure. Each day this couple would strike the flints and endeavor to ignite the wood. Finally, one evening about the time of the setting of the sun, the secret of the technique was unraveled when it occurred to Fonta to climb a near-by tree to secure an abandoned bird's nest. The nest was dry and highly inflammable and consequently flared right up into a full blaze the moment the spark fell upon it. They were so surprised and startled at their success that they almost lost the fire, but they saved it by the addition of suitable fuel, and then began the first search for firewood by the parents of all mankind.

First Human Family 712:5

Andon and Fonta had nineteen children in all, and they lived to enjoy the association of almost half a hundred grandchildren and half a dozen great - grandchildren. The family was domiciled in four adjoining rock shelters, or semicaves, three of which were interconnected by hallways which had been excavated in the soft limestone with flint tools devised by Andon's children.

First Human Family 713:2

As time passed, the Andonic clans grew in number, and the contact of the expanding families developed friction and misunderstandings. Only two things came to occupy the minds of these peoples: hunting to obtain food and fighting to avenge themselves against some real or supposed injustice or insult at the hands of the neighboring tribes.

Family feuds increased, tribal wars broke out, and serious losses were sustained among the very best elements of the more able and advanced groups. Some of these losses were irreparable; some of the most valuable strains of ability and intelligence were forever lost to the world. This early race and its primitive civilization were threatened with extinction by this incessant warfare of the clans.

It is impossible to induce such primitive beings long to live together in peace. Man is the descendant of fighting animals, and when closely associated, uncultured people irritate and offend each other. The Life Carriers know this tendency among evolutionary creatures and accordingly make provision for the eventual separation of developing human beings into at least three, and more often six, distinct and separate races.

First Human Family 714:5-7

To the east of the Badonan peoples, in the Siwalik Hills of northern India, may be found fossils that approach nearer to transition types between man and the various prehuman groups than any others on earth.

850,000 years ago the superior Badonan tribes began a warfare of extermination directed against their inferior and animalistic neighbors. In less than one thousand years most of the borderland animal groups of these regions had been either destroyed or driven back to the southern forests. This campaign for the extermination of inferiors brought about a slight improvement in the hill tribes of that age. And the mixed descendants of this improved Badonite stock appeared on the stage of action as an apparently new people—the *Neanderthal* race.

The Neanderthalers were excellent fighters, and they traveled extensively. They gradually spread from the highland centers in northwest India to France on the west, China on the east, and even down into northern Africa. They dominated the world for almost half a million years until the times of the migration of the evolutionary races of color.

Evolutionary Races of Color 720:5-7

And now, among these highland Badonites there was a new and strange occurrence. A man and woman living in the northeastern part of the then inhabited highland region began suddenly to produce a family of unusually intelligent children. This was the Sangik family, the ancestors of all of the six colored races of Urantia.

Soyoko Ceremony , Hopi Photograph by James Mooney (1893);
© AZUSA Publishing Englewood Colorado

These Sangik children, nineteen in number, were not only intelligent above their fellows, but their skins manifested a unique tendency to turn various colors upon exposure to sunlight. Among these nineteen children were five red, two orange, four yellow, two green, four blue, and two indigo. These colors became more pronounced as the children grew older, and when these youths later mated with their fellow tribesmen, all of their offspring tended toward the skin color of the Sangik parent.

Evolutionary Races of Color 722:3,4

In this way the life that was planted on Urantia evolved until the ice age, when man himself first appeared and began his eventful planetary career. And this appearance of primitive man on earth during the ice age was not just an accident; it was by design. The rigors and climatic severity of the glacial era were in every way adapted to the purpose of fostering the production of a hardy type of human being with tremendous survival endowment.

Overcontrol of Evolution 733:6

The story of man's ascent from seaweed to the lordship of earthly creation is indeed a romance of biologic struggle and mind survival. Man's primordial ancestors were literally the slime and ooze of the ocean bed in the sluggish and warm-water bays and lagoons of the vast shore lines of the ancient inland seas, those very waters in which the Life Carriers established the three independent life implantations on Urantia.

Overcontrol of Evolution 731:5

It is impossible accurately to determine, simultaneously, the exact location and the velocity of a moving object; any attempt at measurement of either inevitably involves change in the other. The same sort of a paradox confronts mortal man when he undertakes the chemical analysis of protoplasm. The chemist can elucidate the chemistry of *dead* protoplasm, but he cannot discern either the physical organization or the dynamic performance of *living* protoplasm. Ever will the scientist come nearer and nearer the secrets of life, but never will he find them and for no other reason than that he must kill protoplasm in order to analyze it. Dead protoplasm weighs the same as living protoplasm, but it is not the same.

There is original endowment of adaptation in living things and beings. In every *living* plant or animal cell, in every *living* organism—material or spiritual—there is an insatiable craving for the attainment of ever-increasing perfection of environmental adjustment, organismal adaptation, and augmented life realization. These interminable efforts of all living things evidence the existence within them of an innate striving for perfection.

Overcontrol of Evolution 737:1,2

~ II ~

Life's Tribulations

In addition to the emergence of humanity, which we will return to in Chapter 3, The Urantia Book espouses a rich philosophy of living.

Here we find the value of the trials and conflicting emotions that beset us in life. Read this chapter slowly, and as you do, absorb how your soul has been shaped by each experience.

All evolutionary creature life is beset by certain *inevitabilities.* Consider the following:

1. Is *courage*—strength of character—desirable? Then must man be reared in an environment which necessitates grappling with hardships and reacting to disappointments.

2. Is *altruism*—service of one's fellows—desirable? Then must life experience provide for encountering situations of social inequality.

3. Is *hope*—the grandeur of trust—desirable? Then human existence must constantly be confronted with insecurities and recurrent uncertainties.

4. Is *faith*—the supreme assertion of human thought—desirable? Then must the mind of man find itself in that troublesome predicament where it ever knows less than it can believe.

5. Is the *love of truth* and the willingness to go wherever it leads, desirable? Then must man grow up in a world where error is present and falsehood always possible.

6. Is *idealism*—the approaching concept of the divine—desirable? Then must man struggle in an environment of relative goodness and beauty, surroundings stimulative of the irrepressible reach for better things.

7. Is *loyalty*—devotion to highest duty—desirable? Then must man carry on amid the possibilities of betrayal and desertion. The valor of devotion to duty consists in the implied danger of default.

8. Is *unselfishness*—the spirit of self-forgetfulness—desirable? Then must mortal man live face to face with the incessant clamoring of an inescapable self for recognition and honor. Man could not dynamically choose the divine life if there were no self-life to forsake. Man could never lay saving hold on righteousness if there were no potential evil to exalt and differentiate the good by contrast.

9. Is *pleasure*—the satisfaction of happiness—desirable? Then must man live in a world where the alternative of pain and the likelihood of suffering are ever-present experiential possibilities.   Attributes of God   51:1-9

1. Anxiety and Tension

Anxiety and tension are among the most unwanted by-products of modern civilization. To relieve a state of anxiety or tension, people must come to like themselves and be comfortable when they are alone. Towards this end they must find the center within themselves that is at peace, for that center is the piece of God within.

As you read the passages that follow, move into a state of meditation. The relaxation derived from worshipful meditation will carry you over the greatest hurdles of worry and frustration.

The angels really find it hard to understand why you will so persistently allow your higher intellectual powers, even your religious faith, to be so dominated by fear, so thoroughly demoralized by the thoughtless panic of dread and anxiety.   Seraphic Guardians of Destiny 1243:2

Anxiety must be abandoned. The disappointments hardest to bear are those which never come.   The Morontia Life 556:5

About this time a state of great nervous and emotional tension developed among the apostles and their immediate disciple associates. They had hardly become accustomed to living and working together. They were experiencing increasing difficulties in maintaining harmonious relations with John's disciples. The contact with the gentiles and the Samaritans was a great trial to these Jews. And besides all this, the recent utterances of Jesus had augmented their disturbed state of mind. Andrew was almost beside himself; he did not know what next to do, and so he went to the

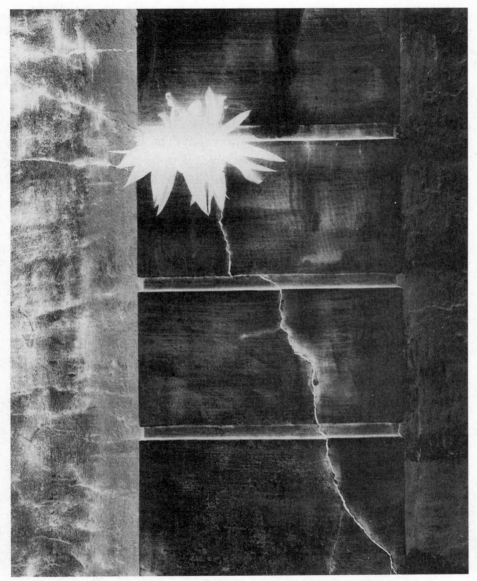

Lotus on a Cement wall ; ©Harriet Blum (1997)
Santa Fe, New Mexico

Master with his problems and perplexities. When Jesus had listened to the apostolic chief relate his troubles, he said: "Andrew, you cannot talk men out of their perplexities when they reach such a stage of involvement, and when so many persons with strong feelings are concerned. I cannot do

what you ask of me—I will not participate in these personal social difficulties—but I will join you in the enjoyment of a three-day period of rest and
relaxation. Go to your brethren and announce that all of you are to go
with me up on Mount Sartaba, where I desire to rest for a day or two.

Going through Samaria 1610:4

    This was a marvelous occasion in the experience of each of them; they
never forgot the day going up the mountain. Throughout the entire trip
hardly a word was said about their troubles. Upon reaching the top of the
mountain, Jesus seated them about him while he said: "My brethren, you
must all learn the value of rest and the efficacy of relaxation. You must
realize that the best method of solving some entangled problems is to
forsake them for a time. Then when you go back fresh from your rest or
worship, you are able to attack your troubles with a clearer head and a
steadier hand, not to mention a more resolute heart. Again, many times
your problem is found to have shrunk in size and proportions while you
have been resting your mind and body."

    The third day when they started down the mountain and back to their
camp, a great change had come over them. They had made the important
discovery that many human perplexities are in reality nonexistent, that
many pressing troubles are the creations of exaggerated fear and the offspring of augmented apprehension. They had learned that all such perplexities are best handled by being forsaken; by going off they had left
such problems to solve themselves.

    There is always danger that monotony of human contact will greatly
multiply perplexities and magnify difficulties. Going to Samaria 1611:3-5

    But the greatest of all methods of problem solving I have learned from
Jesus, your Master. I refer to that which he so consistently practices,
and which he has so faithfully taught you, the isolation of worshipful meditation. In this habit of Jesus' going off so frequently by himself to commune with the Father in heaven is to be found the technique, not only of
gathering strength and wisdom for the ordinary conflicts of living, but also
of appropriating the energy for the solution of the higher problems of a
moral and spiritual nature. But even correct methods of solving problems
will not compensate for inherent defects of personality or atone for the
absence of the hunger and thirst for true righteousness.

I am deeply impressed with the custom of Jesus in going apart by himself to engage in these seasons of solitary survey of the problems of living; to seek for new stores of wisdom and energy for meeting the manifold demands of social service; to quicken and deepen the supreme purpose of living by actually subjecting the total personality to the consciousness of contacting with divinity; to grasp for possession of new and better methods of adjusting oneself to the ever-changing situations of living existence; to effect those vital reconstructions and readjustments of one's personal attitudes which are so essential to enhanced insight into everything worth while and real; and to do all of this with an eye single to the glory of God—to breathe in sincerity your Master's favorite prayer, "Not my will, but yours, be done."

This worshipful practice of your Master brings that relaxation which renews the mind; that illumination which inspires the soul; that courage which enables one bravely to face one's problems; that self-understanding which obliterates debilitating fear; and that consciousness of union with divinity which equips man with the assurance that enables him to dare to be Godlike. The relaxation of worship, or spiritual communion as practiced by the Master, relieves tension, removes conflicts, and mightily augments the total resources of the personality. And all this philosophy, plus the gospel of the kingdom, constitutes the new religion as I understand it.

Rodan of Alexandria 1774:2-4

2. Anger

Is anger your personal demon? When confronted with the slightest perceived injustice do you rise up, red in the face, in self-righteous indignation? Does your sharp tongue lash out to the unwary with bitter invectives.

If so, you are not alone. Know, too, that self-control is within reach. We must be ever vigilant to tame the angry beast that lies sleeping within us, all the while ever ready to awaken in our animal mind.

The eternal God is incapable of wrath and anger in the sense of these human emotions and as man understands such reactions. These sentiments are mean and despicable; they are hardly worthy of being called human, much less divine; and such attitudes are utterly foreign to the perfect nature and gracious character of the Universal Father.

God's Relation to the Universe 57:7

Cupid Chastised; Bartolommeo Manfredi (1595)
© Art Institute of Chicago

Impatience is a spirit poison; anger is like a stone hurled into a hornet's nest.   The Morontia Life 557:4

"Anger is a material manifestation which represents, in a general way, the measure of the failure of the spiritual nature to gain control of the combined intellectual and physical natures. Anger indicates your lack of tolerant brotherly love plus your lack of self-respect and self-control. Anger depletes the health, debases the mind, and handicaps the spirit teacher of man's soul. Have you not read in the Scriptures that `wrath kills the foolish man,' and that man `tears himself in his anger'? That `he who is slow of wrath is of great understanding,' while `he who is hasty of temper exalts folly'? You all know that `a soft answer turns away wrath,' and how `grievous words stir up anger.' `Discretion defers anger,' while `he who has no control over his own self is like a defenseless city without walls.' `Wrath is cruel and anger is outrageous.' `Angry men stir up strife, while the furious multiply their transgressions.' `Be not hasty in spirit, for anger rests in the bosom of fools.'" Before Jesus ceased speaking, he said further: "Let your hearts be so dominated by love that your spirit guide will have little trouble in delivering you from the tendency to give vent to those outbursts of animal anger which are inconsistent with the status of divine sonship."   Second Preaching Tour 1673:2

3. Disappointment

Disappointment lies at the crux of life. To rise from defeat and take on a new day teaches us that each experience, no matter how disappointing it may be, is but a step in our inexorable journey to higher levels of reality.

But long before reaching Havona, these ascendant children of time have learned to feast upon uncertainty, to fatten upon disappointment, to enthuse over apparent defeat, to invigorate in the presence of difficulties, to exhibit indomitable courage in the face of immensity, and to exercise unconquerable faith when confronted with the challenge of the inexplicable. Long since, the battle cry of these pilgrims became: "In liaison with God, nothing—absolutely nothing—is impossible."
                               Ministering Spirits of the Central Universe 291:3

Modele dans l'atelier de l'artiste; Pierre Bonnard(1912)

© Musee d'Orsay, Paris

It is the plan of your superiors to advance you by augmented trusts just as fast as your character is sufficiently developed to gracefully bear these added responsibilities, but to overload the individual only courts disaster and insures disappointment.

Ministering Spirits of the Superuniverse 316:2

Even as mortals, so have these angels been father to many disappointments, and they will point out that sometimes your most disappointing disappointments have become your greatest blessings. Sometimes the planting of a seed necessitates its death, the death of your fondest hopes, before it can be reborn to bear the fruits of new life and new opportunity. And from them you will learn to suffer less through sorrow and disappointment, first, by making fewer personal plans concerning other personalities, and then, by accepting your lot when you have faithfully performed your duty.

You will learn that you increase your burdens and decrease the likelihood of success by taking yourself too seriously. Nothing can take precedence over the work of your status sphere—this world or the next. Very important is the work of preparation for the next higher sphere, but nothing equals the importance of the work of the world in which you are actually living. But though the *work* is important, the *self* is not. When you feel important, you lose energy to the wear and tear of ego dignity so that there is little energy left to do the work. Self-importance, not work-importance, exhausts immature creatures; it is the self element that exhausts, not the effort to achieve. You can do important work if you do not become self-important; you can do several things as easily as one if you leave yourself out. Variety is restful; monotony is what wears and exhausts. Day after day is alike—just life or the alternative of death.

The Morontia Life 555:4,5

Eternal life is the endless quest for infinite values.

Jesus portrayed the profound surety of the God-knowing mortal when he said: "To a God-knowing kingdom believer, what does it matter if all things earthly crash?" Temporal securities are vulnerable, but spiritual sureties are impregnable. When the flood tides of human adversity, selfishness, cruelty, hate, malice, and jealousy beat about the mortal soul, you may rest in the assurance that there is one inner bastion, the citadel of the spirit, which is absolutely unassailable; at least this is true of every human being who has dedicated the keeping of his soul to the indwelling spirit of the eternal God.

After such spiritual attainment, whether secured by gradual growth or specific crisis, there occurs a new orientation of personality as well as the development of a new standard of values. Such spirit-born individuals are so remotivated in life that they can calmly stand by while their fondest ambitions perish and their keenest hopes crash; they positively know that such catastrophes are but the redirecting cataclysms which wreck one's temporal creations preliminary to the rearing of the more noble and enduring realities of a new and more sublime level of universe attainment.

Religion in Human Experience 1096:2,4,5

You humans have begun an endless unfolding of an almost infinite panorama, a limitless expanding of never-ending, ever-widening spheres of opportunity for exhilarating service, matchless adventure, sublime uncertainty, and boundless attainment. When the clouds gather overhead, your faith should accept the fact of the presence of the indwelling Adjuster, and thus you should be able to look beyond the mists of mortal uncertainty into the clear shining of the sun of eternal righteousness on the beckoning heights of the mansion worlds.

Mission and Ministry of Thought Adjusters 1194:1

Much of what a mortal would call good luck might really be bad luck; the smile of fortune that bestows unearned leisure and undeserved wealth may be the greatest of human afflictions; the apparent cruelty of a perverse fate that heaps tribulation upon some suffering mortal may in reality be the tempering fire that is transmuting the soft iron of immature personality into the tempered steel of real character.

Supreme and Ultimate-Time and Space 1305:4

God-knowing individuals are not discouraged by misfortune or downcast by disappointment. Believers are immune to the depression consequent upon purely material upheavals; spirit livers are not perturbed by the episodes of the material world. Candidates for eternal life are practitioners of an invigorating and constructive technique for meeting all of the vicissitudes and harassments of mortal living. Every day a true believer lives, he finds it *easier* to do the right thing.

The measure of the spiritual capacity of the evolving soul is your faith in truth and your love for man, but the measure of your human strength of character is your ability to resist the holding of grudges and your capacity to withstand brooding in the face of deep sorrow. Defeat is the true mirror in which you may honestly view your real self.

The God-conscious mortal is certain of salvation; he is unafraid of life; he is honest and consistent. He knows how bravely to endure unavoidable suffering; he is uncomplaining when faced by inescapable hardship.

The true believer does not grow weary in well-doing just because he is thwarted. Difficulty whets the ardor of the truth lover, while obstacles only challenge the exertions of the undaunted kingdom builder.

Sojourn at Tyre and Sidon 1741:0,4,7,8

But life will become a burden of existence unless you learn how to fail gracefully. There is an art in defeat which noble souls always acquire; you must know how to lose cheerfully; you must be fearless of disappointment. Never hesitate to admit failure. Make no attempt to hide failure under deceptive smiles and beaming optimism. It sounds well always to claim success, but the end results are appalling. Such a technique leads directly to the creation of a world of unreality and to the inevitable crash of ultimate disillusionment.

Success may generate courage and promote confidence, but wisdom comes only from the experiences of adjustment to the results of one's failures. Men who prefer optimistic illusions to reality can never become wise. Only those who face facts and adjust them to ideals can achieve wisdom.   Rodan of Alexandria 1779:5,6

And it is in this business of facing failure and adjusting to defeat that the far-reaching vision of religion exerts its supreme influence. Failure is simply an educational episode—a cultural experiment in the acquirement of wisdom—in the experience of the God-seeking man who has embarked on the eternal adventure of the exploration of a universe. To such men defeat is but a new tool for the achievement of higher levels of universe reality.   Rodan of Alexandria 1780:1

4. Loneliness and Depression

Here you will meet the "Adjuster," the unique piece of God within you. Becoming familiar with your Adjuster is paramount in overcoming loneliness. When you send out a call for help, you will feel his sure hand guide you like a small child to safety. If we have living faith—not only in the human spirit, but in the infinite spirit of our Father in heaven—we will be guided to the sure solution to any depression - through the loving service of our fellow human beings.

May I admonish you to heed the distant echo of the Adjuster's faithful call to your soul? The indwelling Adjuster cannot stop or even materially alter your career struggle of time; the Adjuster cannot lessen the hardships of life as you journey on through this world of toil. The divine indweller can only patiently forbear while you fight the battle of life as it is lived on your planet; but you could, if you only would—as you work and worry, as you fight and toil—permit the valiant Adjuster to fight with you and for you. You could be so comforted and inspired, so enthralled and intrigued, if you would only allow the Adjuster constantly to bring forth the pictures of the real motive, the final aim, and the eternal purpose of all this difficult, uphill struggle with the commonplace problems of your present material world.   The Adjuster and the Soul 1223:4

Personality cannot very well perform in isolation. Man is innately a social creature; he is dominated by the craving of belongingness. It is literally true, "No man lives unto himself."

Personality Survival 1227:6

On Saturday afternoon, December 3, of this year, death for the second time struck at this Nazareth family. Little Amos, their baby brother, died after a week's illness with a high fever. After passing through this time of sorrow with her first-born son as her only support, Mary at last and in the fullest sense recognized Jesus as the real head of the family; and he was truly a worthy head.

For four years their standard of living had steadily declined; year by year they felt the pinch of increasing poverty. By the close of this year they faced one of the most difficult experiences of all their uphill struggles. James had not yet begun to earn much, and the expenses of a funeral on top of everything else staggered them. But Jesus would only say to his anxious and grieving mother: "Mother-Mary, sorrow will not help us; we are all doing our best, and mother's smile, perchance, might even inspire us to do better. Day by day we are strengthened for these tasks by our hope of better days ahead." His sturdy and practical optimism was truly contagious; all the children lived in an atmosphere of anticipation of better times and better things. And this hopeful courage contributed mightily to the development of strong and noble characters, in spite of the depressiveness of their poverty.   The Adolescent Years 1400:5,6

By this time the young man very much desired to talk with Jesus, and he knelt at his feet imploring Jesus to help him, to show him the way of escape from his world of personal sorrow and defeat. Said Jesus: "My friend, arise! Stand up like a man! You may be surrounded with small enemies and be retarded by many obstacles, but the big things and the real things of this world and the universe are on your side. The sun rises every morning to salute you just as it does the most powerful and prosperous man on earth. Look—you have a strong body and powerful muscles— your physical equipment is better than the average. Of course, it is just about useless while you sit out here on the mountainside and grieve over your misfortunes, real and fancied. But you could do great things with your body if you would hasten off to where great things are waiting to be done. You are trying to run away from your unhappy self, but it cannot be done. You and your problems of living are real; you cannot escape them as long as you live. But look again, your mind is clear and capable. Your strong body has an intelligent mind to direct it. Set your mind at work to solve its problems; teach your intellect to work for you; refuse longer to be dominated by fear like an unthinking animal. Your mind should be your courageous ally in the solution of your life problems rather than your being, as you have been, its abject fear-slave and the bond-servant of de- pression and defeat. But most valuable of all, your potential of real achieve- ment is the spirit which lives within you, and which will stimulate and inspire your mind to control itself and activate the body if you will release it from the fetters of fear and thus enable your spiritual nature to begin your deliverance from the evils of inaction by the power-presence of living faith. And then, forthwith, will this faith vanquish fear of men by the compelling presence of that new and all-dominating *love of your fellows* which will so soon fill your soul to overflowing because of the consciousness which has been born in your heart that you are a child of God.

On the Way to Rome 1437:3

Here in Rome also occurred that touching incident in which the Creator of a universe spent several hours restoring a lost child to his anxious mother. This little boy had wandered away from his home, and Jesus found him crying in distress. He and Ganid were on their way to the libraries, but they devoted themselves to getting the child back home. Ganid never forgot Jesus' comment: "You know, Ganid, most human beings are like the lost child. They spend much of their time crying in fear and suffering in sorrow when, in very truth, they are but a short distance from safety and security, even as this child was only a little way from home. And all those who know the way of truth and enjoy the assurance of knowing God should esteem it a privilege, not a duty, to offer guidance to their fellows in their efforts to find the satisfactions of living. Did we not supremely enjoy this ministry of restoring the child to his mother? So do those who lead men to God experience the supreme satisfaction of human service."

The Sojourn at Rome 1465:5

"Simon, some persons are naturally more happy than others. Much, very much, depends upon the willingness of man to be led and directed by the Father's spirit which lives within him. Have you not read in the Scriptures the words of the wise man, 'The spirit of man is the candle of the Lord, searching all the inward parts'?

"Much of man's sorrow is born of the disappointment of his ambitions and the wounding of his pride. Although men owe a duty to themselves to make the best of their lives on earth, having thus sincerely exerted themselves, they should cheerfully accept their lot and exercise ingenuity in making the most of that which has fallen to their hands. All too many of man's troubles take origin in the fear soil of his own natural heart. 'The wicked flee when no man pursues.' 'The wicked are like the troubled sea, for it cannot rest, but its waters cast up mire and dirt; there is no peace, says God, for the wicked.'

"Seek not, then, for false peace and transient joy but rather for the assurance of faith and the sureties of divine sonship which yield composure, contentment, and supreme joy in the spirit."

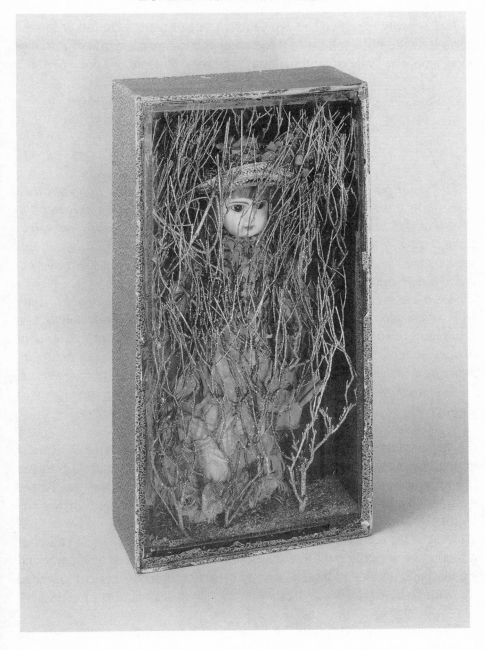

Untitled (Bebe Marie);Joseph Cornell (early 1940's)
© The Museum of
Modern Art New York

Jesus hardly regarded this world as a "vale of tears." He rather looked upon it as the birth sphere of the eternal and immortal spirits of Paradise ascension, the "vale of soul making."   Second Preaching Tour 1674:4-7

5. Pain and Suffering

The great paradox of living is to be truly alive—every now and then something has to die. For us to mature, our fondest hopes may need to perish in defeat. From the ashes of defeat, we can then gather ourselves up and try again, all the while growing stronger and more reliable. In this way, by the time we have completed our trial on earth, we will have become a true asset to the universe.

When the great angel Lucifer revolted against God, declaring himself ruler of the local universe, he took one-third of the angels down with him. Did the majority of evolutionary mortals who had arisen to heaven embrace this great tempter of pride and deceit? No—they knew experientially that God's plan for the universe was infinitely wise and far seeing.

Our universe Father knows the best way to develop loyal subjects is through the sometimes painful climb out of mortality to infinity.

Does the Paradise Father suffer? I do not know. The Creator Sons most certainly can and sometimes do, even as do mortals. The Eternal Son and the Infinite Spirit suffer in a modified sense. I think the Universal Father does, but I cannot understand how; perhaps through the personality circuit or through the individuality of the Thought Adjusters and other bestowals of his eternal nature. He has said of the mortal races, "In all your afflictions I am afflicted." He unquestionably experiences a fatherly and sympathetic understanding; he may truly suffer, but I do not comprehend the nature thereof.   Attributes of God 53:4

The confusion and turmoil of Urantia do not signify that the Paradise Rulers lack either interest or ability to manage affairs differently. The Creators are possessed of full power to make Urantia a veritable paradise, but such an Eden would not contribute to the development of those strong, noble, and experienced characters which the Gods are so surely forging out on your world between the anvils of necessity and the hammers of anguish. Your anxieties and sorrows, your trials and disappointments, are just as much a part of the divine plan on your sphere as are the exquisite perfection and infinite adaptation of all things to their supreme purpose on the worlds of the central and perfect universe.

The Solitary Messengers 258:11

L'arbe aux corbeaux; David Friedrich
(1774-1849) © Louvre, Paris

Many are the pilgrims who, at such a time, look back upon the long, long struggle with a joyous envy, really wishing they might somehow go back to the worlds of time and begin it all over again, just as you mortals, in approaching advanced age, sometimes look back over the struggles of youth and early life and truly wish you might live your lives over once again.   *Ministering Spirits of the Central Universe* 296:1

The greatest affliction of the cosmos is never to have been afflicted. Mortals only learn wisdom by experiencing tribulation.

The Morontia Life 556:14

Because of your planetary misfortunes, Urantians are prevented from understanding very much about the culture of normal worlds. But you should not envisage the evolutionary worlds, even the most ideal, as spheres whereon life is a flowery bed of ease. The initial life of the mortal races is always attended by struggle. Effort and decision are an essential part of the acquirement of survival values.

On first thought it might appear that Urantia and its associated isolated worlds are most unfortunate in being deprived of the beneficent presence and influence of such superhuman personalities as a Planetary Prince and a Material Son and Daughter. But isolation of these spheres affords their races a unique opportunity for the exercise of faith and for the development of a peculiar quality of confidence in cosmic reliability which is not dependent on sight or any other material consideration. It may turn out, eventually, that mortal creatures hailing from the worlds quarantined in consequence of rebellion are extremely fortunate. We have discovered that such ascenders are very early intrusted with numerous special assignments to cosmic undertakings where unquestioned faith and sublime confidence are essential to achievement.   The Planetary Princes 578:3,6

The moral will creatures of the evolutionary worlds are always bothered with the unthinking question as to why the all-wise Creators permit evil and sin. They fail to comprehend that both are inevitable if the creature is to be truly free. The free will of evolving man or exquisite angel is not a mere philosophic concept, a symbolic ideal. Man's ability to choose good or evil is a universe reality. This liberty to choose for oneself is an endowment of the Supreme Rulers, and they will not permit any being or group of beings to deprive a single personality in the wide universe of this divinely bestowed liberty—not even to satisfy such misguided and ignorant beings in the enjoyment of this misnamed personal liberty.

Problems of the Lucifer Rebellion 615:3

At another of these private interviews in the garden Nathaniel asked Jesus: "Master, though I am beginning to understand why you refuse to practice healing indiscriminately, I am still at a loss to understand why the loving Father in heaven permits so many of his children on earth to suffer so many afflictions." The Master answered Nathaniel, saying:

"Nathaniel, you and many others are thus perplexed because you do not comprehend how the natural order of this world has been so many times upset by the sinful adventures of certain rebellious traitors to the Father's will. And I have come to make a beginning of setting these things in order. But many ages will be required to restore this part of the universe to former paths and thus release the children of men from the extra burdens of sin and rebellion. The presence of evil alone is sufficient test for the ascension of man—sin is not essential to survival.

"But, my son, you should know that the Father does not purposely afflict his children. Man brings down upon himself unnecessary affliction as a result of his persistent refusal to walk in the better ways of the divine will. Affliction is potential in evil, but much of it has been produced by sin and iniquity. Many unusual events have transpired on this world, and it is not strange that all thinking men should be perplexed by the scenes of suffering and affliction which they witness. But of one thing you may be sure: The Father does not send affliction as an arbitrary punishment for wrongdoing. The imperfections and handicaps of evil are inherent; the penalties of sin are inevitable; the destroying consequences of iniquity are inexorable. Man should not blame God for those afflictions which are the natural result of the life which he chooses to live; neither should man complain of those experiences which are a part of life as it is lived on this world. It is the Father's will that mortal man should work persistently and consistently toward the betterment of his estate on earth. Intelligent application would enable man to overcome much of his earthly misery.   Training the Evangelist 1661:3-5

Worship—contemplation of the spiritual—must alternate with service, contact with material reality. Work should alternate with play; religion should be balanced by humor. Profound philosophy should be relieved by rhythmic poetry. The strain of living—the time tension of personality—should be relaxed by the restfulness of worship.

Going to Samaria 1616:5

6. Temptation and Addiction

"Lead us not into temptation and deliver us from evil" is a phrase often repeated from the Lord's prayer. "Save us in temptation, deliver us from evil" would be a more accurate translation of the prayer according to The Urantia Book. This supplication to God recognizes that we are responsible for our vices and excesses, and asks for the strength to overcome them.

When we have succumbed to human weakness, the devil hasn't made us misbehave; nor has God tempted us to test our faith. Instead, we have allowed the animal nature of the mind to overcome the spiritual leadings of the soul.

Were you ever tempted to do something you knew was wrong? If so, how did you handle it? Did you embrace a lesser evil, thinking it would at least be better than the more iniquitous one? To surmount such temptations, we can turn to living faith and begin to see the beauty of life overcoming all the ugliness.

On this same occasion the Master talked to the group about the desirability of possessing well-balanced characters. He recognized that it was necessary for most men to devote themselves to the mastery of some vocation, but he deplored all tendency toward overspecialization, toward becoming narrow-minded and circumscribed in life's activities. He called attention to the fact that any virtue, if carried to extremes, may become a vice. Jesus always preached temperance and taught consistency—proportionate adjustment of life problems. He pointed out that overmuch sympathy and pity may degenerate into serious emotional instability; that enthusiasm may drive on into fanaticism. He discussed one of their former associates whose imagination had led him off into visionary and impractical undertakings. At the same time he warned them against the dangers of the dullness of overconservative mediocrity.

Second Preaching Tour 1673:3

On the evening of this same day Nathaniel asked Jesus: "Master, why do we pray that God will lead us not into temptation when we well know from your revelation of the Father that he never does such things?" Jesus answered Nathaniel:

"It is not strange that you ask such questions seeing that you are beginning to know the Father as I know him, and not as the early Hebrew

Temptation of St Anthony; Grunewald (1470-1528),
© Unterlinden Museum, Colmar, France

prophets so dimly saw him. You well know how our forefathers were disposed to see God in almost everything that happened. They looked for the hand of God in all natural occurrences and in every unusual episode of human experience. They connected God with both good and evil. They thought he softened the heart of Moses and hardened the heart of Pharaoh. When man had a strong urge to do something, good or evil, he was in the habit of accounting for these unusual emotions by remarking: 'The Lord spoke to me saying, do thus and so, or go here and there.' Accordingly, since men so often and so violently ran into temptation, it became the habit of our forefathers to believe that God led them thither for testing, punishing, or strengthening. But you, indeed, now know better. You know that men are all too often led into temptation by the urge of their own selfishness and by the impulses of their animal natures. When you are in this way tempted, I admonish you that, while you recognize temptation honestly and sincerely for just what it is, you intelligently redirect the energies of spirit, mind, and body, which are seeking expression, into higher channels and toward more idealistic goals. In this way may you transform your temptations into the highest types of uplifting mortal ministry while you almost wholly avoid these wasteful and weakening conflicts between the animal and spiritual natures.

"But let me warn you against the folly of undertaking to surmount temptation by the effort of supplanting one desire by another and supposedly superior desire through the mere force of the human will. If you would be truly triumphant over the temptations of the lesser and lower nature, you must come to that place of spiritual advantage where you have really and truly developed an actual interest in, and love for, those higher and more idealistic forms of conduct which your mind is desirous of substituting for these lower and less idealistic habits of behavior that you recognize as temptation. You will in this way be delivered through spiritual transformation rather than be increasingly overburdened with the deceptive suppression of mortal desires. The old and the inferior will be forgotten in the love for the new and the superior. Beauty is always triumphant over ugliness in the hearts of all who are illuminated by the love of truth. There is mighty power in the expulsive energy of a new and sincere spiritual affection. And again I say to you, be not overcome by evil but rather overcome evil with good."
                                           Sojourn at Tyre 1738:2-4

The Adjuster remains with you in all disaster and through every sickness which does not wholly destroy the mentality. But how unkind knowingly to defile or otherwise deliberately to pollute the physical body, which must serve as the earthly tabernacle of this marvelous gift from God. All physical poisons greatly retard the efforts of the Adjuster to exalt the material mind, while the mental poisons of fear, anger, envy, jealousy, suspicion, and intolerance likewise tremendously interfere with the spiritual progress of the evolving soul.   Relation of Adjusters to Individuals 1204:3

7. Forgiveness

To forgive others, we must first must learn to forgive ourselves. This capacity is powerfully rendered by the painting of Mary Magdalen on page fifty-one. The intensity with which she looks inside herself bends the candle flame before her.

To forgive others, we must also learn to love them. Loving the caveman in the passage that follows only occurs when we understand his intent: to courageously protect his family from the saber-toothed tiger.

Everyone we meet is a child of God and has the gift of personality—a special treasure he has shared with us. We are each a unique expression of God's infinite character, with a one-of-a-kind talent waiting for a chance to blossom. The more we come to know others and to recognize their true worth, the closer we come to love and forgiveness.

If you love your fellow men, you must have discovered their values. Jesus loved men so much because he placed such a high value upon them. You can best discover values in your associates by discovering their motivation. If some one irritates you, causes feelings of resentment, you should sympathetically seek to discern his viewpoint, his reasons for such objectionable conduct. If once you understand your neighbor, you will become tolerant, and this tolerance will grow into friendship and ripen into love.

In the mind's eye conjure up a picture of one of your primitive ancestors of cave-dwelling times—a short, misshapen, filthy, snarling hulk of a man standing, legs spread, club upraised, breathing hate and animosity as he looks fiercely just ahead. Such a picture hardly depicts the divine dignity of man. But allow us to enlarge the picture. In front of this animated human crouches a saber-toothed tiger. Behind him, a woman and two children. Immediately you recognize that such a picture stands for the beginnings of much that is fine and noble in the human race, but the man is the same in both pictures. Only in the second sketch you are favored with a widened horizon. You therein discern the motivation of this evolving mortal. His attitude becomes praiseworthy because you understand him. If you could only fathom the motives of your associates, how much better you would understand them. If you could only know your fellows, you would eventually fall in love with them.

You cannot truly love your fellows by a mere act of the will. Love is only born of thoroughgoing understanding of your neighbor's motives and sentiments. It is not so important to love all men today as it is that each day you learn to love one more human being. If each day or each week you achieve an understanding of one more of your fellows, and if this is the limit of your ability, then you are certainly socializing and truly spiritualizing your personality. Love is infectious, and when human devotion is intelligent and wise, love is more catching than hate. But only genuine and unselfish love is truly contagious. If each mortal could only become a focus of dynamic affection, this benign virus of love would soon pervade the sentimental emotion-stream of humanity to such an extent that all civilization would be encompassed by love, and that would be the realization of the brotherhood of man.   Religion in Human Experience 1098:1-3

On this particular occasion at Simon's house, among those who came in off the street was a woman of unsavory reputation who had recently become a believer in the good news of the gospel of the kingdom. This woman was well known throughout all Jerusalem as the former keeper of one of the so-called high-class brothels located hard by the temple court of the gentiles. She had, on accepting the teachings of Jesus, closed up her nefarious place of business and had induced the majority of the women associated with her to accept the gospel and change their mode of living; notwithstanding this, she was still held in great disdain by the Pharisees and was compelled to wear her hair down—the badge of harlotry. This unnamed woman had brought with her a large flask of perfumed anointing lotion and, standing behind Jesus as he reclined at meat, began to anoint his feet while she also wet his feet with her tears of gratitude, wiping them with the hair of her head. And when she had finished this anointing, she continued weeping and kissing his feet.

The Repentant Magdalen; Georges de la Tour (1640) National
Gallery of Art, Washington

When Simon saw all this, he said to himself: "This man, if he were a
prophet, would have perceived who and what manner of woman this is
who thus touches him; that she is a notorious sinner." And Jesus, knowing
what was going on in Simon's mind, spoke up, saying: "Simon, I have
something which I would like to say to you." Simon answered, "Teacher,
say on." Then said Jesus: "A certain wealthy moneylender had two debt-

ors. The one owed him five hundred denarii and the other fifty. Now, when neither of them had wherewith to pay, he forgave them both. Which of them do you think, Simon, would love him most?" Simon answered, "He, I suppose, whom he forgave the most." And Jesus said, "You have rightly judged," and pointing to the woman, he continued: "Simon, take a good look at this woman. I entered your house as an invited guest, yet you gave me no water for my feet. This grateful woman has washed my feet with tears and wiped them with the hair of her head. You gave me no kiss of friendly greeting, but this woman, ever since she came in, has not ceased to kiss my feet. My head with oil you neglected to anoint, but she has anointed my feet with precious lotions. And what is the meaning of all this? Simply that her many sins have been forgiven, and this has led her to love much. But those who have received but little forgiveness sometimes love but little." And turning around toward the woman, he took her by the hand and, lifting her up, said: "You have indeed repented of your sins, and they are forgiven. Be not discouraged by the thoughtless and unkind attitude of your fellows; go on in the joy and liberty of the kingdom of heaven."

Interlude at Jerusalem 1651:7, 1652:1

That same evening Jesus made the long-to-be-remembered address to the apostles regarding the relative value of status with God and progress in the eternal ascent to Paradise. Said Jesus: "My children, if there exists a true and living connection between the child and the Father, the child is certain to progress continuously toward the Father's ideals. True, the child may at first make slow progress, but the progress is none the less sure. The important thing is not the rapidity of your progress but rather its certainty. Your actual achievement is not so important as the fact that the direction of your progress is Godward. What you are becoming day by day is of infinitely more importance than what you are today.

"This transformed woman whom some of you saw at Simon's house today is, at this moment, living on a level which is vastly below that of Simon and his well-meaning associates; but while these Pharisees are occupied with the false progress of the illusion of traversing deceptive circles of meaningless ceremonial services, this woman has, in dead earnest, started out on the long and eventful search for God, and her path toward heaven is not blocked by spiritual pride and moral self-satisfaction. The woman is, humanly speaking, much farther away from God than Simon, but her soul is in progressive motion; she is on the way toward an eternal goal. There are present in this woman tremendous spiritual possibilities for the future. Some of you may not stand high in actual levels of soul and spirit, but you are making daily progress on the living way opened up, through faith, to God. There are tremendous possibilities in each of you for the future. Better by far to have a small but living and growing faith than to be possessed of a great intellect with its dead stores of worldly wisdom and spiritual unbelief." Interlude at Jerusalem 1653:1,2

"When a wise man understands the inner impulses of his fellows, he will love them. And when you love your brother, you have already forgiven him. This capacity to understand man's nature and forgive his apparent wrongdoing is Godlike. If you are wise parents, this is the way you will love and understand your children, even forgive them when transient misunderstanding has apparently separated you. The child, being immature and lacking in the fuller understanding of the depth of the child-father relationship, must frequently feel a sense of guilty separation from a father's full approval, but the true father is never conscious of any such separation. Sin is an experience of creature consciousness; it is not a part of God's consciousness.

"Your inability or unwillingness to forgive your fellows is the measure of your immaturity, your failure to attain adult sympathy, understanding, and love. You hold grudges and nurse vengefulness in direct proportion to your ignorance of the inner nature and true longings of your children and your fellow beings. Love is the outworking of the divine and inner urge of life. It is founded on understanding, nurtured by unselfish service, and perfected in wisdom." Tuesday in the Temple 1898:4,5

~ III ~

Ancient History

In normal evolutionary worlds, a young civilization receives guidance with the first appearance of humans capable of free - will decisions. From age to age, repeated revelations of the Father are presented, each of which gives people a more advanced and progressive concept of God.

On our backwater planet at the edge of the Milky Way galaxy, however, civilization has greatly diverged from this normal pattern of evolutionary development. Why? Because the first two representatives from heaven, destined to guide our planet through its critical early years, became mixed up in the Lucifer rebellion and defaulted.

The first emissary was the archdeceiver Caligastia (500,000 BC- 200,000 BC); the second Adam and Eve (35,984 BC - 35,384 BC). Both defaulted in their commission to step up our world into the realities of the universe and the nature of God. Only later did the Melchizedek (1980 BC—1886 BC) begin the task of returning our world to the universe track. The excerpts that follow reveal these divine visitations, as well as the origin of the Bible.

1. Calagastia and Lucifer

The Planetary Prince Caligastia, dispatched from Jerusem—the local universe system capital, arrived almost a half a million years after the first appearance of humans. Through the efforts of the prince's staff, early civilization began slowly developing with the introduction of animal husbandry, irrigation, treating skins, the first alphabet, and primitive hygiene. But then Caligastia wholeheartedly joined Lucifer in a repudiation of God, an action that launched earth onto a path of rebellion against the universe. The fragile civilization the prince had come to guide soon collapsed.

About five hundred thousand years ago and concurrent with the appearance of the six colored or Sangik races, Caligastia, the Planetary Prince,
arrived on Urantia. There were almost one-half billion primitive human
beings on earth at the time of the Prince's arrival, and they were well scattered over Europe, Asia, and Africa. The Prince's headquarters, established
in Mesopotamia, was at about the center of world population.

The Planetary Prince of Urantia 741:2

On going to a young world, a Planetary Prince usually takes with him a
group of volunteer ascending beings from the local system headquarters.
These ascenders accompany the prince as advisers and helpers in the work
of early race improvement. This corps of material helpers constitutes the
connecting link between the prince and the world races. The Urantia Prince,
Caligastia, had a corps of one hundred such helpers.

The Planetary Princes 574:3

Down through the ages of world's history, the revelations of religion are
ever-expanding and successively more enlightening. If revelation is to exalt and upstep the religions of evolution, then must such divine visitations
portray teachings which are not too far removed from the thought and reactions of the age in which they are presented.

Later Evolution of Religion 1007:1

In the headquarters settlement on your world every human habitation
was provided with abundance of land. Although the remote tribes continued in hunting and food foraging, the students and teachers in the Prince's
schools were all agriculturists and horticulturists. The time was about
equally divided between the following pursuits:

1. *Physical labor.* Cultivation of the soil, associated with home building
and embellishment.

2. *Social activities.* Play performances and cultural social groupings.

3. *Educational application.* Individual instruction in connection with fam-
ily-group teaching, supplemented by specialized class training.

4. *Vocational training.* Schools of marriage and homemaking, the schools
of art and craft training, and the classes for the training of teachers—secular, cultural, and religious.

5. *Spiritual culture.* The teacher brotherhood, the enlightenment of childhood and youth groups, and the training of adopted native children as
missionaries to their people.

A Planetary Prince is not visible to mortal beings; it is a test of faith to believe the representations of the semimaterial beings of his staff. But these schools of culture and training are well adapted to the needs of each planet, and there soon develops a keen and laudatory rivalry among the races of men in their efforts to gain entrance to these various institutions of learning.

From such a world center of culture and achievement there gradually radiates to all peoples an uplifting and civilizing influence which slowly and certainly transforms the evolutionary races. Meantime the educated and spiritualized children of the surrounding peoples who have been adopted and trained in the prince's schools are returning to their native groups and, to the best of their ability, are there establishing new and potent centers of learning and culture which they carry on according to the plan of the prince's schools.

On Urantia these plans for planetary progress and cultural advancement were well under way, proceeding most satisfactorily, when the whole enterprise was brought to a rather sudden and most inglorious end by Caligastia's adherence to the Lucifer rebellion.

The Planetary Princes 575:4-11

From the arrival of Prince Caligastia, planetary civilization progressed in a fairly normal manner for almost three hundred thousand years. Aside from being a life-modification sphere and therefore subject to numerous irregularities and unusual episodes of evolutionary fluctuation, Urantia progressed very satisfactorily in its planetary career up to the times of the Lucifer rebellion and the concurrent Caligastia betrayal. All subsequent history has been definitely modified by this catastrophic blunder as well as by the later failure of Adam and Eve to fulfill their planetary mission.

The Planetary Prince of Urantia 752:4

The problems associated with human existence on Urantia are impossible of understanding without a knowledge of certain great epochs of the past, notably the occurrence and consequences of the planetary rebellion. Although this upheaval did not seriously interfere with the progress of organic evolution, it did markedly modify the course of social evolution and of spiritual development.

For three hundred thousand years Caligastia had been in charge of Urantia when Satan, Lucifer's assistant, made one of his periodic inspection calls.

And when Satan arrived on the planet, his appearance in no way resembled your caricatures of his nefarious majesty. He was, and still is, a Lanonandek Son of great brilliance. "And no marvel, for Satan himself is a brilliant creature of light."

The Great Red Dragon and the Woman Clothed with the Sun; William Blake(1805), © National Gallery of Art, Washington

In the course of this inspection Satan informed Caligastia of Lucifer's then proposed "Declaration of Liberty," and as we now know, the Prince agreed to betray the planet upon the announcement of the rebellion. The loyal universe personalities look with peculiar disdain upon Prince Caligastia because of this premeditated betrayal of trust. The Creator Son voiced this contempt when he said: "You are like your leader, Lucifer, and you have sinfully perpetuated his iniquity. He was a falsifier from the beginning of his self-exaltation because he abode not in the truth." The Planetary Rebellion 754:1-3

Whatever the early origins of trouble in the hearts of Lucifer and Satan, the final outbreak took form as the Lucifer Declaration of Liberty. The cause of the rebels was stated under three heads:

1. *The reality of the Universal Father.* Lucifer charged that the Universal Father did not really exist, that physical gravity and space-energy were inherent in the universe, and that the Father was a myth invented by the Paradise Sons to enable them to maintain the rule of the universes in the Father's name. He denied that personality was a gift of the Universal Father. He even intimated that the finaliters were in collusion with the Paradise Sons to foist fraud upon all creation since they never brought back a very clear-cut idea of the Father's actual personality as it is discernible on Paradise. He traded on reverence as ignorance. The charge was sweeping, terrible, and blasphemous.

2. *The universe government of the Creator Son—Michael.* Lucifer contended that the local systems should be autonomous. He protested against the right of Michael, the Creator Son, to assume sovereignty of Nebadon in the name of a hypothetical Paradise Father and require all personalities to acknowledge allegiance to this unseen Father. He asserted that the whole plan of worship was a clever scheme to aggrandize the Paradise Sons. He was willing to acknowledge Michael as his Creator-father but not as his God and rightful ruler.

3. *The attack upon the universal plan of ascendant mortal training.* Lucifer maintained that far too much time and energy were expended upon the scheme of so thoroughly training ascending mortals in the principles of universe administration, principles which he alleged were unethical and unsound. He protested against the agelong program for preparing the mortals of space for some unknown destiny and pointed to the presence of the finaliter corps on Jerusem as proof that these mortals had spent ages of preparation for some destiny of pure fiction.

And it was with such a Declaration of Liberty that Lucifer launched his orgy of darkness and death.   The Lucifer Rebellion 603:2-4, 604:1,2

But this war in heaven was very terrible and very real. While displaying none of the barbarities so characteristic of physical warfare on the immature worlds, this conflict was far more deadly; material life is in jeopardy in material combat, but the war in heaven was fought in terms of life eternal.

The Lucifer Rebellion 606:3

Shortly after Satan's inspection and when the planetary administration was on the eve of the realization of great things on Urantia, one day, midwinter of the northern continents, Caligastia held a prolonged conference with his associate, Daligastia, after which the latter called the ten councils of Urantia in session extraordinary. This assembly was opened with the statement that Prince Caligastia was about to proclaim himself absolute sovereign of Urantia.

Meantime the system circuits had been severed; Urantia was isolated. Every group of celestial life on the planet found itself suddenly and without warning isolated, utterly cut off from all outside counsel and advice.

The Planetary Rebellion 755:3,5

On first thought it might appear that Urantia and its associated isolated worlds are most unfortunate in being deprived of the beneficent presence and influence of such superhuman personalities as a Planetary Prince and a Material Son and Daughter. But isolation of these spheres affords their races a unique opportunity for the exercise of faith and for the development of a peculiar quality of confidence in cosmic reliability which is not dependent on sight or any other material consideration. It may turn out, eventually, that mortal creatures hailing from the worlds quarantined in consequence of rebellion are extremely fortunate. We have discovered that such ascenders are very early intrusted with numerous special assignments to cosmic undertakings where unquestioned faith and sublime confidence are essential to achievement.

The Planetary Princes 578:6

The bestowal of Michael terminated the Lucifer rebellion in all Satania aside from the planets of the apostate Planetary Princes. And this was the significance of Jesus' personal experience, just before his death in the flesh, when he one day exclaimed to his disciples, "And I beheld Satan fall as lightning from heaven." He had come with Lucifer to Urantia for the last crucial struggle.   The Lucifer Rebellion 609:6

2. Adam and Eve

When human beings reached the limit of evolutionary development, the Life Carriers signaled Jerusem to dispatch to this world a Material Son and Daughter: Adam and Eve. The chief business of this imported pair was to multiply, spread out, and uplift the evolutionary races. More specifically, Adam and Eve were to build up a violet race of about 1 million people before integrating with the native evolutionary mortals of earth.

This outpouring of imported ability was to generate a succession of rapid strides in civilization. As a result more progress was to be made in 100,000 years than in previous million years of struggle.

Like Caligastia, Adam and Eve defaulted in their mission. Succumbing to impatience, they unintentionally assisted Lucifer in a nefarious scheme to lead humanity further into chaos and confusion. The earth has yet to recover.

A Planetary Adam and Eve are, in potential, the full gift of physical grace to the mortal races. The chief business of such an imported pair is to multiply and to uplift the children of time. But there is no immediate inter-breeding between the people of the garden and those of the world; for many generations Adam and Eve remain biologically segregated from the evolutionary mortals while they build up a strong race of their order. This is the origin of the violet race on the inhabited worlds.

The Planetary Princes 583:2

The result of the gift of the Adamic life plasm to the mortal races is an immediate upstepping of intellectual capacity and an acceleration of spiritual progress. There is usually some physical improvement also. On an average world the post-Adamic dispensation is an age of great invention, energy control, and mechanical development. This is the era of the appearance of multiform manufacture and the control of natural forces; it is the golden age of exploration and the final subduing of the planet. Much of the material progress of a world occurs during this time of the inauguration of the development of the physical sciences, just such an epoch as Urantia is now experiencing. Your world is a full dispensation and more behind the average planetary schedule.

By the end of the Adamic dispensation on a normal planet the races are practically blended, so that it can be truly proclaimed that "God has made of one blood all the nations," and that his Son "has made of one color all peoples."   Planetary Mortal Epochs 593:5,6

The committee on location was absent for almost three years. It reported favorably concerning three possible locations: The first was an island in the Persian Gulf; the second, the river location subsequently occupied as the second garden; the third, a long narrow peninsula—almost an island—projecting westward from the eastern shores of the Mediterranean Sea.

The committee almost unanimously favored the third selection. This site was chosen, and two years were occupied in transferring the world's cultural headquarters, including the tree of life, to this Mediterranean peninsula. All but a single group of the peninsula dwellers peaceably vacated when Van and his company arrived.

The site chosen for the Garden was probably the most beautiful spot of its kind in all the world, and the climate was then ideal. Nowhere else was there a location which could have lent itself so perfectly to becoming such a paradise of botanic expression. In this rendezvous the cream of the civilization of Urantia was forgathering. Without and beyond, the world lay in darkness, ignorance, and savagery. Eden was the one bright spot on Urantia; it was naturally a dream of loveliness, and it soon became a poem of exquisite and perfected landscape glory.   The Garden of Eden 823:1,2,6

The first task was the building of the brick wall across the neck of the peninsula. This once completed, the real work of landscape beautification and home building could proceed unhindered.

A zoological garden was created by building a smaller wall just outside the main wall; the intervening space, occupied by all manner of wild beasts, served as an additional defense against hostile attacks.

At the time of Adam's arrival, though the Garden was only one-fourth finished, it had thousands of miles of irrigation ditches and more than twelve thousand miles of paved paths and roads. There were a trifle over five thousand brick buildings in the various sectors, and the trees and plants were almost beyond number.   The Garden of Eden 824:1,2,6

In the center of the Garden temple Van planted the long-guarded tree of life, whose leaves were for the "healing of the nations," and whose fruit had so long sustained him on earth. Van well knew that Adam and Eve would also be dependent on this gift of Edentia for their life maintenance after they once appeared on Urantia in material form.

The "tree of the knowledge of good and evil" may be a figure of speech, a symbolic designation covering a multitude of human experiences, but the "tree of life" was not a myth; it was real and for a long time was present on Urantia.

This superplant stored up certain space-energies which were antidotal to the age-producing elements of animal existence. The fruit of the tree of life was like a superchemical storage battery, mysteriously releasing the life-extension force of the universe when eaten. This form of sustenance was wholly useless to the ordinary evolutionary beings on Urantia
The Garden of Eden 825:6,8, 826:1

Adam and Eve arrived on Urantia, from the year A.D. 1934, 37,848 years ago. It was in midseason when the Garden was in the height of bloom that they arrived.
Adam and Eve 828:1

And now, after their formal installation, Adam and Eve became painfully aware of their planetary isolation. Silent were the familiar broadcasts, and absent were all the circuits of extraplanetary communication. Their Jerusem fellows had gone to worlds running along smoothly with a well-established Planetary Prince and an experienced staff ready to receive them and competent to co-operate with them during their early experience on such worlds. But on Urantia rebellion had changed everything. Here the Planetary Prince was very much present, and though shorn of most of his power to work evil, he was still able to make the task of Adam and Eve difficult and to some extent hazardous. It was a serious and disillusioned Son and Daughter of Jerusem who walked that night through the Garden under the shining of the full moon, discussing plans for the next day.
Adam and Eve 830:4

The third day was devoted to an inspection of the Garden. From the large passenger birds—the fandors—Adam and Eve looked down upon the vast stretches of the Garden while being carried through the air over this, the most beautiful spot on earth. This day of inspection ended with an enormous banquet in honor of all who had labored to create this garden of Edenic beauty and grandeur. And again, late into the night of their third day, the Son and his mate walked in the Garden and talked about the immensity of their problems.

The sixth day was devoted to an inspection of the numerous types of men and animals. Along the walls eastward in Eden, Adam and Eve were escorted all day, viewing the animal life of the planet and arriving at a better understanding as to what must be done to bring order out of the confusion of a world inhabited by such a variety of living creatures.

It greatly surprised those who accompanied Adam on this trip to observe how fully he understood the nature and function of the thousands upon thousands of animals shown him. The instant he glanced at an animal, he would indicate its nature and behavior. Adam could give names descriptive of the origin, nature, and function of all material creatures on sight. Those who conducted him on this tour of inspection did not know that the world's new ruler was one of the most expert anatomists of all Satania; and Eve was equally proficient. Adam amazed his associates by describing hosts of living things too small to be seen by human eyes.

Adam and Eve 831:1,4,5

It was early on the morning of this seventh day and from the mount of their so recent reception that Adam held forth in explanation of the orders of divine sonship and made clear to these earth minds that only the Father and those whom he designates may be worshipped. Adam made it plain that he would accept any honor and receive all respect, but worship never!

Adam and Eve 832:4

Adam made a heroic and determined effort to establish a world government, but he met with stubborn resistance at every turn. Adam had already put in operation a system of group control throughout Eden and had federated all of these companies into the Edenic league. But trouble, serious trouble, ensued when he went outside the Garden and sought to apply these ideas to the outlying tribes. The moment Adam's associates began to work outside the Garden, they met the direct and well-planned resistance of Caligastia and Daligastia. The fallen Prince had been deposed as world ruler, but he had not been removed from the planet. He was still present on earth and able, at least to some extent, to resist all of Adam's plans for the rehabilitation of human society. Adam tried to warn the races against Caligastia, but the task was made very difficult because his archenemy was invisible to the eyes of mortals.   Adam and Eve 833:5

Adamson was the first-born of the violet race of Urantia, being followed by his sister and Eveson, the second son of Adam and Eve. Eve was the mother of five children before the Melchizedeks left—three sons and two daughters. The next two were twins. She bore sixty-three children, thirty-two daughters and thirty-one sons, before the default. When Adam and Eve left the Garden, their family consisted of four generations numbering 1,647 pure-line descendants. They had forty-two children after leaving the Garden besides the two offspring of joint parentage with the mortal stock of earth. And this does not include the Adamic parentage to the Nodite and evolutionary races.

The bodies of Adam and Eve gave forth a shimmer of light, but they always wore clothing in conformity with the custom of their associates. Though wearing very little during the day, at eventide they donned night wraps. The origin of the traditional halo encircling the heads of supposed pious and holy men dates back to the days of Adam and Eve. Since the light emanations of their bodies were so largely obscured by clothing, only the radiating glow from their heads was discernible.

Adam and Eve could communicate with each other and with their immediate children over a distance of about fifty miles. This thought exchange was effected by means of the delicate gas chambers located in close proximity to their brain.   Adam and Eve 834:4,7,8

After more than one hundred years of effort on Urantia, Adam was able to see very little progress outside the Garden; the world at large did not seem to be improving much. The realization of race betterment appeared to be a long way off, and the situation seemed so desperate as to demand something for relief not embraced in the original plans. At least that is what often passed through Adam's mind, and he so expressed himself many times to Eve. Adam and his mate were loyal, but they were isolated from their kind, and they were sorely distressed by the sorry plight of their world.

Under normal conditions the first work of a Planetary Adam and Eve would be the co-ordination and blending of the races. But on Urantia such a project seemed just about hopeless, for the races, while biologically fit, had never been purged of their retarded and defective strains.

The Default of Adam and Eve 839:1,3

Le printemps ou Le paradis terrestre;
Nicholas Poussin(1518-1594),
© Louvre , Paris

Adam had just finished his first one hundred years on earth when Serapatatia, upon the death of his father, came to the leadership of the western or Syrian confederation of the Nodite tribes. Serapatatia was a brown-tinted man, a brilliant descendant of the onetime chief of the Dalamatia commission on health mated with one of the master female minds of the blue race of those distant days. All down through the ages this line had held authority and wielded a great influence among the western Nodite tribes.

Presently, Serapatatia became the associate chairman of the Edenic commission on tribal relations, and many plans were laid for the more vigorous prosecution of the work of winning the remote tribes to the cause of the Garden.

He held many conferences with Adam and Eve—especially with Eve—and they talked over many plans for improving their methods. One day, during a talk with Eve, it occurred to Serapatatia that it would be very helpful if, while awaiting the recruiting of large numbers of the violet race, something could be done in the meantime immediately to advance the needy waiting tribes. Serapatatia contended that, if the Nodites, as the most progressive and co-operative race, could have a leader born to them of part origin in the violet stock, it would constitute a powerful tie binding these peoples more closely to the Garden. And all of this was soberly and honestly considered to be for the good of the world since this child, to be reared and educated in the Garden, would exert a great influence for good over his father's people.

It should again be emphasized that Serapatatia was altogether honest and wholly sincere in all that he proposed. He never once suspected that he was playing into the hands of Caligastia and Daligastia. Serapatatia was entirely loyal to the plan of building up a strong reserve of the violet race before attempting the world-wide upstepping of the confused peoples of Urantia. But this would require hundreds of years to consummate, and he was impatient; he wanted to see some immediate results—something in his own lifetime. He made it clear to Eve that Adam was oftentimes discouraged by the little that had been accomplished toward uplifting the world.

For more than five years these plans were secretly matured. At last they had developed to the point where Eve consented to have a secret conference with Cano, the most brilliant mind and active leader of the near-by colony of friendly Nodites. Cano was very sympathetic with the Adamic regime; in fact, he was the sincere spiritual leader of those neighboring Nodites who favored friendly relations with the Garden.

The fateful meeting occurred during the twilight hours of the autumn evening, not far from the home of Adam. Eve had never before met the beautiful and enthusiastic Cano—and he was a magnificent specimen of the survival of the superior physique and outstanding intellect of his remote progenitors of the Prince's staff. And Cano also thoroughly believed in the righteousness of the Serapatatia project. (Outside of the Garden, multiple mating was a common practice.)

Influenced by flattery, enthusiasm, and great personal persuasion, Eve then and there consented to embark upon the much-discussed enterprise, to add her own little scheme of world saving to the larger and more far-reaching divine plan. Before she quite realized what was transpiring, the fatal step had been taken. It was done.

The celestial life of the planet was astir. Adam recognized that something was wrong, and he asked Eve to come aside with him in the Garden. And now, for the first time, Adam heard the entire story of the long-nourished plan for accelerating world improvement by operating simultaneously in two directions: the prosecution of the divine plan concomitantly with the execution of the Serapatatia enterprise.

And as the Material Son and Daughter thus communed in the moonlit Garden, "the voice in the Garden" reproved them for disobedience. And that voice was none other than my own announcement to the Edenic pair that they had transgressed the Garden covenant; that they had disobeyed the instructions of the Melchizedeks; that they had defaulted in the execution of their oaths of trust to the sovereign of the universe.

The Default of Adam and Eve 841:1,4-7, 842:2-4

Eve's disillusionment was truly pathetic. Adam discerned the whole predicament and, while heartbroken and dejected, entertained only pity and sympathy for his erring mate.

It was in the despair of the realization of failure that Adam, the day after Eve's misstep, sought out Laotta, the brilliant Nodite woman who was head of the western schools of the Garden, and with premeditation committed the folly of Eve. But do not misunderstand; Adam was not beguiled; he knew exactly what he was about; he deliberately chose to share the fate of Eve. He loved his mate with a supermortal affection, and the thought of the possibility of a lonely vigil on Urantia without her was more than he could endure.

When they learned what had happened to Eve, the infuriated inhabitants of the Garden became unmanageable; they declared war on the near-by Nodite settlement. They swept out through the gates of Eden and down upon these unprepared people, utterly destroying them—not a man, woman, or child was spared. And Cano, the father of Cain yet unborn, also perished. The Default of Adam and Eve 843:3-5

Time passed, but Adam was not certain of the nature of their offense until seventy days after the default of Eve, when the Melchizedek receivers returned to Urantia and assumed jurisdiction over world affairs. And then he knew they had failed.

But still more trouble was brewing: The news of the annihilation of the Nodite settlement near Eden was not slow in reaching the home tribes of Serapatatia to the north, and presently a great host was assembling to march on the Garden. And this was the beginning of a long and bitter warfare between the Adamites and the Nodites, for these hostilities kept up long after Adam and his followers emigrated to the second garden in the Euphrates valley. There was intense and lasting "enmity between that man and the woman, between his seed and her seed." The Default of Adam and Eve 844:1,2

It was while the Edenic caravan was halted that Adam and Eve were informed of the nature of their transgressions and advised concerning their fate. Gabriel appeared to pronounce judgment. And this was the verdict: The Planetary Adam and Eve of Urantia are adjudged in default; they have violated the covenant of their trusteeship as the rulers of this inhabited world.

While downcast by the sense of guilt, Adam and Eve were greatly cheered by the announcement that their judges on Salvington had absolved them from all charges of standing in "contempt of the universe government." They had not been held guilty of rebellion.

The Edenic pair were informed that they had degraded themselves to the status of the mortals of the realm; that they must henceforth conduct themselves as man and woman of Urantia, looking to the future of the world races for their future.

Caligastia did succeed in trapping Adam and Eve, but he did not accomplish his purpose of leading them into open rebellion against the universe government. What they had done was indeed evil, but they were never guilty of contempt for truth, neither did they knowingly enlist in rebellion against the righteous rule of the Universal Father and his Creator Son.   The Default of Adam and Eve 845:1-3,7

There has been no "fall of man." The history of the human race is one of progressive evolution, and the Adamic bestowal left the world peoples greatly improved over their previous biologic condition. The more superior stocks of Urantia now contain inheritance factors derived from as many as four separate sources: Andonite, Sangik, Nodite, and Adamic.

Adam should not be regarded as the cause of a curse on the human race. While he did fail in carrying forward the divine plan, while he did transgress his covenant with Deity, while he and his mate were most certainly degraded in creature status, notwithstanding all this, their contribution to the human race did much to advance civilization on Urantia.

Never, in all your ascent to Paradise, will you gain anything by impatiently attempting to circumvent the established and divine plan by short cuts, personal inventions, or other devices for improving on the way of perfection, to perfection, and for eternal perfection.

All in all, there probably never was a more disheartening miscarriage of wisdom on any planet in all Nebadon. But it is not surprising that these missteps occur in the affairs of the evolutionary universes. We are a part of a gigantic creation, and it is not strange that everything does not work in perfection; our universe was not created in perfection. Perfection is our eternal goal, not our origin.   The Default of Adam and Eve 845:1,2,4,5

Adam lived for 530 years; he died of what might be termed old age. His physical mechanism simply wore out; the process of disintegration gradually gained on the process of repair, and the inevitable end came. Eve had died nineteen years previously of a weakened heart. They were both buried in the center of the temple of divine service which had been built in accordance with their plans soon after the wall of the colony had been completed. And this was the origin of the practice of burying noted and pious men and women under the floors of the places of worship.

The supermaterial government of Urantia, under the direction of the Melchizedeks, continued, but direct physical contact with the evolutionary races had been severed. From the distant days of the arrival of the corporeal staff of the Planetary Prince, down through the times of Van and Amadon to the arrival of Adam and Eve, physical representatives of the universe government had been stationed on the planet. But with the Adamic default this regime, extending over a period of more than four hundred and fifty thousand years, came to an end.   The Second Garden 852:4,5

And thus ends the story of the Planetary Adam and Eve of Urantia, a story of trial, tragedy, and triumph, at least personal triumph for your well-meaning but deluded Material Son and Daughter and undoubtedly, in the end, a story of ultimate triumph for their world and its rebellion-tossed and evil-harassed inhabitants. When all is summed up, Adam and Eve made a mighty contribution to the speedy civilization and accelerated biologic progress of the human race. They left a great culture on earth, but it was not possible for such an advanced civilization to survive in the face of the early dilution and the eventual submergence of the Adamic inheritance. It is the people who make a civilization; civilization does not make the people.
[Presented by Solonia, the seraphic "voice in the Garden."]
The Second Garden 854:1,2

3. Melchizedek and Abraham

Melchizedek came to earth approximately 4,000 years ago to keep the fast-disappearing concept of "one God" alive. Working with Abraham, he established the Salem missionaries to fulfill the objective. Later, his followers wrote many of the Old Testament Psalms. In short, Melchizedek laid the groundwork for the eventual appearance of Jesus.

The Melchizedeks are the first order of divine Sons to approach sufficiently near the lower creature life to be able to function directly in the ministry of mortal uplift, to serve the evolutionary races without the necessity of incarnation. These Sons are naturally at the mid-point of the great personality descent, by origin being just about midway between the highest Divinity and the lowest creature life of will endowment.
Local Universe Sons of God 385:4

The Melchizedeks are the first to act in all emergencies of whatever nature on all worlds where will creatures dwell. They sometimes act as temporary custodians on wayward planets, serving as receivers of a defaulting planetary government. In a planetary crisis these Melchizedek Sons serve in many unique capacities. It is easily possible for such a Son to make himself visible to mortal beings, and sometimes one of this order has even incarnated in the likeness of mortal flesh.

The Melchizedek who lived on Urantia during the time of Abraham was locally known as Prince of Salem because he presided over a small colony of truth seekers residing at a place called Salem. He volunteered to incarnate in the likeness of mortal flesh and did so with the approval of the Melchizedek receivers of the planet, who feared that the light of life would become extinguished during that period of increasing spiritual darkness. And he did foster the truth of his day and safely pass it on to Abraham and his associates.   Local Universe Sons of God 389:3,4

It was 1,973 years before the birth of Jesus that Machiventa was bestowed upon the human races of Urantia. His coming was unspectacular; his materialization was not witnessed by human eyes. He was first observed by mortal man on that eventful day when he entered the tent of Amdon, a Chaldean herder of Sumerian extraction. And the proclamation of his mission was embodied in the simple statement which he made to this shepherd, "I am Melchizedek, priest of El Elyon, the Most High, the one and only God."

Within a few years Melchizedek had gathered around himself a group of pupils, disciples, and believers who formed the nucleus of the later community of Salem. He was soon known throughout Palestine as the priest of El Elyon, the Most High, and as the sage of Salem. Among some of the surrounding tribes he was often referred to as the sheik, or king, of Salem. Salem was the site which after the disappearance of Melchizedek became the city of Jebus, subsequently being called Jerusalem.

Machiventa Melchizedek 1015:1,4

Like Jesus, Melchizedek attended strictly to the fulfillment of the mission of his bestowal. He did not attempt to reform the mores, to change the habits of the world, nor to promulgate even advanced sanitary practices or scientific truths. He came to achieve two tasks: to keep alive on earth the truth of the one God and to prepare the way for the subsequent mortal bestowal of a Paradise Son of that Universal Father.

The Meeting of Abraham and Melchizedek; Peter Paul Rubens
(1625) © National Gallery of Art, Washington

Melchizedek taught elementary revealed truth at Salem for ninety-four years, and during this time Abraham attended the Salem school three different times. He finally became a convert to the Salem teachings, becoming one of Melchizedek's most brilliant pupils and chief supporters.

Machiventa Melchizedek 1018:4,5

The teaching of Melchizedek was full and replete, but the records of these days seemed impossible and fantastic to the later Hebrew priests, although many had some understanding of these transactions, at least up to the times of the en masse editing of the Old Testament records in Babylon.

What the Old Testament records describe as conversations between Abraham and God were in reality conferences between Abraham and Melchizedek. Later scribes regarded the term Melchizedek as synonymous with God. The record of so many contacts of Abraham and Sarah with "the angel of the Lord" refers to their numerous visits with Melchizedek.

But one of the writers of the Book of Hebrews understood the mission of Melchizedek, for it is written: "This Melchizedek, priest of the Most High, was also king of peace; without father, without mother, without pedigree, having neither beginning of days nor end of life but made like a Son of God, he abides a priest continually."

Machiventa Melchizedek 1023:3,4 1024,2

The last stand of the dwindling band of Salem believers was made by an earnest group of preachers, the Cynics, who exhorted the Romans to abandon their wild and senseless religious rituals and return to a form of worship embodying Melchizedek's gospel as it had been modified and contaminated through contact with the philosophy of the Greeks. But the people at large rejected the Cynics; they preferred to plunge into the rituals of the mysteries, which not only offered hopes of personal salvation but also gratified the desire for diversion, excitement, and entertainment.

Melchizedek Teachings in the Occident 1081:3

And this is the long story of the teachings of Machiventa Melchizedek on Urantia. It is nearly four thousand years since this emergency Son of Nebadon bestowed himself on Urantia, and in that time the teachings of the "priest of El Elyon, the Most High God," have penetrated to all races and peoples. And Machiventa was successful in achieving the purpose of his unusual bestowal; when Michael made ready to appear on Urantia, the God concept was existent in the hearts of men and women, the same God concept that still flames anew in the living spiritual experience of the manifold children of the Universal Father as they live their intriguing temporal lives on the whirling planets of space.

Melchizedek Teachings in the Occident 1085:1,2

4. Origin of the Old Testament

The best teachings in the Old Testament reflect the influence of Melchizedek. As a result of his teachings, Yahweh—the fearsome, wrathful God of the Hebrews—evolves into a loving deity. The inspiration of the Melchizedek is best given expression in the Psalms which exhibit a wealth of devotional praise to God.

The real revolutionary of the Old Testament is Isaiah. This prophet demolished the idea of a national God and proclaimed him the supreme and universal Creator of the heavens.

Because of the influence of Melchizedek and the work of Isaiah, the Old Testament transformed from a political document affirming the Hebrews as the "Chosen People" to a revelation of the Universal God to all peoples.

The destruction of the Hebrew nation and their captivity in Mesopotamia would have proved of great benefit to their expanding theology had it not been for the determined action of their priesthood. Their nation had fallen before the armies of Babylon, and their nationalistic Yahweh had suffered from the international preachments of the spiritual leaders. It was resentment of the loss of their national god that led the Jewish priests to go to such lengths in the invention of fables and the multiplication of miraculous appearing events in Hebrew history in an effort to restore the Jews as the chosen people of even the new and expanded idea of an internationalized God of all nations.

These Hebrew priests and scribes had a single idea in their minds, and that was the rehabilitation of the Jewish nation, the glorification of Hebrew traditions, and the exaltation of their racial history. If there is resentment of the fact that these priests have fastened their erroneous ideas upon such a large part of the Occidental world, it should be remembered that they did not intentionally do this; they did not claim to be writing by inspiration; they made no profession to be writing a sacred book. They were merely preparing a textbook designed to bolster up the dwindling courage of their fellows in captivity. They were definitely aiming at improving the national spirit and morale of their compatriots. It remained for later-day men to assemble these and other writings into a guide book of supposedly infallible teachings. Evolution of the God Concept 1068:1,3

The custom of looking upon the record of the experiences of the Hebrews as sacred history and upon the transactions of the rest of the world as profane history is responsible for much of the confusion existing in the human mind as to the interpretation of history. And this difficulty arises because there is no secular history of the Jews. After the priests of the Babylonian exile had prepared their new record of God's supposedly miraculous dealings with the Hebrews, the sacred history of Israel as portrayed in the Old Testament, they carefully and completely destroyed the existing records of Hebrew affairs—such books as "The Doings of the Kings of Israel" and "The Doings of the Kings of Judah," together with several other more or less accurate records of Hebrew history.

Evolution of the God Concept 1070:4

The difference between sacred and profane history is well illustrated by the two differing stories concerning making David king as they are found in the Old Testament. A part of the secular story of how his immediate followers (his army) made him king was inadvertently left in the record by the priests who subsequently prepared the lengthy and prosaic account of the sacred history wherein is depicted how the prophet Samuel, by divine direction, selected David from among his brethren and proceeded formally and by elaborate and solemn ceremonies to anoint him king over the Hebrews and then to proclaim him Saul's successor.

So many times did the priests, after preparing their fictitious narratives of God's miraculous dealings with Israel, fail fully to delete the plain and matter-of-fact statements which already rested in the records.

Evolution of the God Concept 1072:6,7

New life appeared as Jehoash and his son Jeroboam delivered Israel from its enemies. But by this time there ruled in Samaria a gangster-nobility whose depredations rivaled those of the Davidic dynasty of olden days. State and church went along hand in hand. The attempt to suppress freedom of speech led Elijah, Amos, and Hosea to begin their secret writing, and this was the real beginning of the Jewish and Christian Bibles.

Evolution of the God Concept 1074:2

Creation

In his early teachings, Moses very wisely did not attempt to go back of Adam's time, and since Moses was the supreme teacher of the Hebrews, the stories of Adam became intimately associated with those of creation. That the earlier traditions recognized pre-Adamic civilization is clearly shown by the fact that later editors, intending to eradicate all reference to human affairs before Adam's time, neglected to remove the telltale reference to Cain's emigration to the "land of Nod," where he took himself a wife.   Adam and Eve 837:7

The Hebrews had no written language in general usage for a long time after they reached Palestine. They learned the use of an alphabet from the neighboring Philistines, who were political refugees from the higher civilization of Crete. The Hebrews did little writing until about 900 B.C., and having no written language until such a late date, they had several different stories of creation in circulation, but after the Babylonian captivity they inclined more toward accepting a modified Mesopotamian version.

Jewish tradition became crystallized about Moses, and because he endeavored to trace the lineage of Abraham back to Adam, the Jews assumed that Adam was the first of all mankind. Yahweh was the creator, and since Adam was supposed to be the first man, he must have made the world just prior to making Adam. And then the tradition of Adam's six days got woven into the story, with the result that almost a thousand years after Moses' sojourn on earth the tradition of creation in six days was written out and subsequently credited to him. When the Jewish priests returned to Jerusalem, they had already completed the writing of their narrative of the beginning of things. Soon they made claims that this recital was a recently discovered story of creation written by Moses. But the contemporary Hebrews of around 500 B.C. did not consider these writings to be divine revelations; they looked upon them much as later peoples regard mythological narratives.   Adam and Eve 838:1-3

Noah and the Flood

Almost five thousand years later, as the Hebrew priests in Babylonian captivity sought to trace the Jewish people back to Adam, they found great difficulty in piecing the story together; and it occurred to one of them to abandon the effort, to let the whole world drown in its wickedness at the time of Noah's flood, and thus to be in a better position to trace Abraham right back to one of the three surviving sons of Noah.

The traditions of a time when water covered the whole of the earth's surface are universal. Many races harbor the story of a world-wide flood some time during past ages. The Biblical story of Noah, the ark, and the flood is an invention of the Hebrew priesthood during the Babylonian captivity. There has never been a universal flood since life was established on Urantia. The only time the surface of the earth was completely covered by water was during those Archeozoic ages before the land had begun to appear.

But Noah really lived; he was a wine maker of Aram, a river settlement near Erech. He kept a written record of the days of the river's rise from year to year. He brought much ridicule upon himself by going up and down the river valley advocating that all houses be built of wood, boat fashion, and that the family animals be put on board each night as the flood season approached. He would go to the neighboring river settlements every year and warn them that in so many days the floods would come. Finally a year came in which the annual floods were greatly augmented by unusually heavy rainfall so that the sudden rise of the waters wiped out the entire village; only Noah and his immediate family were saved in their houseboat.   Violet Race After Adam 874:8 875:1,2

Psalms

The Psalmist knew that Edentia was ruled by three Constellation Fathers and accordingly spoke of their abode in the plural: "There is a river, the streams whereof shall make glad the city of God, the most holy place of the tabernacles of the Most Highs."   The Constellations 488:5

Centrally located in this magnificent garden is the worship shrine of the Most Highs. The Psalmist must have known something about these things, for he wrote: "Who shall ascend the hill of the Most Highs? Who shall stand in this holy place? He who has clean hands and a pure heart, who has not lifted up his soul to vanity nor sworn deceitfully." At this shrine the Most Highs, on every tenth day of relaxation, lead all Edentia in the worshipful contemplation of God the Supreme.   The Constellations 492:3

L'Hiver ou le Deluge;
Nicholas Poussin (1594-1665) ©
Louvre, Paris

It was the Salem missionaries of the period following the rejection of
their teaching who wrote many of the Old Testament Psalms, inscribing
them on stone, where later-day Hebrew priests found them during the
captivity and subsequently incorporated them among the collection of
hymns ascribed to Jewish authorship. These beautiful psalms from Babylon
were not written in the temples of Bel-Marduk; they were the work of the
descendants of the earlier Salem missionaries, and they are a striking contrast to the magical conglomerations of the Babylonian priests.

Melchizedek Teachings if the Levant 1043:5

The concept of judgment in the hereafter for the sins of one's life in the
flesh on earth was carried over into Hebrew theology from Egypt. The
word judgment appears only once in the entire Book of Hebrew Psalms,
and that particular psalm was written by an Egyptian.

Melchizedek Teachings if the Levant 1045:3

The teachings of Amenemope were slowly losing their hold on the Egyptian mind when, through the influence of an Egyptian Salemite physician,
a woman of the royal family espoused the Melchizedek teachings. This
woman prevailed upon her son, Ikhnaton, Pharaoh of Egypt, to accept
these doctrines of One God.

Since the disappearance of Melchizedek in the flesh, no human being
up to that time had possessed such an amazingly clear concept of the
revealed religion of Salem as Ikhnaton. In some respects this young Egyptian king is one of the most remarkable persons in human history. During
this time of increasing spiritual depression in Mesopotamia, he kept alive
the doctrine of El Elyon, the One God, in Egypt, thus maintaining the
philosophic monotheistic channel which was vital to the religious background of the then future bestowal of Michael.

Ikhnaton was wise enough to maintain the outward worship of Aton,
the sun-god, while he led his associates in the disguised worship of the
One God, creator of Aton and supreme Father of all. This young teacher-
king was a prolific writer, being author of the exposition entitled "The
One God," a book of thirty-one chapters, which the priests, when returned
to power, utterly destroyed. Ikhnaton also wrote one hundred and thirty-
seven hymns, twelve of which are now preserved in the Old Testament
Book of Psalms, credited to Hebrew authorship.

Melchizedek Teachings if the Levant 1047:1,2 1048:1

No collection of religious writings gives expression to such a wealth of devotion and inspirational ideas of God as the Book of Psalms. And it would be very helpful if, in the perusal of this wonderful collection of worshipful literature, consideration could be given to the source and chronology of each separate hymn of praise and adoration, bearing in mind that no other single collection covers such a great range of time. This Book of Psalms is the record of the varying concepts of God entertained by the believers of the Salem religion throughout the Levant and embraces the entire period from Amenemope to Isaiah. In the Psalms God is depicted in all phases of conception, from the crude idea of a tribal deity to the vastly expanded ideal of the later Hebrews, wherein Yahweh is pictured as a loving ruler and merciful Father.

Yahweh-God of the Hebrews 1060:3

Book of Job

The variegated picture of Deity presented in the Book of Job was the product of more than a score of Mesopotamian religious teachers extending over a period of almost three hundred years. And when you read the lofty concept of divinity found in this compilation of Mesopotamian beliefs, you will recognize that it was in the neighborhood of Ur of Chaldea that the idea of a real God was best preserved during the dark days in Palestine.

Only at Ur did a voice arise to cry out the mercy of God, saying: "He shall pray to God and shall find favor with him and shall see his face with joy, for God will give to man divine righteousness." Thus from Ur there is preached salvation, divine favor, by faith: "He is gracious to the repentant and says, `Deliver him from going down in the pit, for I have found a ransom.' If any say, `I have sinned and perverted that which was right, and it profited me not,' God will deliver his soul from going into the pit, and he shall see the light." Not since the times of Melchizedek had the Levantine world heard such a ringing and cheering message of human salvation as this extraordinary teaching of Elihu, the prophet of Ur and priest of the Salem believers, that is, the remnant of the onetime Melchizedek colony in Mesopotamia.

Yahweh-God of the Hebrews 1061:5,7

Isaiah II

No prophet or religious teacher from Machiventa to the time of Jesus attained the high concept of God that Isaiah the second proclaimed during

The Triumph of Job; Maerten van Heemskerck (1559),
© National Gallery of Art, Washington

these days of the captivity. It was no small, anthropomorphic, man-made God that this spiritual leader proclaimed. "Behold he takes up the isles as a very little thing." "And as the heavens are higher than the earth, so are my ways higher than your ways and my thoughts higher than your thoughts."   Evolution of the God Concept 1068:5

At last Machiventa Melchizedek beheld human teachers proclaiming a real God to mortal man. Like Isaiah the first, this leader preached a God of universal creation and upholding. "I have made the earth and put man upon it. I have created it not in vain; I formed it to be inhabited." "I am the first and the last; there is no God beside me." Speaking for the Lord God of Israel, this new prophet said: "The heavens may vanish and the earth wax old, but my righteousness shall endure forever and my salvation from generation to generation." "Fear you not, for I am with you; be not dismayed, for I am your God." "There is no God beside me—a just God and a Savior."

This Isaiah conducted a far-flung propaganda of the gospel of the enlarging concept of a supreme Yahweh. He vied with Moses in the eloquence with which he portrayed the Lord God of Israel as the Universal Creator. He was poetic in his portrayal of the infinite attributes of the Universal Father. No more beautiful pronouncements about the heavenly Father have ever been made. Like the Psalms, the writings of Isaiah are among the most sublime and true presentations of the spiritual concept of God ever to greet the ears of mortal man prior to the arrival of Michael on Urantia. Listen to his portrayal of Deity: "I am the high and lofty one who inhabits eternity." "I am the first and the last, and beside me there is no other God." "And the Lord's hand is not shortened that it cannot save, neither his ear heavy that it cannot hear." And it was a new doctrine in Jewry when this benign but commanding prophet persisted in the preachment of divine constancy, God's faithfulness. He declared that "God would not forget, would not forsake."

Hear this great Hebrew demolish the concept of a national God while in glory he proclaims the divinity of the Universal Father, of whom he says, "The heavens are my throne, and the earth is my footstool." And Isaiah's God was none the less holy, majestic, just, and unsearchable. The concept of the angry, vengeful, and jealous Yahweh of the desert Bedouins has almost vanished. A new concept of the supreme and universal Yahweh has appeared in the mind of mortal man, never to be lost to human view. The realization of divine justice has begun the destruction of primitive magic and biologic fear. At last, man is introduced to a universe of law and order and to a universal God of dependable and final attributes.

Evolution of the God Concept 1069:1,4,6

Jonah and the Whale

One day after the evening meal Jesus and the young Philistine strolled down by the sea, and Gadiah, not knowing that this "scribe of Damascus" was so well versed in the Hebrew traditions, pointed out to Jesus the ship landing from which it was reputed that Jonah had embarked on his ill-fated voyage to Tarshish. And when he had concluded his remarks, he asked Jesus this question: "But do you suppose the big fish really did swallow Jonah?" Jesus perceived that this young man's life had been tremendously influenced by this tradition, and that its contemplation had impressed upon him the folly of trying to run away from duty; Jesus therefore said nothing that would suddenly destroy the foundations of Gadiah's present motivation for practical living. In answering this question, Jesus said: "My friend, we are all Jonahs with lives to live in accordance with the will of God, and at all times when we seek to escape the present duty of living by running away to far-off enticements, we thereby put ourselves in the immediate control of those influences which are not directed by the powers of truth and the forces of righteousness. The flight from duty is the sacrifice of truth. The escape from the service of light and life can only result in those distressing conflicts with the difficult whales of selfishness which lead eventually to darkness and death unless such God-forsaking Jonahs shall turn their hearts, even when in the very depths of despair, to seek after God and his goodness. And when such disheartened souls sincerely seek for God—hunger for truth and thirst for righteousness—there is nothing that can hold them in further captivity. No matter into what great depths they may have fallen, when they seek the light with a whole heart, the spirit of the Lord God of heaven will deliver them from their captivity; the evil circumstances of life will spew them out upon the dry land of fresh opportunities for renewed service and wiser living."

On the Way to Rome 1428:2

Jesus Comments on the Old Testament

"Nathaniel, you have rightly judged; I do not regard the Scriptures as do the rabbis. I will talk with you about this matter on condition that you do not relate these things to your brethren, who are not all prepared to receive this teaching. The words of the law of Moses and the teachings of the Scriptures were not in existence before Abraham. Only in recent times have the Scriptures been gathered together as we now have them. While they contain the best of the higher thoughts and longings of the Jewish people, they also contain much that is far from being representative of the character and teachings of the Father in heaven; wherefore must I choose from among the better teachings those truths which are to be gleaned for the gospel of the kingdom.

"These writings are the work of men, some of them holy men, others not so holy. The teachings of these books represent the views and extent of enlightenment of the times in which they had their origin. As a revelation of truth, the last are more dependable than the first. The Scriptures are faulty and altogether human in origin, but mistake not, they do constitute the best collection of religious wisdom and spiritual truth to be found in all the world at this time.

"Many of these books were not written by the persons whose names they bear, but that in no way detracts from the value of the truths which they contain. If the story of Jonah should not be a fact, even if Jonah had never lived, still would the profound truth of this narrative, the love of God for Nineveh and the so-called heathen, be none the less precious in the eyes of all those who love their fellow men. The Scriptures are sacred because they present the thoughts and acts of men who were searching for God, and who in these writings left on record their highest concepts of righteousness, truth, and holiness. The Scriptures contain much that is true, very much, but in the light of your present teaching, you know that these writings also contain much that is misrepresentative of the Father in heaven, the loving God I have come to reveal to all the worlds.

The Decapolis Tour 1767:4-6

"Nathaniel, never permit yourself for one moment to believe the Scripture records which tell you that the God of love directed your forefathers to go forth in battle to slay all their enemies—men, women, and children. Such records are the words of men, not very holy men, and they are not the word of God. The Scriptures always have, and always will, reflect the intellectual, moral, and spiritual status of those who create them. Have you not noted that the concepts of Yahweh grow in beauty and glory as the prophets make their records from Samuel to Isaiah? And you should remember that the Scriptures are intended for religious instruction and spiritual guidance. They are not the works of either historians or philosophers.

"The thing most deplorable is not merely this erroneous idea of the absolute perfection of the Scripture record and the infallibility of its teachings, but rather the confusing misinterpretation of these sacred writings by the tradition-enslaved scribes and Pharisees at Jerusalem. And now will they employ both the doctrine of the inspiration of the Scriptures and their misinterpretations thereof in their determined effort to withstand these newer teachings of the gospel of the kingdom. Nathaniel, never forget, the Father does not limit the revelation of truth to any one generation or to any one people. Many earnest seekers after the truth have been, and will continue to be, confused and disheartened by these doctrines of the perfection of the Scriptures.

"The authority of truth is the very spirit that indwells its living manifestations, and not the dead words of the less illuminated and supposedly inspired men of another generation. And even if these holy men of old lived inspired and spirit-filled lives, that does not mean that their *words* were similarly spiritually inspired.

"Mark you well my words, Nathaniel, nothing which human nature has touched can be regarded as infallible. Through the mind of man divine truth may indeed shine forth, but always of relative purity and partial divinity. The creature may crave infallibility, but only the Creators possess it.

"But the greatest error of the teaching about the Scriptures is the doctrine of their being sealed books of mystery and wisdom which only the wise minds of the nation dare to interpret. The revelations of divine truth are not sealed except by human ignorance, bigotry, and narrow-minded intolerance. The light of the Scriptures is only dimmed by prejudice and darkened by superstition. A false fear of sacredness has prevented religion from being safeguarded by common sense. The fear of the authority of the sacred writings of the past effectively prevents the honest souls of today from accepting the new light of the gospel, the light which these very God-knowing men of another generation so intensely longed to see.

The Decapolis Tour 1768:1-5

5. Origin of the New Testament

The Urantia Book regards the first revelation of God as the lost teachings of Calagastia, and the second one Adam and Eve. The third revelation is Melchizedek, and as we learned in the previous section, some of his teachings are contained in the Old Testament. The fourth revelation of God is Jesus, the Creator Son. His words appear in the New Testament.

If you listen carefully while reading the New Testament, you can hear Mark presenting Jesus as a man among men; Luke describing of the Son of God as a friend of publicans and sinners; and John, the greatest of these writers, depicting the triumphant Jesus as he walked on earth in full consciousness of his divinity.

Christianity, while based on the New Testament, has not been widely accepted around the world. Most Asian and Middle Eastern countries, for instance, look upon it as a Western phenomenon. The reason is, perhaps, that Christianity has evolved into a somewhat institutionalized religion about Jesus' life, rather than a personal religion of his teachings.

These New Testament records had their origin in the following circumstances:

1. *The Gospel by Mark.* John Mark wrote the earliest (excepting the notes of Andrew), briefest, and most simple record of Jesus' life. He presented the Master as a minister, as man among men. Although Mark was a lad lingering about many of the scenes which he depicts, his record is in reality the Gospel according to Simon Peter. He was early associated with Peter; later with Paul. Mark wrote this record at the instigation of Peter and on the earnest petition of the church at Rome. Knowing how consistently the Master refused to write out his teachings when on earth and in the flesh, Mark, like the apostles and other leading disciples, was hesitant to put them in writing. But Peter felt the church at Rome required the assistance of such a written narrative, and Mark consented to undertake its preparation. He made many notes before Peter died in A.D. 67, and in accordance with the outline approved by Peter and for the church at Rome, he began his writing soon after Peter's death. The Gospel was completed near the end of A.D. 68. Mark wrote entirely from his own memory and Peter's memory.

2. *The Gospel of Matthew*. The so-called Gospel according to Matthew is the record of the Master's life which was written for the edification of Jewish Christians. The author of this record constantly seeks to show in Jesus' life that much which he did was that "it might be fulfilled which was spoken by the prophet." Matthew's Gospel portrays Jesus as a son of David, picturing him as showing great respect for the law and the prophets.

The Apostle Matthew did not write this Gospel. It was written by Isador, one of his disciples, who had as a help in his work not only Matthew's personal remembrance of these events but also a certain record which the latter had made of the sayings of Jesus directly after the crucifixion. This record by Matthew was written in Aramaic; Isador wrote in Greek. There was no intent to deceive in accrediting the production to Matthew. It was the custom in those days for pupils thus to honor their teachers.

Times of the Bestowal 1341:3-6

3. *The Gospel by Luke*. Luke, the physician of Antioch in Pisidia, was a gentile convert of Paul, and he wrote quite a different story of the Master's life. He began to follow Paul and learn of the life and teachings of Jesus in A.D. 47. Luke preserves much of the "grace of the Lord Jesus Christ" in his record as he gathered up these facts from Paul and others. Luke presents the Master as "the friend of publicans and sinners." He did not formulate his many notes into the Gospel until after Paul's death. Luke wrote in the year 82 in Achaia. He planned three books dealing with the history of Christ and Christianity but died in A.D. 90 just before he finished the second of these works, the "Acts of the Apostles."

As material for the compilation of his Gospel, Luke first depended upon the story of Jesus' life as Paul had related it to him. Luke's Gospel is, therefore, in some ways the Gospel according to Paul. But Luke had other sources of information. He not only interviewed scores of eyewitnesses to the numerous episodes of Jesus' life which he records, but he also had with him a copy of Mark's Gospel, that is, the first four fifths, Isador's narrative, and a brief record made in the year A.D. 78 at Antioch by a believer named Cedes. Luke also had a mutilated and much-edited copy of some notes purported to have been made by the Apostle Andrew.

4. *The Gospel of John*. The Gospel according to John relates much of Jesus' work in Judea and around Jerusalem which is not contained in the other records. This is the so-called Gospel according to John the son of

Zebedee, and though John did not write it, he did inspire it. Since its first writing it has several times been edited to make it appear to have been written by John himself. When this record was made, John had the other

St. John the Evangelist on Patmos; by Titian (1547)
© National Gallery of Art, Washington

Gospels, and he saw that much had been omitted; accordingly, in the year A.D. 101 he encouraged his associate, Nathan, a Greek Jew from Caesarea, to begin the writing. John supplied his material from memory and by reference to the three records already in existence. He had no written records of his own. The Epistle known as "First John" was written by John himself as a covering letter for the work which Nathan executed under his direction.

All these writers presented honest pictures of Jesus as they saw, remembered, or had learned of him, and as their concepts of these distant events were affected by their subsequent espousal of Paul's theology of Christianity. And these records, imperfect as they are, have been sufficient to change the course of the history of Urantia for almost two thousand years.   Times of the Bestowal 1342:3-6

When in temporary exile on Patmos, John wrote the Book of Revelation, which you now have in greatly abridged and distorted form. This Book of Revelation contains the surviving fragments of a great revelation, large portions of which were lost, other portions of which were removed, subsequent to John's writing. It is preserved in only fragmentary and adulterated form.   The Twelve Apostles 1555:7

John the Revelator saw a vision of the arrival of a class of advancing mortals from the seventh mansion world to their first heaven, the glories of Jerusem. He recorded: "And I saw as it were a sea of glass mingled with fire; and those who had gained the victory over the beast that was originally in them and over the image that persisted through the mansion worlds and finally over the last mark and trace, standing on the sea of glass, having the harps of God, and singing the song of deliverance from mortal fear and death."   Seven Mansion Worlds 539:4

Some day a reformation in the Christian church may strike deep enough to get back to the unadulterated religious teachings of Jesus, the author and finisher of our faith. You may *preach* a religion *about* Jesus, but, perforce, you must *live* the religion *of* Jesus. In the enthusiasm of Pentecost, Peter unintentionally inaugurated a new religion, the religion of the risen and glorified Christ. The Apostle Paul later on transformed this new gospel into Christianity, a religion embodying his own theologic views and portraying his own *personal experience* with the Jesus of the Damascus road. The gospel of the kingdom is founded on the personal religious experience of the Jesus of Galilee; Christianity is founded almost exclusively on the personal religious experience of the Apostle Paul. Almost the whole of the New Testament is devoted, not to the portrayal of the significant and inspiring religious life of Jesus, but to a discussion of Paul's religious experience and to a portrayal of his personal religious convictions. The only notable exceptions to this statement, aside from certain parts of Matthew, Mark, and Luke, are the Book of Hebrews and the Epistle of James. Even Peter, in his writing, only once reverted to the personal religious life of his Master. The New Testament is a superb Christian document, but it is only meagerly Jesusonian.

The Faith of Jesus 2091:10

Mark, Matthew, and Luke retain something of the picture of the human Jesus as he engaged in the superb struggle to ascertain the divine will and to do that will. John presents a picture of the triumphant Jesus as he walked on earth in the full consciousness of divinity. The great mistake that has been made by those who have studied the Master's life is that some have conceived of him as entirely human, while others have thought of him as only divine. Throughout his entire experience he was truly both human and divine, even as he yet is.

At the time of the writing of the New Testament, the authors not only most profoundly believed in the divinity of the risen Christ, but they also devotedly and sincerely believed in his immediate return to earth to consummate the heavenly kingdom. This strong faith in the Lord's immediate return had much to do with the tendency to omit from the record those references which portrayed the purely human experiences and attributes of the Master. The whole Christian movement tended away from the human picture of Jesus of Nazareth toward the exaltation of the risen Christ, the glorified and soon-returning Lord Jesus Christ.

The Faith of Jesus 2092:1,3

~ IV ~

Family

1. Family: The Foundation of Civilization

The family is called the foundation of civilization because humanity's highest values are passed on from parent to child in the course of their day-to-day interactions. A good family reveals to the parents the attitude of the Creator toward his children, while revealing to the children the love of the Paradise Father in heaven.

The concept of God the Father is the highest human concept of divinity. The life of the Father is in his Son—the Creator Son Jesus of Nazareth. The spirit of the Father is in his Son's sons; mortal men.

Almost everything of lasting value in civilization has its roots in the family. The family was the first successful peace group, the man and woman learning how to adjust their antagonisms while at the same time teaching the pursuits of peace to their children.   Dawn of Civilization 765:5

Character of torchbearers. Social inheritance enables man to stand on the shoulders of all who have preceded him, and who have contributed aught to the sum of culture and knowledge. In this work of passing on the cultural torch to the next generation, the home will ever be the basic institution. The play and social life comes next, with the school last but equally indispensable in a complex and highly organized society.

The racial ideals. The ideals of one generation carve out the channels of destiny for immediate posterity. The *quality* of the social torchbearers will determine whether civilization goes forward or backward. The homes, churches, and schools of one generation predetermine the character trend of the succeeding generation. The moral and spiritual momentum of a race

or a nation largely determines the cultural velocity of that civilization.
                                        Development of Modern Civilization 909:4,7

While religious, social, and educational institutions are all essential to
the survival of cultural civilization, the family is the master civilizer. A
child learns most of the essentials of life from his family and the neighbors.
                                        The Evolution of Marriage 913:2

The family is man's greatest purely human achievement, combining as
it does the evolution of the biologic relations of male and female with the
social relations of husband and wife.   Marriage and Family 939:3

Sex mating is instinctive, children are the natural result, and the family
thus automatically comes into existence. As are the families of the race or
nation, so is its society. If the families are good, the society is likewise
good. The great cultural stability of the Jewish and of the Chinese peoples
lies in the strength of their family groups.
                                        Marriage and Family Life 939:4

Modern problems of child culture are rendered increasingly difficult
by:
- Artificial and superficial education.
- Inability of the child to gain culture by imitating parents—the parents
are absent from the family picture so much of the time.
   In the present industrial and urban era the marriage institution is evolving along new economic lines. Family life has become more and more
costly, while children, who used to be an asset, have become economic
liabilities. But the security of civilization itself still rests on the growing
willingness of one generation to invest in the welfare of the next and future generations. And any attempt to shift parental responsibility to state
or church will prove suicidal to the welfare and advancement of civilization.
   Human society would be greatly improved if the civilized races would
more generally return to the family-council practices of the Andites. They
did not maintain the patriarchal or autocratic form of family government.
were very brotherly and associative, freely and frankly discussing every
proposal and regulation of a family nature. They were ideally fraternal in

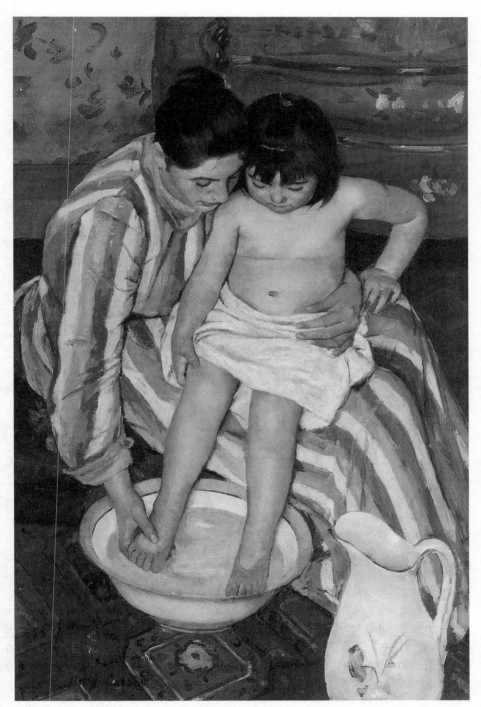

Mary Cassatt; *The Child's Bath* (1891-1892). © Art Institute of Chicago

all their family government. In an ideal family filial and parental affection are both augmented by fraternal devotion.

Marriage and Family Life 941:2,4,5,8,10

But even more, a true family—a good family—reveals to the parental procreators the attitude of the Creator to his children, while at the same time such true parents portray to their children the first of a long series of ascending disclosures of the love of the Paradise parent of all universe children.

The great threat against family life is the menacing rising tide of self-gratification, the modern pleasure mania. The prime incentive to marriage used to be economic; sex attraction was secondary. Marriage, founded on self-maintenance, led to self-perpetuation and concomitantly provided one of the most desirable forms of self-gratification. It is the only institution of human society which embraces all three of the great incentives for living.

Marriage and Family Life 942:1,2

Together with children, religion is the great unifier of family life, provided it is a living and growing faith. Family life cannot be had without children; it can be lived without religion, but such a handicap enormously multiplies the difficulties of this intimate human association. During the early decades of the twentieth century, family life, next to personal religious experience, suffers most from the decadence consequent upon the transition from old religious loyalties to the emerging new meanings and values.

Social Problems of Religion 1089:10

Many noble human impulses die because there is no one to hear their expression. Truly, it is not good for man to be alone. Some degree of recognition and a certain amount of appreciation are essential to the development of human character. Without the genuine love of a home, no child can achieve the full development of normal character. Character is something more than mere mind and morals. Of all social relations calculated to develop character, the most effective and ideal is the affectionate and understanding friendship of man and woman in the mutual embrace of intelligent wedlock. Marriage, with its manifold relations, is best designed to draw forth those precious impulses and those higher motives which are indispensable to the development of a strong character. I do not hesitate thus to glorify family life, for your Master has wisely chosen the father-child relationship as the very cornerstone of this new gospel of the kingdom. And such a matchless community of relationship, man and woman in the fond embrace of the highest ideals of time, is so valuable and satisfying an experience that it is worth any price, any sacrifice, requisite for its possession.   Rodan of Alexandria 1775:7

In the course of this day's visiting with John Mark, Jesus spent considerable time comparing their early childhood and later boyhood experiences. Although John's parents possessed more of this world's goods than had Jesus' parents, there was much experience in their boyhood which was very similar. Jesus said many things which helped John better to understand his parents and other members of his family. When the lad asked the Master how he could know that he would turn out to be a "mighty messenger of the kingdom," Jesus said:

"I know you will prove loyal to the gospel of the kingdom because I can depend upon your present faith and love when these qualities are grounded upon such an early training as has been your portion at home. You are the product of a home where the parents bear each other a sincere affection, and therefore you have not been overloved so as injuriously to exalt your concept of self-importance. Neither has your personality suffered distortion in consequence of your parents' loveless maneuvering for your confidence and loyalty, the one against the other. You have enjoyed that parental love which insures laudable self-confidence and which fosters normal feelings of security. But you have also been fortunate in that your parents possessed wisdom as well as love; and it was wisdom which led them to withhold most forms of indulgence and many luxuries which wealth can buy while they sent you to the synagogue school along with your neighborhood playfellows, and they also encouraged you to learn how to live in this world by permitting you to have original experience. You came over to the Jordan, where we preached and John's disciples baptized, with your young friend Amos. Both of you desired to go with us. When you returned to Jerusalem, your parents consented; Amos's parents refused; they loved their son so much that they denied him the blessed experience which you have had, even such as you this day enjoy. By running away from home, Amos could have joined us, but in so doing he would have wounded love and sacrificed loyalty. Even if such a course had been wise, it would have been a terrible price to pay for experience, independence, and liberty. Wise parents, such as yours, see to it that their children do not have to wound love or stifle loyalty in order to develop independence and enjoy invigorating liberty when they have grown up to your age.

"Love, John, is the supreme reality of the universe when bestowed by all-wise beings, but it is a dangerous and oftentimes semiselfish trait as it is manifested in the experience of mortal parents. When you get married and have children of your own to rear, make sure that your love is admonished by wisdom and guided by intelligence.

"Your young friend Amos believes this gospel of the kingdom just as much as you, but I cannot fully depend upon him; I am not certain about what he will do in the years to come. His early home life was not such as would produce a wholly dependable person. Amos is too much like one of the apostles who failed to enjoy a normal, loving, and wise home training. Your whole afterlife will be more happy and dependable because you spent your first eight years in a normal and well-regulated home. You possess a strong and well-knit character because you grew up in a home where love prevailed and wisdom reigned. Such a childhood training produces a type of loyalty which assures me that you will go through with the course you have begun."

For more than an hour Jesus and John continued this discussion of home life. The Master went on to explain to John how a child is wholly dependent on his parents and the associated home life for all his early concepts of everything intellectual, social, moral, and even spiritual since the family represents to the young child all that he can first know of either human or divine relationships. The child must derive his first impressions of the universe from the mother's care; he is wholly dependent on the earthly father for his first ideas of the heavenly Father. The child's subsequent life is made happy or unhappy, easy or difficult, in accordance with his early mental and emotional life, conditioned by these social and spiritual relationships of the home. A human being's entire afterlife is enormously influenced by what happens during the first few years of existence.

Wednesday the Rest Day 1921:5,6 & 1922:1-3

Neither do genuine believers trouble themselves so much about the future punishment of sin. The real believer is only concerned about present separation from God. True, wise fathers may chasten their sons, but they do all this in love and for corrective purposes. They do not punish in anger, neither do they chastise in retribution.

The Time of the Tomb 2017:5

2. Education

Our main task on this planet is to educate our souls through experience. The more experience the soul acquires, the more receptive the individual becomes to the ideas and knowledge of others, and the more the soul evolves.

How do we best impart this hard-earned wisdom to our children? Simply by example. Rather than deliver negative reproachments in the form of "don't do this," it is more effective to get down on the floor with your little one and show genuine interest. Instead of shouting instructions over your shoulder, try saying, "Come with me and I will show you the way." Children exposed to these approaches will quickly brighten up and listen.

When Jesus taught children about religion, he preferred to commune with the heavenly Father amid the trees and animals of the natural world. He would go out at night and gaze at the inspiring spectacle of the starry heavens. You too, can initiate discussions with even a young child by taking a blanket out on a cool, clear crisp night and snuggling up, looking into the sky for shooting stars. Ask the child which star he likes best. Which one would he like to visit first? Which star system did Uncle Pierre go to when he died?

The goal of education is to aid children in developing a majestic and well-balanced personality. Parents and teachers alike can assist in this task by placing more emphasis on life planning and character progression. Investing more taxes in schools alone won't improve a child's education without the personal interest and attention of the parent in the student's progress.

The higher a creature's education, the more respect he has for the knowledge, experience, and opinions of others.

Messenger Hosts of Space 278:3

All sex instruction is administered in the home by parents or by legal guardians. Moral instruction is offered by teachers during the rest periods in the school shops, but not so with religious training, which is deemed to be the exclusive privilege of parents, religion being looked upon as an integral part of home life. Purely religious instruction is given publicly only in the temples of philosophy, no such exclusively religious institutions as the Urantia churches having developed among this people. In their philosophy, religion is the striving to know God and to manifest love for one's fellows through service for them, but this is not typical of the religious status of the other nations on this planet. Religion is so entirely a family matter among these people that there are no public places devoted exclusively to religious assembly. Politically, church and state, as Urantians are wont to say, are entirely separate, but there is a strange overlapping of religion and philosophy.   Government on a Neighboring Planet 811:5

The educational system of this nation is compulsory and coeducational in the precollege schools that the student attends from the ages of five to eighteen. These schools are vastly different from those of Urantia. There are no classrooms, only one study is pursued at a time, and after the first three years all pupils become assistant teachers, instructing those below them. Books are used only to secure information that will assist in solving the problems arising in the school shops and on the school farms.
Government on a Neighboring Planet 812:3

Social inheritance enables man to stand on the shoulders of all who have preceded him, and who have contributed aught to the sum of culture and knowledge. In this work of passing on the cultural torch to the next generation, the home will ever be the basic institution. The play and social life comes next, with the school last but equally indispensable in a complex and highly organized society.
Development of Modern Civilization 909:4

A child learns most of the essentials of life from his family and the neighbors.   The Evolution of Marriage 913:2

The mortal career, the soul's evolution, is not so much a probation as an education. Faith in the survival of supreme values is the core of religion.
Mind knows quantity, reality, meanings. But quality—values—is felt.
The Adjuster and the Soul 1219:4,5

Any civilization is in jeopardy when three quarters of its youth enter materialistic professions and devote themselves to the pursuit of the sensory activities of the outer world. Civilization is in danger when youth neglect to interest themselves in ethics, sociology, philosophy, the fine arts, religion, and cosmology.   The Adjuster and the Soul 1220:3

Jesus received his moral training and spiritual culture chiefly in his own home. He secured much of his intellectual and theological education from the chazan. But his real education—that equipment of mind and heart for the actual test of grappling with the difficult problems of life—he obtained by mingling with his fellow men. It was this close association with his fellow men, young and old, Jew and gentile, that afforded him the opportunity to know the human race. Jesus was highly educated in that he thoroughly understood men and devotedly loved them.
Early Childhood of Jesus 1363:1

The apostolic steward was not a good public speaker, but he was a very persuasive and successful personal worker. He was not easily discouraged; he was a plodder and very tenacious in anything he undertook. He had that great and rare gift of saying, "Come." When his first convert, Nathaniel, wanted to argue about the merits and demerits of Jesus and Nazareth, Philip's effective reply was, "Come and see." He was not a dogmatic preacher who exhorted his hearers to "Go"—do this and do that. He met all situations as they arose in his work with "Come"—"come with me; I will show you the way." And that is always the effective technique in all forms and phases of teaching. Even parents may learn from Philip the better way of saying to their children not "Go do this and go do that," but rather, "Come with us while we show and share with you the better way."   The Twelve Apostles 1557:2

"Happy are the pure in heart, for they shall see God." Spiritual purity is not a negative quality, except that it does lack suspicion and revenge. In discussing purity, Jesus did not intend to deal exclusively with human sex attitudes. He referred more to that faith which man should have in his fellow man; that faith which a parent has in his child, and which enables him to love his fellows even as a father would love them. A father's love need not pamper, and it does not condone evil, but it is always anticynical. Fatherly love has singleness of purpose, and it always looks for the best in man; that is the attitude of a true parent.

It is easy to teach this admonition even to a child. Children are naturally trustful, and parents should see to it that they do not lose that simple faith.

A Young Girl Reading; Jean-Honore Fragonard (1776).

© National Gallery of Art, Washington

In dealing with children, avoid all deception and refrain from suggesting suspicion. Wisely help them to choose their heroes and select their lifework.

Ordination of the Twelve 1574:5,7

"Happy are they who mourn, for they shall be comforted." So-called common sense or the best of logic would never suggest that happiness could be derived from mourning. But Jesus did not refer to outward or ostentatious mourning. He alluded to an emotional attitude of tenderheartedness. It is a great error to teach boys and young men that it is unmanly to show tenderness or otherwise to give evidence of emotional feeling or physical suffering. Sympathy is a worthy attribute of the male as well as the female. It is not necessary to be calloused in order to be manly. This is the wrong way to create courageous men. The world's great men have not been afraid to mourn. Moses, the mourner, was a greater man than either Samson or Goliath. Moses was a superb leader, but he was also a man of meekness. Being sensitive and responsive to human need creates genuine and lasting happiness, while such kindly attitudes safeguard the soul from the destructive influences of anger, hate, and suspicion.   Ordination of the Twelve 1575:1

Following that, came the memorable discussion of the fundamental characteristics of family life and their application to the relationship existing between God and man. Jesus stated that a true family is founded on the following seven facts:

1. *The fact of existence.* The relationships of nature and the phenomena of mortal likenesses are bound up in the family: Children inherit certain parental traits. The children take origin in the parents; personality existence depends on the act of the parent. The relationship of father and child is inherent in all nature and pervades all living existences.

2. *Security and pleasure.* True fathers take great pleasure in providing for the needs of their children. Many fathers are not content with supplying the mere wants of their children but enjoy making provision for their pleasures also.

3. *Education and training.* Wise fathers carefully plan for the education and adequate training of their sons and daughters. When young they are prepared for the greater responsibilities of later life.

4. *Discipline and restraint.* Farseeing fathers also make provision for the necessary discipline, guidance, correction, and sometimes restraint of their young and immature offspring.

5. *Companionship and loyalty.* The affectionate father holds intimate and loving intercourse with his children. Always is his ear open to their petitions; he is ever ready to share their hardships and assist them over their difficulties. The father is supremely interested in the progressive welfare of his progeny.

6. *Love and mercy.* A compassionate father is freely forgiving; fathers do not hold vengeful memories against their children. Fathers are not like judges, enemies, or creditors. Real families are built upon tolerance, patience, and forgiveness.   Passover at Jerusalem 1604:3-6

It was also at Jericho, in connection with the discussion of the early religious training of children in habits of divine worship, that Jesus impressed upon his apostles the great value of beauty as an influence leading to the urge to worship, especially with children. The Master by precept and example taught the value of worshiping the Creator in the midst of the natural surroundings of creation. He preferred to commune with the heavenly Father amidst the trees and among the lowly creatures of the natural world. He rejoiced to contemplate the Father through the inspiring spectacle of the starry realms of the Creator Sons.

When it is not possible to worship God in the tabernacles of nature, men should do their best to provide houses of beauty, sanctuaries of appealing simplicity and artistic embellishment, so that the highest of human emotions may be aroused in association with the intellectual approach to spiritual communion with God. Truth, beauty, and holiness are powerful and effective aids to true worship. But spirit communion is not promoted by mere massive ornateness and overmuch embellishment with man's elaborate and ostentatious art. Beauty is most religious when it is most simple and naturelike. How unfortunate that little children should have their first introduction to concepts of public worship in cold and barren rooms so devoid of the beauty appeal and so empty of all suggestion of good cheer and inspiring holiness! The child should be introduced to worship in nature's outdoors and later accompany his parents to public houses of religious assembly which are at least as materially attractive and artistically beautiful as the home in which he is daily domiciled.

                                                Visit to Philadelphia 1840:4,5

Even secular education could help in this great spiritual renaissance if it would pay more attention to the work of teaching youth how to engage in life planning and character progression. The purpose of all education should be to foster and further the supreme purpose of life, the development of a majestic and well-balanced personality. There is great need for the teaching of moral discipline in the place of so much self-gratification. Upon such a foundation religion may contribute its spiritual incentive to the en-

largement and enrichment of mortal life, even to the security and enhancement of life eternal. After Pentecost 2086:3

3. Marriage and Divorce

Ah, the sweet pleasure of being curled up in bed with a loving spouse on a cold winter night! As it is recounted in the Old Testament:

> How beautiful you are and how
> pleasing,
> O love, with your delights!
> Your stature is like that of the palm,
> and your breasts like clusters of
> fruit.
> I said, "I will climb the palm tree;
> I will take hold of its fruit."
> May your breasts be like the clusters
> of the vine,
> the fragrance of your breath like
> apples,
> and your mouth like the best wine.
>
> May the wine go straight to my
> lover,
> flowing gently over lips and teeth.
> I belong to my lover,
> and his desire is for me.
> Come, my lover, let us go to the
> countryside,
> let us spend the night in the
> henna bushes.
> Let us go early to the vineyards
> to see if the vines have budded,
> if their blossoms have opened,
> and if the pomegranates are in
> bloom—

there I will give you my love.
The mandrakes send out their
    fragrance,
and at our door is every delicacy,
both new and old,
    that I have stored up for you, my
    lover.
Song of Songs 7:6-13 Old Testament (NIV)

Marriage is a choice gift and a source of pleasure. Divorce on the other hand, is a shattering and devastating blow.

Through the example of a faithful marriage, we pass down to our children a lasting impression of caring for a spouse and raising a family. Children raised without this basic guidance, particularly those in a household of terror—with a siege mentality—may have a hard time establishing a stable marriage later in life. To break the vicious cycle of shattered families, we must turn to education. High schools, especially, could offer classes in premarital instruction.

These primitive trial marriages were entirely free from all semblance of license; they were simply sincere tests of fecundity. The contracting individuals married permanently just as soon as fertility was established. When modern couples marry with the thought of convenient divorce in the background of their minds if they are not wholly pleased with their married life, they are in reality entering upon a form of trial marriage and one that is far beneath the status of the honest adventures of their less civilized ancestors.   Evolution of Marriage 917:3

But just so long as society fails to properly educate children and youths, so long as the social order fails to provide adequate premarital training, and so long as unwise and immature youthful idealism is to be the arbiter of the entrance upon marriage, just so long will divorce remain prevalent. And in so far as the social group falls short of providing marriage preparation for youths, to that extent must divorce function as the social safety valve which prevents still worse situations during the ages of the rapid growth of the evolving mores.   The Marriage Institution 929:2

The Storm; Pierre Auguste Cot (1837-1883), © The Metropolitan
Museum of Art, New York

Jesus was minded to go on discussing the other commandments when James Zebedee interrupted him, asking: "Master, what shall we teach the people regarding divorcement? Shall we allow a man to divorce his wife as Moses has directed?" And when Jesus heard this question, he said: "I have not come to legislate but to enlighten. I have come not to reform the kingdoms of this world but rather to establish the kingdom of heaven. It is not the will of the Father that I should yield to the temptation to teach you rules of government, trade, or social behavior, which, while they might be good for today, would be far from suitable for the society of another age. I am on earth solely to comfort the minds, liberate the spirits, and save the souls of men. But I will say, concerning this question of divorcement, that, while Moses looked with favor upon such things, it was not so in the days of Adam and in the Garden."   Ordination of the Twelve 1576:6

I repeat, such inspiring and ennobling association finds its ideal possibilities in the human marriage relation. True, much is attained out of marriage, and many, many marriages utterly fail to produce these moral and spiritual fruits. Too many times marriage is entered by those who seek other values which are lower than these superior accompaniments of human maturity. Ideal marriage must be founded on something more stable than the fluctuations of sentiment and the fickleness of mere sex attraction; it must be based on genuine and mutual personal devotion. And thus, if you can build up such trustworthy and effective small units of human association, when these are assembled in the aggregate, the world will behold a great and glorified social structure, the civilization of mortal maturity. Such a race might begin to realize something of your Master's ideal of "peace on earth and good will among men." While such a society would not be perfect or entirely free from evil, it would at least approach the stabilization of maturity.   Rodan of Alexandria 1777:1

Though Jesus refused to be drawn into a controversy with the Pharisees concerning divorce, he did proclaim a positive teaching of the highest ideals regarding marriage. He exalted marriage as the most ideal and highest of all human relationships. Likewise, he intimated strong disapproval of the lax and unfair divorce practices of the Jerusalem Jews, who at that time permitted a man to divorce his wife for the most trifling of reasons, such as being a poor cook, a faulty housekeeper, or for no better reason than that he had become enamoured of a better-looking woman.

The Pharisees had even gone so far as to teach that divorce of this easy variety was a special dispensation granted the Jewish people, particularly the Pharisees. And so, while Jesus refused to make pronouncements dealing with marriage and divorce, he did most bitterly denounce these shameful floutings of the marriage relationship and pointed out their injustice to women and children. He never sanctioned any divorce practice which gave man any advantage over woman; the Master countenanced only those teachings which accorded women equality with men.

Visit to Philadelphia 1838:4 & 1839:1

4. Raising a Family: An Invaluable Experience

According to The Urantia Book, an evolving mortal must acquire the experience of raising children. To truly comprehend the concept of God, our Father in heaven, one must come to know firsthand the feeling of nurturing and love for a growing child. In so doing, one learns to love unconditionally despite all the youngster's inadequacies and mistakes, just as God loves us despite all the wrong paths we have taken.

Parents who have lost a young child are given heartening news. Guess who helps to raise that child in heaven? You do.

No surviving mortal may ascend to Paradise, attain the Father, and be mustered into the Corps of the Finality without having passed through that sublime experience of achieving parental relationship to an evolving child of the worlds or some other experience analogous and equivalent thereto. The relationship of child and parent is fundamental to the essential concept of the Universal Father and his universe children. Therefore does such an experience become indispensable to the experiential training of all ascenders.

All mortal survivors who have not experienced parenthood on the evolutionary worlds must also obtain this necessary training while sojourning in the homes of the Jerusem Material Sons and as parental associates of these superb fathers and mothers.   Local System Administration 516:2,4

But irrespective of parental experience, mansion world parents who have growing children in the probation nursery are given every opportunity to collaborate with the morontia custodians of such children regarding their instruction and training. These parents are permitted to journey there for visits as often as four times a year. And it is one of the most touchingly

Venus Consoling Love; Francois Boucher (1751) National
Gallery of Art, Washington

beautiful scenes of all the ascending career to observe the mansion world
parents embrace their material offspring on the occasions of their periodic
pilgrimages to the finaliter world. While one or both parents may leave a
mansion world ahead of the child, they are quite often contemporary for a
season.

No ascending mortal can escape the experience of rearing children—their own or others—either on the material worlds or subsequently on the finaliter world or on Jerusem. Fathers must pass through this essential experience just as certainly as mothers. It is an unfortunate and mistaken notion of modern peoples on Urantia that child culture is largely the task of mothers. Children need fathers as well as mothers, and fathers need this parental experience as much as do mothers.

Seven Mansion Worlds 531:3,4

Mortals of the probationary-dependent orders of ascension. The arrival of an Adjuster constitutes identity in the eyes of the universe, and all indwelt beings are on the roll calls of justice. But temporal life on the evolutionary worlds is uncertain, and many die in youth before choosing the Paradise career. Such Adjuster-indwelt children and youths follow the parent of most advanced spiritual status, thus going to the system finaliter world (the probationary nursery) on the third day, at a special resurrection, or at the regular millennial and dispensational roll calls.

Children who die when too young to have Thought Adjusters are repersonalized on the finaliter world of the local systems concomitant with the arrival of either parent on the mansion worlds. A child acquires physical entity at mortal birth, but in the matter of survival all Adjusterless children are reckoned as still attached to their parents.

The Inhabited Worlds 569:6 & 570:1

~ V ~

The Life and Teachings of Jesus

Who is Jesus? Why did he come here? Did he really die on the cross to appease God's wrath toward humanity?

Jesus is the Creator Son of the local universe, home to 4 million inhabited planets. He visited our world 2,000 years ago for three primary reasons:

- *To reveal a more advanced concept of God to his children on earth.*
- *To face Lucifer and the blasphemous pretensions of his heavenly rebellion against God. As it turned out, Jesus did not face Lucifer in his full raiment as Creator Son, but in the likeness of the lowliest creature of his realm—a mortal human being.*
- *To gain complete sovereignty of his creation, Jesus was required by God to experience first hand all levels of life. Jesus had to select a planet on which to live a human life and after reviewing all the planets in his domain, he chose earth as the one most in need of attention. Jesus knew that if he could live a perfect life in this confused world, it would serve as a thrilling example to mortals struggling on the more stable planets.*

The religion of Jesus would quickly revive if we could cut through the mists of the past 2,000 years of painful history and dispel the fog produced by competing sects, commercialism, and institutionalized Christianity. By embracing the core teachings of this magnificent God-man, our civilization would truly flourish.

The Master placed emphasis on the following five points as representing the cardinal features of the gospel of the kingdom:

1. The pre-eminence of the individual.
2. The will as the determining factor in man's experience.
3. Spiritual fellowship with God the Father.
4. The supreme satisfactions of the loving service of man.
5. The transcendency of the spiritual over the material in human personality. The Kingdom of Heaven 1863:6-11

1. Jesus' Early Years

Jesus was challenged early in life. His father died when Jesus was fourteen years old, leaving him in charge of caring for his widowed mother and seven brothers and sisters. When he reached his mid-twenties, however, he gradually turned over the caretaking of the family to his younger brothers. Then, in his twenty-ninth year, he began to travel around the Mediterranean and Mesopotamian regions. While in Rome, Jesus became acquainted with at least thirty individuals—among them were Stoics, Cynics, and mystery cultists. Although they knew him only as the scribe of Damascus, his teachings there laid fertile ground for the Romans to receive the Apostles and disciples who followed in his footsteps.

Many of the great highways joining the nations of antiquity passed through Palestine, which thus became the meeting place, or crossroads, of three continents. The travel, trade, and armies of Babylonia, Assyria, Egypt, Syria, Greece, Parthia, and Rome successively swept over Palestine. From time immemorial, many caravan routes from the Orient passed through some part of this region to the few good seaports of the eastern end of the Mediterranean, whence ships carried their cargoes to all the maritime Occident. And more than half of this caravan traffic passed through or near the little town of Nazareth in Galilee.

Greece provided a language and a culture, Rome built the roads and unified an empire, but the dispersion of the Jews, with their more than two hundred synagogues and well-organized religious communities scattered hither and yon throughout the Roman world, provided the cultural centers in which the new gospel of the kingdom of heaven found initial reception, and from which it subsequently spread to the uttermost parts of the world.

Times of the Bestowal 1333:4,6

The home of Jesus was not far from the high hill in the northerly part of Nazareth, some distance from the village spring, which was in the eastern section of the town. Jesus' family dwelt in the outskirts of the city, and this made it all the easier for him subsequently to enjoy frequent strolls in the country and to make trips up to the top of this near-by highland, the highest of all the hills of southern Galilee save the Mount Tabor range to the east and the hill of Nain, which was about the same height. Their home was located a little to the south and east of the southern promontory of this hill and about midway between the base of this elevation and the road leading out of Nazareth toward Cana. Aside from climbing the hill, Jesus' favorite stroll was to follow a narrow trail winding about the base of the hill in a northeasterly direction to a point where it joined the road to Sepphoris.

The home of Joseph and Mary was a one-room stone structure with a flat roof and an adjoining building for housing the animals. The furniture consisted of a low stone table, earthenware and stone dishes and pots, a loom, a lampstand, several small stools, andmats for sleeping on the stone floor. In the back yard, near the animal annex, was the shelter which covered the oven and the mill for grinding grain. It required two persons to operate this type of mill, one to grind and another to feed the grain. As a small boy Jesus often fed grain to this mill while his mother turned the grinder.   Birth and Infancy 1349:8 & 1350:1

The inn was overcrowded, and Joseph accordingly sought lodgings with distant relatives, but every room in Bethlehem was filled to overflowing. On returning to the courtyard of the inn, he was informed that the caravan stables, hewn out of the side of the rock and situated just below the inn, had been cleared of animals and cleaned up for the reception of lodgers. Leaving the donkey in the courtyard, Joseph shouldered their bags of clothing and provisions and with Mary descended the stone steps to their lodgings below. They found themselves located in what had been a grain storage room to the front of the stalls and mangers. Tent curtains had been hung, and they counted themselves fortunate to have such comfortable quarters.

All that night Mary was restless so that neither of them slept much. By the break of day the pangs of childbirth were well in evidence, and at noon, August 21, 7 B.C., with the help and kind ministrations of women fellow travelers, Mary was delivered of a male child. Jesus of Nazareth was born into the world, was wrapped in the clothes which Mary had brought along for such a possible contingency, and laid in a near-by manger.

In just the same manner as all babies before that day and since have come into the world, the promised child was born; and on the eighth day,

The Holy Family with St. Elizabeth and John and a Dove;
Peter Paul Rubens (1577-1640), © The Metropolitan Museum of Art,
New York

according to the Jewish practice, he was circumcised and formally named
Joshua (Jesus).   Birth and Infancy 1351:3,5,6

These wise men saw no star to guide them to Bethlehem. The beautiful
legend of the star of Bethlehem originated in this way: Jesus was born
August 21 at noon, 7 B.C. On May 29, 7 B.C., there occurred an extraordinary conjunction of Jupiter and Saturn in the constellation of Pisces.
And it is a remarkable astronomic fact that similar conjunctions occurred
on September 29 and December 5 of the same year. Upon the basis of
these extraordinary but wholly natural events the well-meaning zealots of
the succeeding generation constructed the appealing legend of the star of
Bethlehem and the adoring Magi led thereby to the manger, where they
beheld and worshiped the newborn babe. Oriental and near-Oriental minds
delight in fairy stories, and they are continually spinning such beautiful
myths about the lives of their religious leaders and political heroes. In the
absence of printing, when most human knowledge was passed by word of
mouth from one generation to another, it was very easy for myths to become traditions and for traditions eventually to become accepted as facts.
                                                   Birth and Infancy 1352:3

The most serious trouble as yet to come up at school occurred in late
winter when Jesus dared to challenge the chazan regarding the teaching
that all images, pictures, and drawings were idolatrous in nature. Jesus
delighted in drawing landscapes as well as in modeling a great variety of
objects in potter's clay. Everything of that sort was strictly forbidden by
Jewish law, but up to this time he had managed to disarm his parents'
objection to such an extent that they had permitted him to continue in
these activities.

But trouble was again stirred up at school when one of the more backward pupils discovered Jesus drawing a charcoal picture of the teacher on
the floor of the schoolroom. There it was, plain as day, and many of the
elders had viewed it before the committee went to call on Joseph to demand that something be done to suppress the lawlessness of his eldest son.
And though this was not the first time complaints had come to Joseph and
Mary about the doings of their versatile and aggressive child, this was the
most serious of all the accusations which had thus far been lodged against
him. Jesus listened to the indictment of his artistic efforts for some time,
being seated on a large stone just outside the back door. He resented their

blaming his father for his alleged misdeeds; so in he marched, fearlessly confronting his accusers. The elders were thrown into confusion. Some were inclined to view the episode humorously, while one or two seemed to think the boy was sacrilegious if not blasphemous. Joseph was nonplused, Mary indignant, but Jesus insisted on being heard. He had his say, courageously defended his viewpoint, and with consummate self-control announced that he would abide by the decision of his father in this as in all other matters controversial. And the committee of elders departed in silence.

Mary endeavored to influence Joseph to permit Jesus to model in clay at home, provided he promised not to carry on any of these questionable activities at school, but Joseph felt impelled to rule that the rabbinical interpretation of the second commandment should prevail. And so Jesus no more drew or modeled the likeness of anything from that day as long as he lived in his father's house. But he was unconvinced of the wrong of what he had done, and to give up such a favorite pastime constituted one of the great trials of his young life.

Later Childhood of Jesus 1366:4,5 & 1367:1

The only time Jesus ever saw his father angry with him was that night in their room at the inn when, in the course of their discussions, the boy so far forgot the trends of Jewish thought as to suggest that they go back home and work for the building of an amphitheater at Nazareth. When Joseph heard his first-born son express such un-Jewish sentiments, he forgot his usual calm demeanor and, seizing Jesus by the shoulder, angrily exclaimed, "My son, never again let me hear you give utterance to such an evil thought as long as you live." Jesus was startled by his father's display of emotion; he had never before been made to feel the personal sting of his father's indignation and was astonished and shocked beyond expression. He only replied, "Very well, my father, it shall be so." And never again did the boy even in the slightest manner allude to the games and other athletic activities of the Greeks as long as his father lived.

Later on, Jesus saw the Greek amphitheater at Jerusalem and learned how hateful such things were from the Jewish point of view. Nevertheless, throughout his life he endeavored to introduce the idea of wholesome recreation into his personal plans and, as far as Jewish practice would permit, into the later program of regular activities for his twelve apostles.

From this time on he became more successful in getting along with his brothers and sisters. He was increasingly tactful, always compassionate

and considerate of their welfare and happiness, and enjoyed good relations with them up to the beginning of his public ministry. To be more
explicit: He got along with James, Miriam, and the two younger (as yet
unborn) children, Amos and Ruth, most excellently. He always got along
with Martha fairly well. What trouble he had at home largely arose out
of friction with Joseph and Jude, particularly the latter.

Later Childhood of Jesus 1371:1,2,6

(The Journey to Jerusalem)
The road now led immediately down into the tropical Jordan valley,
and soon Jesus was to have exposed to his wondering gaze the crooked
and ever-winding Jordan with its glistening and rippling waters as it
flowed down toward the Dead Sea. They laid aside their outer garments
as they journeyed south in this tropical valley, enjoying the luxurious
fields of grain and the beautiful oleanders laden with their pink blos-
soms, while massive snow-capped Mount Hermon stood far to the north,
in majesty looking down on the historic valley. A little over three hours'
travel from opposite Scythopolis they came upon a bubbling spring,
and here they camped for the night, out under the starlit heavens.

Later Childhood of Jesus 1374:5

He passed through the consecration rituals but was disappointed by
their perfunctory and routine natures. He missed that personal interest
which characterized the ceremonies of the synagogue at Nazareth. He
then returned to greet his mother and prepared to accompany his father
on his first trip about the temple and its various courts, galleries, and
corridors. The temple precincts could accommodate over two hundred
thousand worshipers at one time, and while the vastness of these buildings—in comparison with any he had ever seen—greatly impressed his
mind, he was more intrigued by the contemplation of the spiritual significance of the temple ceremonies and their associated worship.

Though many of the temple rituals very touchingly impressed his sense
of the beautiful and the symbolic, he was always disappointed by the explanation of the real meanings of these ceremonies which his parents would
offer in answer to his many searching inquiries. Jesus simply would not
accept explanations of worship and religious devotion which involved belief
in the wrath of God or the anger of the Almighty. In further discussion of

these questions, after the conclusion of the temple visit, when his father became mildly insistent that he acknowledge acceptance of the orthodox Jewish beliefs, Jesus turned suddenly upon his parents and, looking appealingly into the eyes of his father, said: "My father, it cannot be true—the Father in heaven cannot so regard his erring children on earth. The heavenly Father cannot love his children less than you love me. And I well know, no matter what unwise thing I might do, you would never pour out wrath upon me nor vent anger against me. If you, my earthly father, possess such human reflections of the Divine, how much more must the heavenly Father be filled with goodness and overflowing with mercy. I refuse to believe that my Father in heaven loves me less than my father on earth."

When Joseph and Mary heard these words of their first-born son, they held their peace. And never again did they seek to change his mind about the love of God and the mercifulness of the Father in heaven.

Everywhere Jesus went throughout the temple courts, he was shocked and sickened by the spirit of irreverence which he observed. He deemed the conduct of the temple throngs to be inconsistent with their presence in "his Father's house." But he received the shock of his young life when his father escorted him into the court of the gentiles with its noisy jargon, loud talking and cursing, mingled indiscriminately with the bleating of sheep and the babble of noises which betrayed the presence of the money-changers and the vendors of sacrificial animals and sundry other commercial commodities.

But most of all was his sense of propriety outraged by the sight of the frivolous courtesans parading about within this precinct of the temple, just such painted women as he had so recently seen when on a visit to Sepphoris. This profanation of the temple fully aroused all his youthful indignation, and he did not hesitate to express himself freely to Joseph.

Jesus admired the sentiment and service of the temple, but he was shocked by the spiritual ugliness which he beheld on the faces of so many of the unthinking worshipers.

They now passed down to the priests' court beneath the rock ledge in front of the temple, where the altar stood, to observe the killing of the droves of animals and the washing away of the blood from the hands of the officiating slaughter priests at the bronze fountain. The bloodstained pavement, the gory hands of the priests, and the sounds of the dying animals were more than this nature-loving lad could stand. The terrible sight sickened this boy of Nazareth; he clutched his father's arm and begged to be taken away. They walked back through the court of the gentiles, and even the coarse laughter and profane jesting which he there heard were a relief from the sights he had just beheld.

Jesus at Jerusalem 1377:5-1378:6

Jesus' third day with the scribes and teachers in the temple witnessed the gathering of many spectators who, having heard of this youth from Galilee, came to enjoy the experience of seeing a lad confuse the wise men of the law. Simon also came down from Bethany to see what the boy was up to. Throughout this day Joseph and Mary continued their anxious search for Jesus, even going several times into the temple but never thinking to scrutinize the several discussion groups, although they once came almost within hearing distance of his fascinating voice.

Before the day had ended, the entire attention of the chief discussion group of the temple had become focused upon the questions being asked by Jesus. Among his many questions were:

1. What really exists in the holy of holies, behind the veil?

2. Why should mothers in Israel be segregated from the male temple worshipers?

3. If God is a father who loves his children, why all this slaughter of animals to gain divine favor—has the teaching of Moses been misunderstood?

4. Since the temple is dedicated to the worship of the Father in heaven, is it consistent to permit the presence of those who engage in secular barter and trade?

5. Is the expected Messiah to become a temporal prince to sit on the throne of David, or is he to function as the light of life in the establishment of a spiritual kingdom?

And all the day through, those who listened marveled at these questions, and none was more astonished than Simon. For more than four hours this Nazareth youth plied these Jewish teachers with thought-provoking and heart-searching questions. He made few comments on the remarks of his elders. He conveyed his teaching by the questions he would ask. By the deft and subtle phrasing of a question he would at one and the same time challenge their teaching and suggest his own. In the manner of

Christ among the Doctors; Bernaert van Orly (1513)
© National Gallery of Art, Washington (Right)

his asking a question there was an appealing combination of sagacity and humor which endeared him even to those who more or less resented his youthfulness. He was always eminently fair and considerate in the asking of these penetrating questions. On this eventful afternoon in the temple he exhibited that same reluctance to take unfair advantage of an opponent which characterized his entire subsequent public ministry. As a youth, and later on as a man, he seemed to be utterly free from all egoistic desire to win an argument merely to experience logical triumph over his fellows, being interested supremely in just one thing: to proclaim everlasting truth and thus effect a fuller revelation of the eternal God.

Jesus at Jerusalem 1382:3-1393:1

All did go well until that fateful day of Tuesday, September 25, when a runner from Sepphoris brought to this Nazareth home the tragic news that Joseph had been severely injured by the falling of a derrick while at work on the governor's residence. The messenger from Sepphoris had stopped at the shop on the way to Joseph's home, informing Jesus of his father's accident, and they went together to the house to break the sad news to Mary. Jesus desired to go immediately to his father, but Mary would hear to nothing but that she must hasten to her husband's side. She directed that James, then ten years of age, should accompany her to
Sepphoris while Jesus remained home with the younger children until she should return, as she did not know how seriously Joseph had been injured. But Joseph died of his injuries before Mary arrived. They brought him to Nazareth, and on the following day he was laid to rest with his fathers.

Just at the time when prospects were good and the future looked bright, an apparently cruel hand struck down the head of this Nazareth household, the affairs of this home were disrupted, and every plan for Jesus and his future education was demolished. This carpenter lad, now just past fourteen years of age, awakened to the realization that he had not only to fulfill the commission of his heavenly Father to reveal the divine nature on earth and in the flesh, but that his young human nature must also shoulder the responsibility of caring for his widowed mother and seven brothers and sisters—and another yet to be born. This lad of Nazareth now became the sole support and comfort of this so suddenly bereaved family.

Jesus cheerfully accepted the responsibilities so suddenly thrust upon him, and he carried them faithfully to the end. At least one great problem and anticipated difficulty in his life had been tragically solved—he would not now be expected to go to Jerusalem to study under the rabbis. It remained always true that Jesus "sat at no man's feet." He was ever willing to learn from even the humblest of little children, but he never derived authority to teach truth from human sources.

Still he knew nothing of the Gabriel visit to his mother before his birth; he only learned of this from John on the day of his baptism, at the beginning of his public ministry.   Two Crucial Years 1388:1-4

By this time Jesus and Mary were getting along much better. She regarded him less as a son; he had become to her more a father to her children. Each day's life swarmed with practical and immediate difficulties. Less frequently they spoke of his lifework, for, as time passed, all their thought was mutually devoted to the support and upbringing of their family of four boys and three girls.

By the beginning of this year Jesus had fully won his mother to the acceptance of his methods of child training—the positive injunction to do good in the place of the older Jewish method of forbidding to do evil. In his home and throughout his public-teaching career Jesus invariably employed the positive form of exhortation. Always and everywhere did he say, "You shall do this—you ought to do that." Never did he employ the negative mode of teaching derived from the ancient taboos. He refrained from placing emphasis on evil by forbidding it, while he exalted the good by commanding its performance. Prayer time in this household was the occasion for discussing anything and everything relating to the welfare of the

Jesus began wise discipline upon his brothers and sisters at such an early age that little or no punishment was ever required to secure their prompt and wholehearted obedience. The only exception was Jude, upon whom on sundry occasions Jesus found it necessary to impose penalties for his infractions of the rules of the home. On three occasions when it was deemed wise to punish Jude for self-confessed and deliberate violations of the family rules of conduct, his punishment was fixed by the unanimous decree of the older children and was assented to by Jude himself before it was inflicted.

While Jesus was most methodical and systematic in everything he did, there was also in all his administrative rulings a refreshing elasticity of

Jerusalem from the Mount of Olives, Sunrise;
Edward Lear (1859)

interpretation and an individuality of adaptation that greatly impressed all
the children with the spirit of justice which actuated their father-brother.
He never arbitrarily disciplined his brothers and sisters, and such uniform
fairness and personal consideration greatly endeared Jesus to all his family.   The Adolescent Years 1401:1-4

The tour of the Roman world consumed most of the twenty-eighth and
the entire twenty-ninth year of Jesus' life on earth. Jesus and the two na-
tives from India—Gonod and his son Ganid—left Jerusalem on a Sunday
morning, April 26, A.D. 22. They made their journey according to schedule, and Jesus said good-bye to the father and son in the city of Charax on
the Persian Gulf on the tenth day of December the following year, A.D.
23.

From Jerusalem they went to Caesarea by way of Joppa. At Caesarea
they took a boat for Alexandria. From Alexandria they sailed for Lasea in
Crete. From Crete they sailed for Carthage, touching at Cyrene. At Carthage
they took a boat for Naples, stopping at Malta, Syracuse, and Messina.
From Naples they went to Capua, whence they traveled by the Appian
Way to Rome.

After their stay in Rome they went overland to Tarentum, where they set
sail for Athens in Greece, stopping at Nicopolis and Corinth. From Athens
they went to Ephesus by way of Troas. From Ephesus they sailed for
Cyprus, putting in at Rhodes on the way. They spent considerable time
visiting and resting on Cyprus and then sailed for Antioch in Syria. From
Antioch they journeyed south to Sidon and then went over to Damascus.
From there they traveled by caravan to Mesopotamia, passing through
Thapsacus and Larissa. They spent some time in Babylon, visited Ur and
other places, and then went to Susa. From Susa they journeyed to Charax,
from which place Gonod and Ganid embarked for India.

                                    On the Way to Rome 1427:1-3

At this time the Roman Empire included all of southern Europe, Asia
Minor, Syria, Egypt, and northwest Africa; and its inhabitants embraced
the citizens of every country of the Eastern Hemisphere. His desire to
study and mingle with this cosmopolitan aggregation of Urantia mortals
was the chief reason why Jesus consented to make this journey.

Jesus learned much about men while in Rome, but the most valuable of
all the manifold experiences of his six months' sojourn in that city was his

contact with, and influence upon, the religious leaders of the empire's capital. Before the end of the first week in Rome Jesus had sought out, and had made the acquaintance of, the worth-while leaders of the Cynics, the Stoics, and the mystery cults, in particular the Mithraic group. Whether or not it was apparent to Jesus that the Jews were going to reject his mission, he most certainly foresaw that his messengers were presently coming to Rome to proclaim the kingdom of heaven; and he therefore set about, in the most amazing manner, to prepare the way for the better and more certain reception of their message. He selected five of the leading Stoics, eleven of the Cynics, and sixteen of the mystery-cult leaders and spent much of his spare time for almost six months in intimate association with these religious teachers. And this was his method of instruction: Never once did he attack their errors or even mention the flaws in their teachings. In each case he would select the truth in what they taught and then proceed so to embellish and illuminate this truth in their minds that in a very short time this enhancement of the truth effectively crowded out the associated error; and thus were these Jesus-taught men and women prepared for the subsequent recognition of additional and similar truths in the teachings of the early Christian missionaries. It was this early acceptance of the teachings of the gospel preachers which gave that powerful impetus to the rapid spread of Christianity in Rome and from there throughout the empire.

The significance of this remarkable doing can the better be understood when we record the fact that, out of this group of thirty-two Jesus-taught religious leaders in Rome, only two were unfruitful; the thirty became pivotal individuals in the establishment of Christianity in Rome, and certain of them also aided in turning the chief Mithraic temple into the first Christian church of that city. We who view human activities from behind the scenes and in the light of nineteen centuries of time recognize just three factors of paramount value in the early setting of the stage for the rapid spread of Christianity throughout Europe, and they are:

1. The choosing and holding of Simon Peter as an apostle.

2. The talk in Jerusalem with Stephen, whose death led to the winning of Saul of Tarsus.

3. The preliminary preparation of these thirty Romans for the subsequent leadership of the new religion in Rome and throughout the empire.

The Sojourn at Rome 1455:3-1456:3

2. The Apostles

This is a compelling story of ordinary men—the "Joe Six-packs" of 2,000 years ago who, upon hearing the progressive truths of Jesus, cast aside their fishing nets and looked courageously beyond the religion of their parents .

It is said that one of the people involved in publishing the Urantia Papers first believed that he was reading truth when he came upon Paper 139 - "The Twelve Apostles." Why?—because the story of the Apostle's lives is so human, so compelling, and so real. The more these commoners followed the call of spirit, the more they found that nothing was impossible. In fact, this handful of men, who embraced Jesus' radical teachings of love and brotherhood, went out and turned the Roman Empire upside down.

It is an eloquent testimony to the charm and righteousness of Jesus' earth life that, although he repeatedly dashed to pieces the hopes of his apostles and tore to shreds their every ambition for personal exaltation, only one deserted him.

The apostles learned from Jesus about the kingdom of heaven, and Jesus learned much from them about the kingdom of men, human nature as it lives on Urantia and on the other evolutionary worlds of time and space. These twelve men represented many different types of human temperament, and they had not been made alike by schooling. Many of these Galilean fishermen carried heavy strains of gentile blood as a result of the forcible conversion of the gentile population of Galilee one hundred years previously.

Do not make the mistake of regarding the apostles as being altogether ignorant and unlearned. All of them, except the Alpheus twins, were graduates of the synagogue schools, having been thoroughly trained in the Hebrew scriptures and in much of the current knowledge of that day. Seven were graduates of the Capernaum synagogue schools, and there were no better Jewish schools in all Galilee.   The Twelve Apostles 1548:1-3

Andrew and Peter were very unlike in character and temperament, but it must be recorded everlastingly to their credit that they got along together splendidly. Andrew was never jealous of Peter's oratorical ability. Not often will an older man of Andrew's type be observed exerting such a profound influence over a younger and talented brother. Andrew and Peter never seemed to be in the least jealous of each other's abilities or achievements. Late on the evening of the day of Pentecost, when, largely through the energetic and inspiring preaching of Peter, two thousand souls were added to the kingdom, Andrew said to his brother: "I could not do that, but I am glad I have a brother who could." To which Peter replied: "And but for your bringing me to the Master and by your steadfastness keeping me with him, I should not have been here to do this." Andrew and Peter were the exceptions to the rule, proving that even brothers can live together peaceably and work together effectively.

After Pentecost Peter was famous, but it never irritated the older Andrew to spend the rest of his life being introduced as "Simon Peter's brother."

When the later persecutions finally scattered the apostles from Jerusalem, Andrew journeyed through Armenia, Asia Minor, and Macedonia and, after bringing many thousands into the kingdom, was finally apprehended and crucified in Patrae in Achaia. It was two full days before this robust man expired on the cross, and throughout these tragic hours he continued effectively to proclaim the glad tidings of the salvation of the kingdom of heaven.   The Twelve Apostles 1549:4,5 & 1550:3

When Simon joined the apostles, he was thirty years of age. He was married, had three children, and lived at Bethsaida, near Capernaum. His brother, Andrew, and his wife's mother lived with him. Both Peter and Andrew were fisher partners of the sons of Zebedee.

Peter was a fluent speaker, eloquent and dramatic. He was also a natural and inspirational leader of men, a quick thinker but not a deep reasoner. He asked many questions, more than all the apostles put together, and while the majority of these questions were good and relevant, many of them were thoughtless and foolish. Peter did not have a deep mind, but he knew his mind fairly well. He was therefore a man of quick decision and sudden action. While others talked in their astonishment at seeing Jesus on the beach, Peter jumped in and swam ashore to meet the Master.

Simon Peter was distressingly vacillating; he would suddenly swing from one extreme to the other.   First he refused to let Jesus wash his feet and then, on hearing the Master's reply, begged to be washed all over. But, after all, Jesus knew that Peter's faults were of the head and not of the heart. He was one of the most inexplicable combinations of courage and cowardice that ever lived on earth. His great strength of character was loyalty, friendship. Peter really and truly loved Jesus. And yet despite this towering strength of devotion he was so unstable and inconstant that he permitted a servant girl to tease him into denying his Lord and Master. Peter could withstand persecution and any other form of direct assault, but he withered and shrank before ridicule. He was a brave soldier when facing a frontal attack, but he was a fear-cringing coward when surprised with an assault from the rear.

After leaving Jerusalem and before Paul became the leading spirit among the gentile Christian churches, Peter traveled extensively, visiting all the churches from Babylon to Corinth. He even visited and ministered to many of the churches which had been raised up by Paul. Although Peter and Paul differed much in temperament and education, even in theology, they worked together harmoniously for the upbuilding of the churches during their later years.

Peter's wife was a very able woman. For years she labored acceptably as a member of the women's corps, and when Peter was driven out of Jerusalem, she accompanied him upon all his journeys to the churches as well as on all his missionary excursions. And the day her illustrious husband yielded up his life, she was thrown to the wild beasts in the arena at Rome.

And so this man Peter, an intimate of Jesus, one of the inner circle, went forth from Jerusalem proclaiming the glad tidings of the kingdom with power and glory until the fullness of his ministry had been accomplished; and he regarded himself as the recipient of high honors when his captors informed him that he must die as his Master had died—on the cross. And thus was Simon Peter crucified in Rome.

The Twelve Apostles 1550:4,7 & 1551:2,7 & 1552:3,4

James, the older of the two apostle sons of Zebedee, whom Jesus nicknamed "sons of thunder," was thirty years old when he became an apostle. He was married, had four children, and lived near his parents in the outskirts of Capernaum, Bethsaida. He was a fisherman, plying his calling in company with his younger brother John and in association with Andrew and Simon. James and his brother John enjoyed the advantage of having known Jesus longer than any of the other apostles.

When Jesus asked if they were ready to drink the cup, they replied that they were. And as concerns James, it was literally true—he did drink the cup with the Master, seeing that he was the first of the apostles to experience martyrdom, being early put to death with the sword by Herod Agrippa. James was thus the first of the twelve to sacrifice his life upon the new battle line of the kingdom. Herod Agrippa feared James above all the other apostles. He was indeed often quiet and silent, but he was brave and determined when his convictions were aroused and challenged.

James lived his life to the full, and when the end came, he bore himself with such grace and fortitude that even his accuser and informer, who attended his trial and execution, was so touched that he rushed away from the scene of James's death to join himself to the disciples of Jesus.

The Twelve Apostles 1553:4,5

When he became an apostle, John was twenty-four years old and was the youngest of the twelve. He was unmarried and lived with his parents at Bethsaida; he was a fisherman and worked with his brother James in partnership with Andrew and Peter. Both before and after becoming an apostle, John functioned as the personal agent of Jesus in dealing with the Master's family, and he continued to bear this responsibility as long as Mary the mother of Jesus lived.

Since John was the youngest of the twelve and so closely associated with Jesus in his family affairs, he was very dear to the Master, but it cannot be truthfully said that he was "the disciple whom Jesus loved." You would hardly suspect such a magnanimous personality as Jesus to be guilty of showing favoritism, of loving one of his apostles more than the others. The fact that John was one of the three personal aides of Jesus lent further color to this mistaken idea, not to mention that John, along with his brother James, had known Jesus longer than the others.

The strongest trait in John's character was his dependability; he was prompt and courageous, faithful and devoted. His greatest weakness was this characteristic conceit. He was the youngest member of his father's family and the youngest of the apostolic group. Perhaps he was just a bit spoiled; maybe he had been humored slightly too much. But the John of after years was a very different type of person than the self-admiring and arbitrary young man who joined the ranks of Jesus' apostles when he was twenty-four.

John had a cool and daring courage which few of the other apostles possessed. He was the one apostle who followed right along with Jesus the night of his arrest and dared to accompany his Master into the very jaws of death. He was present and near at hand right up to the last earthly hour and was found faithfully carrying out his trust with regard to Jesus' mother and ready to receive such additional instructions as might be given during the last moments of the Master's mortal existence. One thing is certain, John was thoroughly dependable. John usually sat on Jesus' right hand when the twelve were at meat. He was the first of the twelve really and fully to believe in the resurrection, and he was the first to recognize the Master when he came to them on the seashore after his resurrection.

John traveled much, labored incessantly, and after becoming bishop of the Asia churches, settled down at Ephesus. He directed his associate, Nathan, in the writing of the so-called "Gospel according to John," at Ephesus, when he was ninety-nine years old. Of all the twelve apostles, John Zebedee eventually became the outstanding theologian. He died a natural death at Ephesus in A.D. 103 when he was one hundred and one years of age.   The Twelve Apostles 1553:6,7 & 1554:3 & 1555:3,8

Philip was twenty-seven years of age when he joined the apostles; he had recently been married, but he had no children at this time. The nickname which the apostles gave him signified "curiosity." Philip was always wanting to be shown. He never seemed to see very far into any proposition. He was not necessarily dull, but he lacked imagination. This lack of imagination was the great weakness of his character. He was a commonplace and matter-of-fact individual.

He was also greatly lacking in spiritual insight. He would not hesitate to interrupt Jesus in the midst of one of the Master's most profound discourses to ask an apparently foolish question. But Jesus never reprimanded him for such thoughtlessness; he was patient with him and considerate of his inability to grasp the deeper meanings of the teaching. Jesus well knew that, if he once rebuked Philip for asking these annoying questions, he would not only wound this honest soul, but such a reprimand would so hurt Philip that he would never again feel free to ask questions. Jesus knew that on his worlds of space there were untold billions of similar slow-thinking mortals, and he wanted to encourage them all to look to him and always to feel free to come to him with their questions and problems. After all, Jesus was really more interested in Philip's foolish questions than in the sermon he might be preaching. Jesus was supremely interested in men, all kinds of men.

Philip went on through the trying times of the Master's death, participated in the reorganization of the twelve, and was the first to go forth to win souls for the kingdom outside of the immediate Jewish ranks, being most successful in his work for the Samaritans and in all his subsequent labors in behalf of the gospel.

Philip's wife, who was an efficient member of the women's corps, became actively associated with her husband in his evangelistic work after their flight from the Jerusalem persecutions. His wife was a fearless woman. She stood at the foot of Philip's cross encouraging him to proclaim the glad tidings even to his murderers, and when his strength failed, she began the recital of the story of salvation by faith in Jesus and was silenced only when the irate Jews rushed upon her and stoned her to death. Their eldest daughter, Leah, continued their work, later on becoming the renowned prophetess of Hierapolis.   The Twelve Apostles 1556:2 & 1557:1,4,5

When Nathaniel joined the apostles, he was twenty-five years old and was the next to the youngest of the group. He was the youngest of a family of seven, was unmarried, and the only support of aged and infirm parents, with whom he lived at Cana; his brothers and sister were either married or deceased, and none lived there. Nathaniel and Judas Iscariot were the two best educated men among the twelve. Nathaniel had thought to become a merchant.

In many respects Nathaniel was the odd genius of the twelve. He was the apostolic philosopher and dreamer, but he was a very practical sort of dreamer. He alternated between seasons of profound philosophy and periods of rare and droll humor; when in the proper mood, he was probably the best storyteller among the twelve. Jesus greatly enjoyed hearing Nathaniel discourse on things both serious and frivolous. Nathaniel progressively took Jesus and the kingdom more seriously, but never did he take himself seriously.

Nathaniel's father (Bartholomew) died shortly after Pentecost, after which this apostle went into Mesopotamia and India proclaiming the glad tidings of the kingdom and baptizing believers. His brethren never knew what became of their onetime philosopher, poet, and humorist. But he also was a great man in the kingdom and did much to spread his Master's

Christ at the Sea of Galilee; Jacopo Tintoretto (1575/1580) © National Gallery of Art, Washington

teachings, even though he did not participate in the organization of the subsequent Christian church. Nathaniel died in India.

The Twelve Apostles 1558:3,5 & 1559:4

Matthew, the seventh apostle, was chosen by Andrew. Matthew belonged to a family of tax gatherers, or publicans, but was himself a customs collector in Capernaum, where he lived. He was thirty-one years old and married and had four children. He was a man of moderate wealth, the only one of any means belonging to the apostolic corps. He was a good business man, a good social mixer, and was gifted with the ability to make friends and to get along smoothly with a great variety of people.

Though Matthew was a man with a past, he gave an excellent account of himself, and as time went on, his associates became proud of the publican's performances. He was one of the apostles who made extensive notes on the sayings of Jesus, and these notes were used as the basis of Isador's subsequent narrative of the sayings and doings of Jesus, which has become known as the Gospel according to Matthew.

Matthew received freely tendered offerings from believing disciples and the immediate auditors of the Master's teachings, but he never openly solicited funds from the multitudes. He did all his financial work in a quiet and personal way and raised most of the money among the more substantial class of interested believers. He gave practically the whole of his modest fortune to the work of the Master and his apostles, but they never knew of this generosity, save Jesus, who knew all about it. Matthew hesitated openly to contribute to the apostolic funds for fear that Jesus and his associates might regard his money as being tainted; so he gave much in the names of other believers.

When these persecutions caused the believers to forsake Jerusalem, Matthew journeyed north, preaching the gospel of the kingdom and baptizing believers. He was lost to the knowledge of his former apostolic associates, but on he went, preaching and baptizing, through Syria, Cappadocia, Galatia, Bithynia, and Thrace. And it was in Thrace, at Lysimachia, that certain unbelieving Jews conspired with the Roman soldiers to encompass his death. And this regenerated publican died triumphant in the faith of a salvation he had so surely learned from the teachings of the Master during his recent sojourn on earth.

The Twelve Apostles 1559:5 & 1560:1,4,6

When Thomas joined the apostles, he was twenty-nine years old, was married, and had four children. Formerly he had been a carpenter and stone mason, but latterly he had become a fisherman and resided at Tarichea, situated on the west bank of the Jordan where it flows out of the Sea of Galilee, and he was regarded as the leading citizen of this little village. He had little education, but he possessed a keen, reasoning mind and was the son of excellent parents, who lived at Tiberias. Thomas had the one truly analytical mind of the twelve; he was the real scientist of the apostolic group.

The early home life of Thomas had been unfortunate; his parents were not altogether happy in their married life, and this was reflected in Thomas's adult experience. He grew up having a very disagreeable and quarrelsome disposition. Even his wife was glad to see him join the apostles; she was relieved by the thought that her pessimistic husband would be away from home most of the time. Thomas also had a streak of suspicion which made it very difficult to get along peaceably with him. Peter was very much upset by Thomas at first, complaining to his brother, Andrew, that Thomas was "mean, ugly, and always suspicious." But the better his associates knew Thomas, the more they liked him. They found he was superbly honest and unflinchingly loyal.

In the councils of the twelve Thomas was always cautious, advocating a policy of safety first, but if his conservatism was voted down or overruled, he was always the first fearlessly to move out in execution of the program decided upon. Again and again would he stand out against some project as being foolhardy and presumptuous; he would debate to the bitter end, but when Andrew would put the proposition to a vote, and after the twelve would elect to do that which he had so strenuously opposed, Thomas was the first to say, "Let's go!" He was a good loser. He did not hold grudges nor nurse wounded feelings. Time and again did he oppose letting Jesus expose himself to danger, but when the Master would decide to take such risks, always was it Thomas who rallied the apostles with his courageous words, "Come on, comrades, let's go and die with him."

Sometimes Thomas would get permission from Andrew to go off by himself for a day or two. But he soon learned that such a course was not wise; he early found that it was best, when he was downhearted, to stick close to his work and to remain near his associates. But no matter what happened in his emotional life, he kept right on being an apostle. When the time actually came to move forward, it was always Thomas who said, "Let's go!"

Thomas had a trying time during the days of the trial and crucifixion. He was for a season in the depths of despair, but he rallied his courage, stuck to the apostles, and was present with them to welcome Jesus on the Sea of Galilee. For a while he succumbed to his doubting depression but eventually rallied his faith and courage. He gave wise counsel to the apostles after Pentecost and, when persecution scattered the believers, went to Cyprus, Crete, the North African coast, and Sicily, preaching the glad tidings of the kingdom and baptizing believers. And Thomas continued preaching and baptizing until he was apprehended by the agents of the Roman government and was put to death in Malta. Just a few weeks before his death he had begun the writing of the life and teachings of Jesus.

The Twelve Apostles 1561:2,3 & 1562:2,5 & 1563:1

James and Judas the sons of Alpheus, the twin fishermen living near Kheresa, were the ninth and tenth apostles and were chosen by James and John Zebedee. They were twenty-six years old and married, James having three children, Judas two.

There is not much to be said about these two commonplace fisherfolk. They loved their Master and Jesus loved them, but they never interrupted his discourses with questions. They understood very little about the philosophical discussions or the theological debates of their fellow apostles, but they rejoiced to find themselves numbered among such a group of mighty men.

Andrew assigned them to the work of policing the multitudes. They were the chief ushers of the preaching hours and, in fact, the general servants and errand boys of the twelve. They helped Philip with the supplies, they carried money to the families for Nathaniel, and always were they ready to lend a helping hand to any one of the apostles.

The multitudes of the common people were greatly encouraged to find two like themselves honored with places among the apostles. By their very acceptance as apostles these mediocre twins were the means of bringing a host of faint-hearted believers into the kingdom. And, too, the common people took more kindly to the idea of being directed and managed by official ushers who were very much like themselves.

The twins served faithfully until the end, until the dark days of trial, crucifixion, and despair. They never lost their heart faith in Jesus, and (save John) they were the first to believe in his resurrection. But they could not comprehend the establishment of the kingdom. Soon after their Master was crucified, they returned to their families and nets; their work was done. They had not the ability to go on in the more complex battles of the kingdom. But they lived and died conscious of having been honored and blessed with four years of close and personal association with a Son of God, the sovereign maker of a universe.

The Twelve Apostles 1563:3-5 & 1564:5

Simon Zelotes, the eleventh apostle, was chosen by Simon Peter. He was an able man of good ancestry and lived with his family at Capernaum. He was twenty-eight years old when he became attached to the apostles. He was a fiery agitator and was also a man who spoke much without thinking. He had been a merchant in Capernaum before he turned his entire attention to the patriotic organization of the Zealots.

Simon's strength was his inspirational loyalty. When the apostles found a man or woman who floundered in indecision about entering the kingdom, they would send for Simon. It usually required only about fifteen minutes for this enthusiastic advocate of salvation through faith in God to settle all doubts and remove all indecision, to see a new soul born into the "liberty of faith and the joy of salvation."

Although Simon was a rabid revolutionist, a fearless firebrand of agitation, he gradually subdued his fiery nature until he became a powerful and effective preacher of "Peace on earth and good will among men." Simon was a great debater; he did like to argue. And when it came to dealing with the legalistic minds of the educated Jews or the intellectual quibblings of the Greeks, the task was always assigned to Simon.

After the dispersion because of the Jerusalem persecutions, Simon went into temporary retirement. He was literally crushed. As a nationalist patriot he had surrendered in deference to Jesus' teachings; now all was lost. He was in despair, but in a few years he rallied his hopes and went forth to proclaim the gospel of the kingdom.

He went to Alexandria and, after working up the Nile, penetrated into the heart of Africa, everywhere preaching the gospel of Jesus and baptizing believers. Thus he labored until he was an old man and feeble. And he died and was buried in the heart of Africa.

The Twelve Apostles 1564:6,8 & 1565:3,7,8

When Nathaniel met Judas at Tarichea, he was seeking employment with a fish-drying enterprise at the lower end of the Sea of Galilee. He was thirty years of age and unmarried when he joined the apostles. He was probably the best-educated man among the twelve and the only Judean in the Master's apostolic family. Judas had no outstanding trait of personal strength, though he had many outwardly appearing traits of culture and habits of training. He was a good thinker but not always a truly *honest* thinker. Judas did not really understand himself; he was not really sincere in dealing with himself.

The apostles loved Judas; he was really one of them. He must have *believed* in Jesus, but we doubt whether he really *loved* the Master with a whole heart. The case of Judas illustrates the truthfulness of that saying: "There is a way that seems right to a man, but the end thereof is death." It is altogether possible to fall victim to the peaceful deception of pleasant adjustment to the paths of sin and death. Be assured that Judas was always financially loyal to his Master and his fellow apostles. Money could never have been the motive for his betrayal of the Master.

To Jesus, Judas was a faith adventure. From the beginning the Master fully understood the weakness of this apostle and well knew the dangers of admitting him to fellowship. But it is the nature of the Sons of God to give every created being a full and equal chance for salvation and survival. Jesus wanted not only the mortals of this world but the onlookers of innumerable other worlds to know that, when doubts exist as to the sincerity and wholeheartedness of a creature's devotion to the kingdom, it is the invariable practice of the Judges of men fully to receive the doubtful candidate. The door of eternal life is wide open to all; "whosoever will may come"; there are no restrictions or qualifications save the *faith* of the one who comes.

When the sordid and sinful business was all over, this renegade mortal, who thought lightly of selling his friend for thirty pieces of silver to satisfy his long-nursed craving for revenge, rushed out and committed the final act in the drama of fleeing from the realities of mortal existence—suicide.

The eleven apostles were horrified, stunned. Jesus regarded the betrayer only with pity. The worlds have found it difficult to forgive Judas, and his name has become eschewed throughout a far-flung universe.

The Twelve Apostles 1566:1,4,6 & 1567:6,7

3. Jesus' Method of Teaching

Jesus was the consummate teacher for many reasons. First, he was deeply interested in his students. Second, he avoided negative instruction. He taught the Apostles to seed truths into people's souls, to refrain from taking anything out of their hearts and to rest assured that the living truth would eventually drive out any error. Third, Jesus advised the populace to be as wise and resourceful in fostering their eternal lives as they were in managing their business affairs.

Always the burden of his message was: the fact of the heavenly Father's love and the truth of his mercy, coupled with the good news that man is a faith-son of this same God of love. Jesus' usual technique of social contact was to draw people out and into talking with him by asking them questions. The interview would usually begin by his asking them questions and end by their asking him questions. He was equally adept in teaching by either asking or answering questions. As a rule, to those he taught the most, he said the least. Those who derived most benefit from his personal ministry were overburdened, anxious, and dejected mortals who gained much relief because of the opportunity to unburden their souls to a sympathetic and understanding listener, and he was all that and more. And when these maladjusted human beings had told Jesus about their troubles, always was he able to offer practical and immediately helpful suggestions looking toward the correction of their real difficulties, albeit he did not neglect to speak words of present comfort and immediate consolation. And invariably would he tell these distressed mortals about the love of God and impart the information, by various and sundry methods, that they were the children of this loving Father in heaven.

The Sojourn at Rome 1460:6

What he aimed at in his life appears to have been a superb self-respect. He only advised man to humble himself that he might become truly exalted; what he really aimed at was true humility toward God. He placed great value upon sincerity—a pure heart. Fidelity was a cardinal virtue in his estimate of character, while courage was the very heart of his teachings. "Fear not" was his watchword, and patient endurance his ideal of strength of character. The teachings of Jesus constitute a religion of valor, courage, and heroism. And this is just why he chose as his personal representatives twelve commonplace men, the majority of whom were rugged, virile, and manly fishermen.

Jesus had little to say about the social vices of his day; seldom did he make reference to moral delinquency. He was a positive teacher of true virtue. He studiously avoided the negative method of imparting instruction; he refused to advertise evil. He was not even a moral reformer. He well knew, and so taught his apostles, that the sensual urges of mankind are not suppressed by either religious rebuke or legal prohibitions. His few denunciations were largely directed against pride, cruelty, oppression, and hypocrisy.

James grasped the thrilling truth that Jesus wanted his children on earth to live as though they were already citizens of the completed heavenly kingdom.

Jesus knew men were different, and he so taught his apostles. He constantly exhorted them to refrain from trying to mold the disciples and believers according to some set pattern. He sought to allow each soul to develop in its own way, a perfecting and separate individual before God.

Ordination of the Twelve 1582:1,2,6,7

One of the most eventful of all the evening conferences at Amathus was the session having to do with the discussion of spiritual unity. James Zebedee had asked, "Master, how shall we learn to see alike and thereby enjoy more harmony among ourselves?" When Jesus heard this question, he was stirred within his spirit, so much so that he replied: "James, James, when did I teach you that you should all see alike? I have come into the world to proclaim spiritual liberty to the end that mortals may be empowered to live individual lives of originality and freedom before God. I do not desire that social harmony and fraternal peace shall be purchased by the sacrifice of free personality and spiritual originality. What I require of you, my apostles, is spirit unity—and that you can experience in the joy of your united dedication to the wholehearted doing of the will of my Father in heaven. You do not have to see alike or feel alike or even think alike in order spiritually to be alike. Spiritual unity is derived from the consciousness that each of you is indwelt, and increasingly dominated, by the spirit gift of the heavenly Father. Your apostolic harmony must grow out of the fact that the spirit hope of each of you is identical in origin, nature, and destiny.   Beginning of Public Work 1591:6

Many times during the training of the twelve Jesus reverted to this theme. Repeatedly he told them it was not his desire that those who believed in him should become dogmatized and standardized in accordance with the religious interpretations of even good men. Again and again he warned his apostles against the formulation of creeds and the establishment of traditions as a means of guiding and controlling believers in the gospel of the kingdom.

Near the end of the last week at Amathus, Simon Zelotes brought to Jesus one Teherma, a Persian doing business at Damascus. Teherma had heard of Jesus and had come to Capernaum to see him, and there learning that Jesus had gone with his apostles down the Jordan on the way to Jerusalem, he set out to find him. Andrew had presented Teherma to Simon for instruction. Simon looked upon the Persian as a "fire worshiper," although Teherma took great pains to explain that fire was only the visible symbol of the Pure and Holy One. After talking with Jesus, the Persian signified his intention of remaining for several days to hear the teaching and listen to the preaching.

When Simon Zelotes and Jesus were alone, Simon asked the Master: "Why is it that I could not persuade him? Why did he so resist me and so readily lend an ear to you?" Jesus answered: "Simon, Simon, how many times have I instructed you to refrain from all efforts to take something out of the hearts of those who seek salvation? How often have I told you to labor only to put something into these hungry souls? Lead men into the kingdom, and the great and living truths of the kingdom will presently drive out all serious error. When you have presented to mortal man the good news that God is his Father, you can the easier persuade him that he is in reality a son of God. And having done that, you have brought the light of salvation to the one who sits in darkness. Simon, when the Son of Man came first to you, did he come denouncing Moses and the prophets and proclaiming a new and better way of life? No. I came not to take away that which you had from your forefathers but to show you the perfected vision of that which your fathers saw only in part. Go then, Simon, teaching and preaching the kingdom, and when you have a man safely and securely within the kingdom, then is the time, when such a one shall come to you with inquiries, to impart instruction having to do with the progressive advancement of the soul within the divine kingdom."

Simon was astonished at these words, but he did as Jesus had instructed him, and Teherma, the Persian, was numbered among those who entered the kingdom.   Beginning Public Work 1592:2-5

The Baptism of Christ; Alessandro Magnasco (1740)
© National Gallery of Art, Washington

In teaching the apostles the value of parables, Jesus called attention to the following points:

The parable provides for a simultaneous appeal to vastly different levels of mind and spirit. The parable stimulates the imagination, challenges the discrimination, and provokes critical thinking; it promotes sympathy without arousing antagonism.

The parable proceeds from the things which are known to the discernment of the unknown. The parable utilizes the material and natural as a means of introducing the spiritual and the supermaterial.

Parables favor the making of impartial moral decisions. The parable evades much prejudice and puts new truth gracefully into the mind and does all this with the arousal of a minimum of the self-defense of personal resentment.   Tarrying by the Seaside 1692:3-7

Jesus continued to teach the twenty-four, saying: "The heathen are not without excuse when they rage at us. Because their outlook is small and narrow, they are able to concentrate their energies enthusiastically. Their goal is near and more or less visible; wherefore do they strive with valiant and effective execution. You who have professed entrance into the kingdom of heaven are altogether too vacillating and indefinite in your teaching conduct. The heathen strike directly for their objectives; you are guilty of too much chronic yearning. If you desire to enter the kingdom, why do you not take it by spiritual assault even as the heathen take a city they lay siege to? You are hardly worthy of the kingdom when your service consists so largely in an attitude of regretting the past, whining over the present, and vainly hoping for the future. Why do the heathen rage? Because they know not the truth. Why do you languish in futile yearning? Because you obey not the truth. Cease your useless yearning and go forth bravely doing that which concerns the establishment of the kingdom.
Fleeing Through Northern Galilee 1725:4

"Some of you, before you entered the kingdom, were very shrewd in dealing with your business associates. If you were unjust and often unfair, you were nonetheless prudent and farseeing in that you transacted your business with an eye single to your present profit and future safety. Likewise should you now so order your lives in the kingdom as to provide for your present joy while you also make certain of your future enjoyment of treasures laid up in heaven. If you were so diligent in making gains for yourselves when in the service of self, why should you show less diligence in gaining souls for the kingdom since you are now servants of the brotherhood of man and stewards of God?   Last Teaching at Pella 1853:5

Do not forget that you are commissioned to go forth preaching only the good news. You are not to attack the old ways; you are skillfully to put the leaven of new truth in the midst of the old beliefs. Let the Spirit of Truth do his own work. Let controversy come only when they who despise the truth force it upon you. But when the willful unbeliever attacks you, do not hesitate to stand in vigorous defense of the truth which has saved and sanctified you.

Throughout the vicissitudes of life, remember always to love one another. Do not strive with men, even with unbelievers. Show mercy even to those who despitefully abuse you. Show yourselves to be loyal citizens, upright artisans, praiseworthy neighbors, devoted kinsmen, understanding parents, and sincere believers in the brotherhood of the Father's kingdom. And my spirit shall be upon you, now and even to the end of the world.   Last Day at the Camp 1932:1,2

4. Jesus' Personality

What do you think it would have been like to meet Jesus in Nazareth? For me, two pictures come to mind. I have an impression of Jesus being led by the village children to their favorite rock, behind the carpenter shed, to sit and tell stories that bring a giggle to their hearts and a shine to their eyes. Here is the Creator of the universe enjoying the company and love of his lowliest creatures.

My second impression is of Jesus the fine craftsman, carefully sawing, shaping, and sanding the rich wood in the interior of a boat under construction. The care he is taking and the satisfaction he is deriving from a job well done show the joy of living a perfect human life on earth. Hearing the call of John the Baptist, Jesus the God-man lays down his tools, removes his apron, and calmly takes on the task of revealing the loving personality of his Father in heaven.

Although the average mortal of Urantia cannot hope to attain the high perfection of character which Jesus of Nazareth acquired while sojourning in the flesh, it is altogether possible for every mortal believer to develop a strong and unified personality along the perfected lines of the Jesus personality. The unique feature of the Master's personality was not so much its perfection as its symmetry, its exquisite and balanced unification. The most effective presentation of Jesus consists in following the example of the one who said, as he gestured toward the Master standing before his accusers, "Behold the man!"

The unfailing kindness of Jesus touched the hearts of men, but his stalwart strength of character amazed his followers. He was truly sincere; there was nothing of the hypocrite in him. He was free from affectation; he was always so refreshingly genuine. He never stooped to pretense, and he never resorted to shamming. He lived the truth, even as he taught it. He was the truth. He was constrained to proclaim saving truth to his generation, even though such sincerity sometimes caused pain. He was unquestioningly loyal to all truth.

But the Master was so reasonable, so approachable. He was so practical in all his ministry, while all his plans were characterized by such sanctified common sense. He was so free from all freakish, erratic, and eccentric tendencies. He was never capricious, whimsical, or hysterical. In all his teaching and in everything he did there was always an exquisite discrimination associated with an extraordinary sense of propriety.

Religion in Human Experience 1101:5-7

Jesus was an unusually cheerful person, but he was not a blind and unreasoning optimist. His constant word of exhortation was, "Be of good cheer." He could maintain this confident attitude because of his unswerving trust in God and his unshakable confidence in man. He was always touchingly considerate of all men because he loved them and believed in them. Still he was always true to his convictions and magnificently firm in his devotion to the doing of his Father's will.

The Master was always generous. He never grew weary of saying, "It is more blessed to give than to receive." Said he, "Freely you have received, freely give." And yet, with all of his unbounded generosity, he was never wasteful or extravagant. He taught that you must believe to receive salvation. "For every one who seeks shall receive."

He was candid, but always kind. Said he, "If it were not so, I would have told you." He was frank, but always friendly. He was outspoken in his love for the sinner and in his hatred for sin. But throughout all this amazing frankness he was unerringly *fair*.

Religion in Human Experience 1102:6-8

Jesus was great because he was good, and yet he fraternized with the little children. He was gentle and unassuming in his personal life, and yet he was the perfected man of a universe. His associates called him Master unbidden.

Jesus was the perfectly unified human personality. And today, as in Galilee, he continues to unify mortal experience and to co-ordinate human endeavors. He unifies life, ennobles character, and simplifies experience. He enters the human mind to elevate, transform, and transfigure it. It is literally true: "If any man has Christ Jesus within him, he is a new creature; old things are passing away; behold, all things are becoming new."

Religion in Human Experience 1103:5,6

Jesus derived much of his unusual gentleness and marvelous sympathetic understanding of human nature from his father; he inherited his gift as a great teacher and his tremendous capacity for righteous indignation from his mother. In emotional reactions to his adult-life environment, Jesus was at one time like his father, meditative and worshipful, sometimes characterized by apparent sadness; but more often he drove forward in the manner of his mother's optimistic and determined disposition. All in all, Mary's temperament tended to dominate the career of the divine Son as he grew up and swung into the momentous strides of his adult life. In some particulars Jesus was a blending of his parents' traits; in other respects he exhibited the traits of one in contrast with those of the other.

Birth and Infancy 1348:3

This year his seasons of deep meditation were often broken into by Ruth and her playmates. And always was Jesus ready to postpone the contemplation of his future work for the world and the universe that he might share in the childish joy and youthful gladness of these youngsters, who never tired of listening to Jesus relate the experiences of his various trips to Jerusalem. They also greatly enjoyed his stories about animals and nature.

The children were always welcome at the repair shop. Jesus provided sand, blocks, and stones by the side of the shop, and bevies of youngsters

Suffer not the Children; Thomas Sully   (1783-1872)
© National Gallery of Art, Washington

flocked there to amuse themselves. When they tired of their play, the more intrepid ones would peek into the shop, and if its keeper were not busy, they would make bold to go in and say, "Uncle Joshua, come out and tell us a big story." Then they would lead him out by tugging at his hands until he was seated on the favorite rock by the corner of the shop, with the children on the ground in a semicircle before him. And how the little folks did enjoy their Uncle Joshua. They were learning to laugh, and to laugh heartily. It was customary for one or two of the smallest of the children to climb upon his knees and sit there, looking up in wonderment at his expressive features as he told his stories. The children loved Jesus, and Jesus loved the children.

It was difficult for his friends to comprehend the range of his intellectual activities, how he could so suddenly and so completely swing from the profound discussion of politics, philosophy, or religion to the lighthearted and joyous playfulness of these tots of from five to ten years of age.

Jesus' Early Manhood 1416:3-5

During this final period of Jesus' work at the boatshop, he spent most of his time on the interior finishing of some of the larger craft. He took great pains with all his handiwork and seemed to experience the satisfaction of human achievement when he had completed a commendable piece of work. Though he wasted little time upon trifles, he was a painstaking workman when it came to the essentials of any given undertaking.

As time passed, rumors came to Capernaum of one John who was preaching while baptizing penitents in the Jordan, and John preached: "The kingdom of heaven is at hand; repent and be baptized." Jesus listened to these reports as John slowly worked his way up the Jordan valley from the ford of the river nearest to Jerusalem. But Jesus worked on, making boats, until John had journeyed up the river to a point near Pella in the month of January of the next year, A.D. 26, when he laid down his tools, declaring, "My hour has come," and presently presented himself to John for baptism.

But a great change had been coming over Jesus. Few of the people who had enjoyed his visits and ministrations as he had gone up and down in the land ever subsequently recognized in the public teacher the same person they had known and loved as a private individual in former years. And there was a reason for this failure of his early beneficiaries to recognize him in his later role of public and authoritative teacher. For long years this transformation of mind and spirit had been in progress, and it was finished during the eventful sojourn on Mount Hermon.

The Transition Years 1495:4-6

Jesus of Nazareth was indeed a strong and forceful personality; he was an intellectual power and a spiritual stronghold. His personality not only appealed to the spiritually minded women among his followers, but also to the educated and intellectual Nicodemus and to the hardy Roman soldier, the captain stationed on guard at the cross, who, when he had finished watching the Master die, said, "Truly, this was a Son of God." And red-blooded, rugged Galilean fishermen called him Master.

The pictures of Jesus have been most unfortunate. These paintings of the Christ have exerted a deleterious influence on youth; the temple merchants would hardly have fled before Jesus if he had been such a man as your artists usually have depicted. His was a dignified manhood; he was good, but natural. Jesus did not pose as a mild, sweet, gentle, and kindly mystic. His teaching was thrillingly dynamic. He not only *meant well*, but he went about actually *doing good*.

Beginning Public Work 1589:6-1590:1

Jesus spread good cheer everywhere he went. He was full of grace and truth. His associates never ceased to wonder at the gracious words that proceeded out of his mouth. You can cultivate gracefulness, but graciousness is the aroma of friendliness which emanates from a love-saturated soul.

Jesus was never in a hurry. He had time to comfort his fellow men "as he passed by." And he always made his friends feel at ease. He was a charming listener. He never engaged in the meddlesome probing of the souls of his associates. As he comforted hungry minds and ministered to thirsty souls, the recipients of his mercy did not so much feel that they were confessing to him as that they were conferring with him. They had unbounded confidence in him because they saw he had so much faith in them.

On the Way to Jerusalem 1874:4,8

Most of the really important things which Jesus said or did seemed to happen casually, "as he passed by." There was so little of the professional, the well-planned, or the premeditated in the Master's earthly ministry. He dispensed health and scattered happiness naturally and gracefully as he journeyed through life. It was literally true, "He went about doing good."

On the Way to Jerusalem 1875:4

5. Jesus: Divine and Human

The following passages introduce a number of perhaps unfamiliar names and concepts. These terms and their meanings are spelled out in the glossary, but here is a brief introduction nonetheless. The Urantia Book defines Jesus as the Creator Son of the local universe named Nebadon. Currently, Nebadon is known to encompass 4 million inhabited planets and to have the capacity for containing up to 10 million. Jesus resides on the sphere called Salvington.

Jesus, the "only begotten Son" of God, personalizes the 611,121st universal concept of God. He is not the Eternal Son of the Paradise Trinity referred to in Chapter 8, but rather an infinite deity personality who, along with his Creative Mother Spirit associate, is the creator parent of the local universe.

Above all, Jesus was both divine and human. He came to earth not only to teach us about his Father, but also to gain firsthand experience in what the life of a mortal is like in the evolutionary worlds of time and space. Indeed, he became a living example to mortals throughout the universe of ways to learn from life's challenges. In keeping with the infinitely wise plan of the Universal Father, a Creator Son must experience all levels of life before he is declared the sovereign of his creation—a task Jesus completed while he was on earth.

Our Creator Son is the personification of the 611,121st original concept of infinite identity of simultaneous origin in the Universal Father and the Eternal Son. The Michael of Nebadon is the "only-begotten Son" personalizing this 611,121st universal concept of divinity and infinity. His headquarters is in the threefold mansion of light on Salvington. And this dwelling is so ordered because Michael has experienced the living of all three phases of intelligent creature existence: spiritual, morontial, and material. Because of the name associated with his seventh and final bestowal on Urantia, he is sometimes spoken of as Christ Michael.

Our Creator Son is not the Eternal Son, the existential Paradise associate of the Universal Father and the Infinite Spirit. Michael of Nebadon is not a member of the Paradise Trinity. Nevertheless our Master Son possesses in his realm all of the divine attributes and powers that the Eternal Son himself would manifest were he actually to be present on Salvington and functioning in Nebadon. Michael possesses even additional power and authority, for he not only personifies the Eternal Son but also fully represents and actually embodies the personality presence of the Universal Father to and in this local universe. He even represents the Father-Son. These relationships constitute a Creator Son the most powerful, versatile, and influential of all divine beings who are capable of direct administration of evolutionary universes and of personality contact with immature creature beings.

Our Creator Son exerts the same spiritual drawing power, spirit gravity, from the headquarters of the local universe that the Eternal Son of Paradise would exert if he were personally present on Salvington, and more; this Universe Son is also the personification of the Universal Father to the universe of Nebadon. Creator Sons are personality centers for the spiritual forces of the Paradise Father-Son. Creator Sons are the final power-personality focalizations of the mighty time-space attributes of God the Sevenfold.

The Creator Son is the vicegerent personalization of the Universal Father, the divinity co-ordinate of the Eternal Son, and the creative associate of the Infinite Spirit. To our universe and all its inhabited worlds the Sovereign Son is, to all practical intents and purposes, God. He personifies all of the Paradise Deities which evolving mortals can discerningly comprehend. This Son and his Spirit associate are your creator parents. To you, Michael, the Creator Son, is the supreme personality; to you, the Eternal Son is supersupreme—an infinite Deity personality.

In the person of the Creator Son we have a ruler and divine parent who is just as mighty, efficient, and beneficent as would be the Universal Father and the Eternal Son if both were present on Salvington and engaged in the administration of the affairs of the universe of Nebadon.

Administration of the Local Universe 366:2 - 367:2

Of his human nature he was never in doubt; it was self-evident and always present in his consciousness. But of his divine nature there was always room for doubt and conjecture, at least this was true right up to the event of his baptism. The self-realization of divinity was a slow and, from the human standpoint, a natural evolutionary revelation. This revelation and self-realization of divinity began in Jerusalem when he was not quite

he Miracle of Christ Healing the Blind; El Greco (Domenikos Theotokopoulos),(1541-1614) ©The Metropolitan Museum of Art

thirteen years old with the first supernatural occurrence of his human existence; and this experience of effecting the self-realization of his divine nature was completed at the time of his second supernatural experience while in the flesh, the episode attendant upon his baptism by John in the Jordan, which event marked the beginning of his public career of ministry and teaching.

Between these two celestial visitations, one in his thirteenth year and the other at his baptism, there occurred nothing supernatural or superhuman in the life of this incarnated Creator Son. Notwithstanding this, the babe of Bethlehem, the lad, youth, and man of Nazareth, was in reality the incarnated Creator of a universe; but he never once used aught of this power, nor did he utilize the guidance of celestial personalities, aside from that of his guardian seraphim, in the living of his human life up to the day of his baptism by John. And we who thus testify know whereof we speak.

And yet, throughout all these years of his life in the flesh he was truly divine. He was actually a Creator Son of the Paradise Father. When once he had espoused his public career, subsequent to the technical completion of his purely mortal experience of sovereignty acquirement, he did not hesitate publicly to admit that he was the Son of God. He did not hesitate to declare, "I am Alpha and Omega, the beginning and the end, the first and the last." He made no protest in later years when he was called Lord of Glory, Ruler of a Universe, the Lord God of all creation, the Holy One of Israel, the Lord of all, our Lord and our God, God with us, having a name above every name and on all worlds, the Omnipotence of a universe, the Universe Mind of this creation, the One in whom are hid all treasures of wisdom and knowledge, the fullness of Him who fills all things, the eternal Word of the eternal God, the One who was before all things and in whom all things consist, the Creator of the heavens and the earth, the Upholder of a universe, the Judge of all the earth, the Giver of life eternal, the True Shepherd, the Deliverer of the worlds, and the Captain of our salvation.   Jesus' Early Manhood 1408:5-7

As Jesus paused for a moment to look over the congregation, one of the teachers from Jerusalem (a member of the Sanhedrin) rose up and asked: "Do I understand you to say that you are the bread which comes down from heaven, and that the manna which Moses gave to our fathers in the wilderness did not?" And Jesus answered the Pharisee, "You understood aright." Then said the Pharisee: "But are you not Jesus of Nazareth, the son of Joseph, the carpenter? Are not your father and mother, as well as your brothers and sisters, well known to many of us? How then is it that you appear here in God's house and declare that you have come down from heaven?"

By this time there was much murmuring in the synagogue, and such a tumult was threatened that Jesus stood up and said: "Let us be patient; the truth never suffers from honest examination. I am all that you say but more. The Father and I are one; the Son does only that which the Father teaches him, while all those who are given to the Son by the Father, the Son will receive to himself. You have read where it is written in the Prophets, 'You shall all be taught by God,' and that 'Those whom the Father teaches will hear also his Son.' Every one who yields to the teaching of the Father's indwelling spirit will eventually come to me. Not that any man has seen the Father, but the Father's spirit does live within man. And the Son who came down from heaven, he has surely seen the Father. And those who truly believe this Son already have eternal life.

"I am this bread of life. Your fathers ate manna in the wilderness and are dead. But this bread which comes down from God, if a man eats thereof, he shall never die in spirit. I repeat, I am this living bread, and every soul who attains the realization of this united nature of God and man shall live forever. And this bread of life which I give to all who will receive is my own living and combined nature. The Father in the Son and the Son one with the Father—that is my life-giving revelation to the world and my saving gift to all nations."

When Jesus had finished speaking, the ruler of the synagogue dismissed the congregation, but they would not depart. They crowded up around Jesus to ask more questions while others murmured and disputed among themselves. And this state of affairs continued for more than three hours. It was well past seven o'clock before the audience finally dispersed.

Crisis at Capernaum 1711:2-5

The faith of the apostles was at a high point at the time of the feeding of the five thousand, and then it rapidly fell almost to zero. Now, as a result of the Master's admission of his divinity, the lagging faith of the twelve arose in the next few weeks to its highest pitch, only to undergo a progressive decline. The third revival of their faith did not occur until after the Master's resurrection.

When the three had been fast asleep for about half an hour, they were suddenly awakened by a near-by crackling sound, and much to their amazement and consternation, on looking about them, they beheld Jesus in intimate converse with two brilliant beings clothed in the habiliments of the light of the celestial world. And Jesus' face and form shone with the luminosity of a heavenly light. These three conversed in a strange language, but from certain things said, Peter erroneously conjectured that the beings with Jesus were Moses and Elijah; in reality, they were Gabriel and the Father Melchizedek. The physical controllers had arranged for the apostles to witness this scene because of Jesus' request.

The three apostles were so badly frightened that they were slow in collecting their wits, but Peter, who was first to recover himself, said, as the dazzling vision faded from before them and they observed Jesus standing alone: "Jesus, Master, it is good to have been here. We rejoice to see this glory. We are loath to go back down to the inglorious world. If you are willing, let us abide here, and we will erect three tents, one for you, one for Moses, and one for Elijah." And Peter said this because of his confusion, and because nothing else came into his mind at just that moment.

While Peter was yet speaking, a silvery cloud drew near and overshadowed the four of them. The apostles now became greatly frightened, and as they fell down on their faces to worship, they heard a voice, the same that had spoken on the occasion of Jesus' baptism, say: "This is my beloved Son; give heed to him." And when the cloud vanished, again was Jesus alone with the three, and he reached down and touched them, saying: "Arise and be not afraid; you shall see greater things than this." But the apostles were truly afraid; they were a silent and thoughtful trio as they made ready to descend the mountain shortly before midnight.

Mount of Transfiguration 1753:1,4-6

Mark, Matthew, and Luke retain something of the picture of the human Jesus as he engaged in the superb struggle to ascertain the divine will and to do that will. John presents a picture of the triumphant Jesus as he walked on earth in the full consciousness of divinity. The great mistake that has been made by those who have studied the Master's life is that some have conceived of him as entirely human, while others have thought of him as only divine. Throughout his entire experience he was truly both human and divine, even as he yet is.

The Faith of Jesus 2092:1

6. Jesus and Women

Jesus struck some of the first blows in the struggle for women's liberation. The society of his time frowned upon men recognizing their wives in public, and considered it better to burn the Scriptures than have them delivered to women. Even at sixteen years of age, Jesus would not accept his sisters be home schooled in the same lessons he and his brothers received in the synagogue school.

In later life, Jesus continued to advocate for the equal status of women when he appointed ten women as ministers for the work of the kingdom. Most of the Apostles followed this practice after his death. Paul, however, could not accept that Jesus proposed such radical procedures, and went on to make demeaning comments about women, as is illustrated in the New Testament. In subsequent generations, women's equality became lost in the mists of time.

Did Jesus have a girlfriend or a wife? No, procreation was prohibited by the mandates of his home sphere—and fortunately so. Imagine the ancestor worship and cults that would have resulted if Jesus had left offspring on earth! One woman, Rebecca, sought his hand in marriage and was politely refused. Nevertheless, she followed him throughout his years of public ministry and sat at his feet below the cross on the day of his death.

While you will live the normal and average social life of the planet, being a normal individual of the male sex, you will probably not enter the marriage relation, which relation would be wholly honorable and consistent with your bestowal; but I must remind you that one of the incarnation mandates of Sonarington forbids the leaving of human offspring behind on any planet by a bestowal Son of Paradise origin.

The Bestowal of Michael 1330:3

This year Simon started to school, and they were compelled to sell another house. James now took charge of the teaching of his three sisters, two of whom were old enough to begin serious study. As soon as Ruth grew up, she was taken in hand by Miriam and Martha. Ordinarily the girls of Jewish families received little education, but Jesus maintained (and his mother agreed) that girls should go to school the same as boys, and since the synagogue school would not receive them, there was nothing to do but conduct a home school especially for them.

The Adolescent Years 1396:2

Although Jesus was poor, his social standing in Nazareth was in no way impaired. He was one of the foremost young men of the city and very highly regarded by most of the young women. Since Jesus was such a

In the House of Martha and Mary; Jacopo Tintoretto (1518-1594)
©Alte Pinakothek Munchen, Germany

highly regarded by most of the young women. Since Jesus was such a splendid specimen of robust and intellectual manhood, and considering his reputation as a spiritual leader, it was not strange that Rebecca, the eldest daughter of Ezra, a wealthy merchant and trader of Nazareth, should discover that she was slowly falling in love with this son of Joseph. She first confided her affection to Miriam, Jesus' sister, and Miriam in turn talked all this over with her mother. Mary was intensely aroused. Was she about to lose her son, now become the indispensable head of the family? Would troubles never cease? What next could happen? And then she paused to contemplate what effect marriage would have upon Jesus' future career; not often, but at least sometimes, did she recall the fact that Jesus was a "child of promise."

Then began that eventful talk with Rebecca. Thus far in his life, Jesus had made little distinction in his association with boys and girls, with young men and young women. His mind had been altogether too much occupied with the pressing problems of practical earthly affairs and the intriguing contemplation of his eventual career "about his Father's business" ever to have given serious consideration to the consummation of personal love in human marriage. But now he was face to face with another of those problems which every average human being must confront and decide. Indeed was he "tested in all points like as you are."

After listening attentively, he sincerely thanked Rebecca for her expressed admiration, adding, "it shall cheer and comfort me all the days of my life." He explained that he was not free to enter into relations with any woman other than those of simple brotherly regard and pure friendship. He made it clear that his first and paramount duty was the rearing of his father's family, that he could not consider marriage until that was accomplished; and then he added: "If I am a son of destiny, I must not assume obligations of lifelong duration until such a time as my destiny shall be made manifest."

Rebecca was heartbroken. She refused to be comforted and importuned her father to leave Nazareth until he finally consented to move to Sepphoris. In after years, to the many men who sought her hand in marriage, Rebecca had but one answer. She lived for only one purpose—to await the hour when this, to her, the greatest man who ever lived would begin his career as a teacher of living truth. And she followed him devotedly through his eventful years of public labor, being present (unobserved by Jesus) that day when he rode triumphantly into Jerusalem; and she stood "among the other women" by the side of Mary on that fateful and tragic afternoon when the Son of Man hung upon the cross, to her, as well as to countless worlds on high, "the one altogether lovely and the greatest among ten thousand."   The Adolescent Years 1402:4 & 1403:2-4

The most astonishing and the most revolutionary feature of Michael's mission on earth was his attitude toward women. In a day and generation when a man was not supposed to salute even his own wife in a public place, Jesus dared to take women along as teachers of the gospel in connection with his third tour of Galilee. And he had the consummate courage to do this in the face of the rabbinic teaching which declared that it was "better that the words of the law should be burned than delivered to women."

In one generation Jesus lifted women out of the disrespectful oblivion and the slavish drudgery of the ages. And it is the one shameful thing about the religion that presumed to take Jesus' name that it lacked the moral courage to follow this noble example in its subsequent attitude toward women.   Second Preaching Tour 1671:3,4

Of all the daring things which Jesus did in connection with his earth career, the most amazing was his sudden announcement on the evening of January 16: "On the morrow we will set apart ten women for the ministering work of the kingdom." At the beginning of the two weeks' period during which the apostles and the evangelists were to be absent from Bethsaida on their furlough, Jesus requested David to summon his parents back to their home and to dispatch messengers calling to Bethsaida ten devout women who had served in the administration of the former encampment and the tented infirmary. These women had all listened to the instruction given the young evangelists, but it had never occurred to either themselves or their teachers that Jesus would dare to commission women to teach the gospel of the kingdom and minister to the sick. These ten women selected and commissioned by Jesus were: Susanna, the daughter of the former chazan of the Nazareth synagogue; Joanna, the wife of Chuza, the steward of Herod Antipas; Elizabeth, the daughter of a wealthy Jew of Tiberias and Sepphoris; Martha, the elder sister of Andrew and Peter; Rachel, the sister-in-law of Jude, the Master's brother in the flesh; Nasanta, the daughter of Elman, the Syrian physician; Milcha, a cousin of the Apostle Thomas; Ruth, the eldest daughter of Matthew Levi; Celta, the daughter of a Roman centurion; and Agaman, a widow of Damascus. Subsequently, Jesus added two other women to this group—Mary Magdalene and Rebecca, the daughter of Joseph of Arimathea.

Jesus authorized these women to effect their own organization and directed Judas to provide funds for their equipment and for pack animals. The ten elected Susanna as their chief and Joanna as their treasurer. From this time on they furnished their own funds; never again did they draw upon Judas for support.

It was most astounding in that day, when women were not even allowed on the main floor of the synagogue (being confined to the women's gallery), to behold them being recognized as authorized teachers of the new gospel of the kingdom. The charge which Jesus gave these ten women as he set them apart for gospel teaching and ministry was the emancipation proclamation which set free all women and for all time; no more was man to look upon woman as his spiritual inferior. This was a decided shock to even the twelve apostles. Notwithstanding they had many times heard the Master say that "in the kingdom of heaven there is neither rich nor poor, free nor bond, male nor female, all are equally the sons and daughters of God," they were literally stunned when he proposed formally to commission these ten women as religious teachers and even to permit their traveling about with them. The whole country was stirred up by this proceeding, the enemies of Jesus making great capital out of this move, but everywhere the women believers in the good news stood staunchly behind their chosen sisters and voiced no uncertain approval of this tardy acknowledgment of woman's place in religious work. And this liberation of women, giving them due recognition, was practiced by the apostles immediately after the Master's departure, albeit they fell back to the olden customs in subsequent generations. Throughout the early days of the Christian church women teachers and ministers were called *deaconesses* and were accorded general recognition. But Paul, despite the fact that he conceded all this in theory, never really incorporated it into his own attitude and personally found it difficult to carry out in practice.

Third Preaching Tour 1678:5 - 1679:2

7. The Remembrance Supper

The most horrifying event in Jesus' childhood occurred on his first trip to Jerusalem. The sight of priests slaughtering animals and of holy men's arms dripping with blood on the altar of worship to God overwhelmed him with disgust. In response, Jesus was determined to replace the sacrifice of animals in celebration of his people's faith with a bloodless Passover.

Any group of people coming together for a special meal or event can honor this decision by holding a Remembrance Supper. One of the most meaningful worship services I attended was at a conference in Flagstaff, Arizona. People of many faiths had convened in the Northern Arizona University library, whose large windows looked on the setting sun as it dropped behind the San Francisco Peaks.

A violinist and a harpist were playing in the center of the room. Around them were half a dozen tables with chairs, bidding us to participate in a silent self-service communion with God. Each person present was to move from table to table and perform a designated task. One table held a prayer tree, paper, and pencils; we were to write a prayer and tape it to a limb of the tree. Another held a burning candle, readings, and an invitation to meditate. On the third table was a vine with branches, the parable of the vine and branches, and a box of costume jewelry; we were to read the parable, select a stone, and glue it to the shrub. On a fourth table was a large, flat box of smooth sand accompanied by a mind-searching task. We were to read the biblical story of the prostitute who was about to be stoned, then—as Jesus did for each of the women's accusers—write something about ourselves in the sand.

Against the wall facing the mountains were several easy chairs where we could sit and listen to the music, contemplate nature, and plan our eternal future. A table toward the center of the room held a basket of bread and small cups of apple juice; here our assignment was to select someone at random, tell them a story about Jesus' life, and serve them bread and juice.

The room was so quiet you could almost hear your soul speak. There was no set ritual, no same old words to hash through mindlessly, no sense of having to rush out the door to beat the crowd to the parking lot—just

*you and your Maker. Unexpectedly, tears filled my eyes and streamed
down my face. A rare and cleansing moment in my life.*

*Through a Remembrance Supper, you too, can be reborn. Share bread;
think back to the time when God walked the face of our earth; and, if you
wish, read Psalm 118 at the close of this section.*

Even at this early date, though he said nothing about such matters to his
parents, Jesus had begun to turn over in his mind the propriety of celebrat-
ing the Passover without the slaughtered lamb. He felt assured in his own
mind that the Father in heaven was not pleased with this spectacle of sacrificial offerings, and as the years passed, he became increasingly determined someday to establish the celebration of a bloodless Passover.

Jesus at Jerusalem (age 13) 1379:4

As they brought Jesus the third cup of wine, the "cup of blessing," he
arose from the couch and, taking the cup in his hands, blessed it, saying:
"Take this cup, all of you, and drink of it. This shall be the cup of my
remembrance. This is the cup of the blessing of a new dispensation of
grace and truth. This shall be to you the emblem of the bestowal and
ministry of the divine Spirit of Truth. And I will not again drink this cup
with you until I drink in new form with you in the Father's eternal kingdom."

The Last Supper 1941:6

The apostles all sensed that something out of the ordinary was transpiring as they drank of this cup of blessing in profound reverence and perfect
silence. The old Passover commemorated the emergence of their fathers
from a state of racial slavery into individual freedom; now the Master was
instituting a new remembrance supper as a symbol of the new dispensation wherein the enslaved individual emerges from the bondage of cer-
emonialism and selfishness into the spiritual joy of the brotherhood and
fellowship of the liberated faith sons of the living God.

When they had finished drinking this new cup of remembrance, the
Master took up the bread and, after giving thanks, broke it in pieces and,
directing them to pass it around, said: "Take this bread of remembrance
and eat it. I have told you that I am the bread of life. And this bread of life
is the united life of the Father and the Son in one gift. The word of the
Father, as revealed in the Son, is indeed the bread of life." When they had

partaken of the bread of remembrance, the symbol of the living word of truth incarnated in the likeness of mortal flesh, they all sat down.

This supper of remembrance, when it is partaken of by those who are Son-believing and God-knowing, does not need to have associated with its symbolism any of man's puerile misinterpretations regarding the meaning of the divine presence, for upon all such occasions the Master is really present. The remembrance supper is the believer's symbolic rendezvous with Michael. When you become thus spirit-conscious, the Son is actually present, and his spirit fraternizes with the indwelling fragment of his Father.   The Last Supper 1942:1,2,5

When Jesus had thus established the supper of the remembrance, he said to the apostles: "And as often as you do this, do it in remembrance of me. And when you do remember me, first look back upon my life in the flesh, recall that I was once with you, and then, by faith, discern that you shall all some time sup with me in the Father's eternal kingdom. This is the new Passover which I leave with you, even the memory of my bestowal life, the word of eternal truth; and of my love for you, the outpouring of my Spirit of Truth upon all flesh."

And they ended this celebration of the old but bloodless Passover in connection with the inauguration of the new supper of the remembrance, by singing, all together, the one hundred and eighteenth Psalm.
                                                    The Last Supper 1943:2,3

Psalm 118

Give thanks to the Lord, for he is good;
   his love endures forever.

Let Israel say:
   "His love endures forever."
Let the house of Aaron say:
   "His love endures forever."
Let those who fear the LORD say:
   "His love endures forever."

In my anguish I cried to the LORD,
   and he answered by setting me free.
The LORD is with me; I will not be afraid.

Christ washing his Disciples' Feet; by Jacopo Tintoretto (1518-1594)
© National Gallery of London

What can man do to me?
The LORD is with me; he is my helper.
    I will look in triumph on my enemies.

It is better to take refuge in the LORD
        than to trust in man.
It is better to take refuge in the Lord
        than to trust in princes.
All the nations surrounded me,
        but in the name of the LORD
            I cut them off.

They surrounded me on every side,
        but in the name of the LORD
            I cut them off.
They swarmed around me like bees,
        but they died out as quickly as
            burning thorns;
            in the name of the LORD I cut them off.

I was pushed back and about to fall,
        but the LORD helped me.
The LORD is my strength and my song;
        he has become my salvation.

Shouts of joy and victory
            resound in the tents of the righteous:
"The Lord's right hand has done mighty things!
The Lord's right hand is lifted high;
the Lord's right hand has done mighty things!"

I will not die but live,
        and will proclaim what the LORD
            has done.
The LORD has chastened me severely,
        but he has not given me over to death.

Open for me the gates of righteousness;
        I will enter and give thanks to the LORD.
This is the gate of the LORD
        through which the righteous may enter.

I will give you thanks, for you answered me;
    you have become my salvation.

The stone the builders rejected
    has become the capstone;
the LORD has done this,
    and it is marvelous in our eyes.
This is the day the LORD has made;
    let us rejoice and be glad in it.

O LORD, save us;
    O LORD, grant us success.
Blessed is he who comes in the name of the LORD.
    From the house of the LORD we bless you.
The LORD is God,
    and he has made his light shine upon us.
With boughs in hand, join in the festal procession
    up to the horns of the altar.

You are my God, and I will give you thanks;
    you are my God, and I will exalt you.

Give thanks to the LORD, for he is good;
    his love endures forever.
              Psalm 118 Old Testament (NIV)

8. Original Sin(?) and the Crucifixion

The Urantia Book maintains that the concept of original sin is the most ingrained misconception in today's Christian liturgy. The notion that God was vengeful toward humanity because of some distant ancestral sin has hamstrung the teachings of Jesus. Guilt resulting from this sin was first proposed by Paul, a tireless missionary who became the father of modern day Christianity, overlaying the spiritual teachings of Jesus with his own belief in redemption through sacrifice.

Did Adam and Eve err? Yes, yet they acknowledged their mistakes and accepted the consequences. Would God hold their misdeeds against us 37,000 years later? Not according to Jesus' teaching of the loving Father in heaven.

Jesus realized early in life that the concept of a spiritual kingdom would not be embraced by Hebrews who wanted a mighty savior to deliver them from the Roman yoke, erase their age-old oppressions, and set them to their rightful position as the "Chosen People of God." He also knew that most of his family members, as well as residents in his hometown of Nazareth, rejected him as a misguided mystic. Even so, he did not alter his message of faith and hope. He accepted his fate and, honoring his Father's gift of free will to the people of earth, allowed misguided mortals to slay him.

Jesus is not about to die as a sacrifice for sin. He is not going to atone for the inborn moral guilt of the human race. Mankind has no such racial guilt before God. Guilt is purely a matter of personal sin and knowing, deliberate rebellion against the will of the Father and the administration of his Sons.

Just Before the Crucifixion 2003:1

"You are confused, Thomas, by the doctrines of the Greeks and the errors of the Persians. You do not understand the relationships of evil and sin because you view mankind as beginning on earth with a perfect Adam and rapidly degenerating, through sin, to man's present deplorable estate. But why do you refuse to comprehend the meaning of the record which discloses how Cain, the son of Adam, went over into the land of Nod and there got himself a wife? And why do you refuse to interpret the meaning of the record which portrays the sons of God finding wives for themselves among the daughters of men?

"Men are, indeed, by nature evil, but not necessarily sinful. The new birth—the baptism of the spirit—is essential to deliverance from evil and necessary for entrance into the kingdom of heaven, but none of this detracts from the fact that man is the son of God. Neither does this inherent presence of potential evil mean that man is in some mysterious way estranged from the Father in heaven so that, as an alien, foreigner, or stepchild, he must in some manner seek for legal adoption by the Father. All such notions are born, first, of your misunderstanding of the Father and, second, of your ignorance of the origin, nature, and destiny of man."

Training the Evangelists 1660:6,7

Jerusalem from the Mount of Olives (1902) Gustav Bauernfeind

What a travesty upon the infinite character of God! this teaching that his fatherly heart in all its austere coldness and hardness was so untouched by the misfortunes and sorrows of his creatures that his tender mercies were not forthcoming until he saw his blameless Son bleeding and dying upon the cross of Calvary!   God's Relation to the Universe 60:5

But Paul's theory of original sin, the doctrines of hereditary guilt and innate evil and redemption therefrom, was partially Mithraic in origin, having little in common with Hebrew theology, Philo's philosophy, or Jesus' teachings. Some phases of Paul's teachings regarding original sin and the atonement were original with himself.   Times of the Bestowal 1339:1

Paul started out to build a new Christian cult on "the blood of the everlasting covenant." And while he may have unnecessarily encumbered Christianity with teachings about blood and sacrifice, he did once and for all make an end of the doctrines of redemption through human or animal sacrifices. His theologic compromises indicate that even revelation must submit to the graduated control of evolution. According to Paul, Christ became the last and all-sufficient human sacrifice; the divine Judge is now fully and forever satisfied.   Sin, Sacrifice, and Atonement 984:2

Earlier in the evening it had not seemed so difficult to drink the cup, but as the human Jesus bade farewell to his apostles and sent them to their rest, the trial grew more appalling. Jesus experienced that natural ebb and flow of feeling which is common to all human experience, and just now he was weary from work, exhausted from the long hours of strenuous labor and painful anxiety concerning the safety of his apostles. While no mortal can presume to understand the thoughts and feelings of the incarnate Son of God at such a time as this, we know that he endured great anguish and suffered untold sorrow, for the perspiration rolled off his face in great drops. He was at last convinced that the Father intended to allow natural events to take their course; he was fully determined to employ none of his sovereign power as the supreme head of a universe to save himself.

The experience of parting with the apostles was a great strain on the human heart of Jesus; this sorrow of love bore down on him and made it more difficult to face such a death as he well knew awaited him. He realized how weak and how ignorant his apostles were, and he dreaded to leave them. He well knew that the time of his departure had come, but his

Christ on the Mount of Olives; Hendrik Goltzius (1597)
©National Gallery of Art, Washington

human heart longed to find out whether there might not possibly be some legitimate avenue of escape from this terrible plight of suffering and sorrow And when it had thus sought escape, and failed, it was willing to drink the cup. The divine mind of Michael knew he had done his best for the twelve apostles; but the human heart of Jesus wished that more might have been done for them before they should be left alone in the world. Jesus' heart was being crushed; he truly loved his brethren. He was isolated from his family in the flesh; one of his chosen associates was betraying him. His father Joseph's people had rejected him and thereby sealed their doom as a people with a special mission on earth. His soul was tortured by baffled love and rejected mercy. It was just one of those awful human moments when everything seems to bear down with crushing cruelty and terrible agony.

Jesus' humanity was not insensible to this situation of private loneliness, public shame, and the appearance of the failure of his cause. All these sentiments bore down on him with indescribable heaviness. In this great sorrow his mind went back to the days of his childhood in Nazareth and to his early work in Galilee. At the time of this great trial there came up in his mind many of those pleasant scenes of his earthly ministry. And it was from these old memories of Nazareth, Capernaum, Mount Hermon, and of the sunrise and sunset on the shimmering Sea of Galilee, that he soothed himself as he made his human heart strong and ready to encounter the traitor who should so soon betray him.

Before Judas and the soldiers arrived, the Master had fully regained his customary poise; the spirit had triumphed over the flesh; faith had asserted itself over all human tendencies to fear or entertain doubt. The supreme test of the full realization of the human nature had been met and acceptably passed. Once more the Son of Man was prepared to face his enemies with equanimity and in the full assurance of his invincibility as a mortal man unreservedly dedicated to the doing of his Father's will.   In Gethsemane 1969:2,4,5 & 1970:1

Shortly after one o'clock, amidst the increasing darkness of the fierce sandstorm, Jesus began to fail in human consciousness. His last words of mercy, forgiveness, and admonition had been spoken. His last wish—concerning the care of his mother—had been expressed. During this hour of approaching death the human mind of Jesus resorted to the repetition of many passages in the Hebrew scriptures, particularly the Psalms. The last conscious thought of the human Jesus was concerned with the repetition in his mind of a portion of the Book of Psalms now known as the twentieth, twenty-first, and twenty-second Psalms. While his lips would often move, he was too weak to utter the words as these passages, which he so well knew by heart, would pass through his mind. Only a few times did those standing by catch some utterance, such as, "I know the Lord will save his anointed," "Your hand shall find out all my enemies," and "My God, my God, why have you forsaken me?" Jesus did not for one moment entertain the slightest doubt that he had lived in accordance with the Father's will; and he never doubted that he was now laying down his life in the flesh in accordance with his Father's will. He did not feel that the Father had forsaken him; he was merely reciting in his vanishing consciousness many Scriptures, among them this twenty-second Psalm, which begins with "My God, my God, why have you forsaken me?" And this happened to be one of the three passages which were spoken with sufficient clearness to be heard by those standing by.

The sandstorm grew in intensity and the heavens increasingly darkened. Still the soldiers and the small group of believers stood by. The soldiers crouched near the cross, huddled together to protect themselves from the cutting sand. The mother of John and others watched from a distance where they were somewhat sheltered by an overhanging rock. When the Master finally breathed his last, there were present at the foot of his cross John Zebedee, his brother Jude, his sister Ruth, Mary Magdalene, and Rebecca, onetime of Sepphoris.

It was just before three o'clock when Jesus, with a loud voice, cried out, "It is finished! Father, into your hands I commend my spirit." And when he had thus spoken, he bowed his head and gave up the life struggle. When the Roman centurion saw how Jesus died, he smote his smote his breast and said: "This was indeed a righteous man; truly he must have been a Son of God." And from that hour he began to believe in Jesus.

The Crucifixion 2010:3,4 & 2011:1

The apostles never ceased to be shocked by Jesus' willingness to talk with women, women of questionable character, even immoral women. It was very difficult for Jesus to teach his apostles that women, even so-called immoral women, have souls which can choose God as their Father, thereby becoming daughters of God and candidates for life everlasting. Even nineteen centuries later many show the same unwillingness to grasp the Master's teachings. Even the Christian religion has been persistently built up around the fact of the death of Christ instead of around the truth of his life. The world should be more concerned with his happy and God-revealing life than with his tragic and sorrowful death.

Going Through Samaria 1614:5

9. Holy Spirit: The Spirit of Truth

Before Jesus departed, he promised humanity a new gift—the spirit of living truth. On earth he could be in only one place at a time, but through the Spirit of Truth he could be with all people at the same time.

The Spirit of Truth is not the Holy Spirit, regarded as the Third Person of the Trinity. Rather, the Spirit of Truth is the water of life. Those who accept the leadings of spirit will find it flowing into their souls and speaking through them. The joy of this outpoured spirit is a tonic for health, a stimulus for mind, and an unfailing source of energy for the soul.

Having started out on the way of life everlasting, having accepted the assignment and received your orders to advance, do not fear the dangers of human forgetfulness and mortal inconstancy, do not be troubled with doubts of failure or by perplexing confusion, do not falter and question your status and standing, for in every dark hour, at every crossroad in the forward struggle, the Spirit of Truth will always speak, saying, "This is the way."

Local Universe Mother Spirit 383:2

"But take heed, for your enemies will bring you up before their councils, while in their synagogues they will castigate you. Before governors and rulers you will be brought because you believe this gospel, and your very testimony shall be a witness for me to them. And when they lead you to judgment, be not anxious about what you shall say, for the spirit of my Father indwells you and will at such a time speak through you."

Ordination of the Twelve 1584:2

On the last day, the great day of the feast, as the procession from the pool of Siloam passed through the temple courts, and just after the water and the wine had been poured down upon the altar by the priests, Jesus, standing among the pilgrims, said: "If any man thirst, let him come to me and drink. From the Father above I bring to this world the water of life. He who believes me shall be filled with the spirit which this water represents, for even the Scriptures have said, `Out of him shall flow rivers of living waters.' When the Son of Man has finished his work on earth, there shall be poured out upon all flesh the living Spirit of Truth. Those who receive this spirit shall never know spiritual thirst."

At the Feast of the Tabernacles 1795:5

Jesus continued to teach, saying: "When I have gone to the Father, and after he has fully accepted the work I have done for you on earth, and after I have received the final sovereignty of my own domain, I shall say to my Father: Having left my children alone on earth, it is in accordance with my promise to send them another teacher. And when the Father shall approve, I will pour out the Spirit of Truth upon all flesh. Already is my Father's spirit in your hearts, and when this day shall come, you will also have me with you even as you now have the Father. This new gift is the spirit of living truth. The unbelievers will not at first listen to the teachings of this spirit, but the sons of light will all receive him gladly and with a whole heart. And you shall know this spirit when he comes even as you have known me, and you will receive this gift in your hearts, and he will abide with you. You thus perceive that I am not going to leave you without help and guidance. I will not leave you desolate. Today I can be with you only in person. In the times to come I will be with you and all other men who desire my presence, wherever you may be, and with each of you at the same time. Do you not discern that it is better for me to go away; that I leave you in the flesh so that I may the better and the more fully be with you in the spirit?   The Farewell Discourse 1948:2

Jesus looked down upon them all, smiled, and said: "My little children, I am going away, going back to my Father. In a little while you will not see me as you do here, as flesh and blood. In a very short time I am going to send you my spirit, just like me except for this material body. This new teacher is the Spirit of Truth who will live with each one of you, in your hearts, and so will all the children of light be made one and be drawn toward one another. And in this very manner will my Father and I be able to live in the souls of each one of you and also in the hearts of all other men who love us and make that love real in their experiences by loving one another, even as I am now loving you."

Cascade du Herrison, (1995) Jura region France

The new helper which Jesus promised to send into the hearts of believers, to pour out upon all flesh, is the *Spirit of Truth*. This divine endowment is not the letter or law of truth, neither is it to function as the form or expression of truth. The new teacher is the *conviction of truth*, the consciousness and assurance of true meanings on real spirit levels. And this new teacher is the spirit of living and growing truth, expanding, unfolding, and adaptative truth.

The true child of universe insight looks for the living Spirit of Truth in every wise saying. The God-knowing individual is constantly elevating wisdom to the living-truth levels of divine attainment; the spiritually unprogressive soul is all the while dragging the living truth down to the dead levels of wisdom and to the domain of mere exalted knowledge.

The Farewell Discourse 1949:1,3,6

Do not make the mistake of expecting to become strongly intellectually conscious of the outpoured Spirit of Truth. The spirit never creates a consciousness of himself, only a consciousness of Michael, the Son. From the beginning Jesus taught that the spirit would not speak of himself. The proof, therefore, of your fellowship with the Spirit of Truth is not to be found in your consciousness of this spirit but rather in your experience of enhanced fellowship with Michael.

The spirit also came to help men recall and understand the words of the Master as well as to illuminate and reinterpret his life on earth.

Next, the Spirit of Truth came to help the believer to witness to the realities of Jesus' teachings and his life as he lived it in the flesh, and as he now again lives it anew and afresh in the individual believer of each passing generation of the spirit-filled sons of God.

Thus it appears that the Spirit of Truth comes really to lead all believers into all truth, into the expanding knowledge of the experience of the living and growing spiritual consciousness of the reality of eternal and ascending sonship with God.

Bestowal of the Spirit of Truth 2061:2-5

Many queer and strange teachings became associated with the early narratives of the day of Pentecost. In subsequent times the events of this day, on which the Spirit of Truth, the new teacher, came to dwell with mankind, have become confused with the foolish outbreaks of rampant emotionalism. The chief mission of this outpoured spirit of the Father and the Son is to teach men about the truths of the Father's love and the Son's mercy. These are the truths of divinity which men can comprehend more fully than all the other divine traits of character. The Spirit of Truth is concerned primarily with the revelation of the Father's spirit nature and the Son's moral character. The Creator Son, in the flesh, revealed God to men; the Spirit of Truth, in the heart, reveals the Creator Son to men. When man yields the "fruits of the spirit" in his life, he is simply showing forth the traits which the Master manifested in his own earthly life. When Jesus was on earth, he lived his life as one personality—Jesus of Nazareth. As the indwelling spirit of the "new teacher," the Master has, since Pentecost, been able to live his life anew in the experience of every truth-taught believer.   Bestowal of the Spirit of Truth 2062:10

Pentecost was designed to lessen the self-assertiveness of individuals, groups, nations, and races. It is this spirit of self-assertiveness which so increases in tension that it periodically breaks loose in destructive wars. Mankind can be unified only by the spiritual approach, and the Spirit of Truth is a world influence which is universal.

The coming of the Spirit of Truth purifies the human heart and leads the recipient to formulate a life purpose single to the will of God and the welfare of men. The material spirit of selfishness has been swallowed up in this new spiritual bestowal of selflessness. Pentecost, then and now, signifies that the Jesus of history has become the divine Son of living experience. The joy of this outpoured spirit, when it is consciously experienced in human life, is a tonic for health, a stimulus for mind, and an unfailing energy for the soul.   Bestowal of the Spirit of Truth 2065:6,7

10. The Future

Earth is overdue for a spiritual revolution. Humanity has made great strides in technology over the past century, and institutional religions are straining under the weight. What's more, we can no longer control religion by harnessing it with the reins of ritual; people today are simply not willing to be told what to believe. What we seek is a living faith. Just as scientists formulate theories based on the observable mechanics of the universe, so do spiritual seekers turn to the divine spirit within for an understanding of truth and right actions.

Certainly, it is more comfortable to follow a rigid set of guidelines spelling out appropriate beliefs and conduct, and to show up for an hour

a week to recite a prayer heard many times before. But it is not as reward-
ing. Jesus proclaimed that the kingdom of God is within, and the more
meaning we find in these words, the more inclined we will be to draw on
the Spirit of Truth in determining the will of the Father.

This does not mean to abandon the religion of your forebears. To the
contrary, it is exhilarating to attend a religious service among fellow
believers in God and feel his spirit fill the room. When you step back out
into the world, however, trust in his spirit to guide you.

Our primary task for the future is to foster a spiritual renaissance in
ourselves. Only then will it permeate the world.

The early Christians (and all too many of the later ones) generally lost
sight of the Father-and-son idea embodied in Jesus' teaching of the kingdom, while they substituted therefor the well-organized social fellowship
of the church. The church thus became in the main a *social* brotherhood
which effectively displaced Jesus' concept and ideal of a *spiritual* brotherhood.

This world has never seriously or sincerely or honestly tried out these
dynamic ideas and divine ideals of Jesus' doctrine of the kingdom of heaven.
But you should not become discouraged by the apparently slow progress
of the kingdom idea on Urantia. Remember that the order of progressive
evolution is subjected to sudden and unexpected periodical changes in
both the material and the spiritual worlds.

The Kingdom of Heaven 1865:5,1863:12

Sooner or later another and greater John the Baptist is due to arise proclaiming "the kingdom of God is at hand"—meaning a return to the high
spiritual concept of Jesus, who proclaimed that the kingdom is the will of
his heavenly Father dominant and transcendent in the heart of the believer—
and doing all this without in any way referring either to the visible church
on earth or to the anticipated second coming of Christ. There must come
a revival of the *actual* teachings of Jesus, such a restatement as will
undo the work of his early followers who went about to create a
sociophilosophical system of belief regarding the fact of Michael's sojourn
on earth. In a short time the teaching of this story *about* Jesus nearly sup-
planted the preaching of Jesus' gospel of the kingdom. In this way a historical religion displaced that teaching in which Jesus had blended man's

Meeting of Land and Water; © Harriet Blum (1997)
Santa Fe, New Mexico

highest moral ideas and spiritual ideals with man's most sublime hope for the future—eternal life. And that was the gospel of the kingdom.

Mistake not! there is in the teachings of Jesus an eternal nature which will not permit them forever to remain unfruitful in the hearts of thinking men. The kingdom as Jesus conceived it has to a large extent failed on earth; for the time being, an outward church has taken its place; but you should comprehend that this church is only the larval stage of the thwarted spiritual kingdom, which will carry it through this material age and over into a more spiritual dispensation where the Master's teachings may enjoy a fuller opportunity for development. Thus does the so-called Christian church become the cocoon in which the kingdom of Jesus' concept now slumbers. The kingdom of the divine brotherhood is still alive and will eventually and certainly come forth from this long submergence, just as surely as the butterfly eventually emerges as the beautiful unfolding of its less attractive creature of metamorphic development.

The Kingdom of Heaven 1866:2-4

Religion is now confronted by the challenge of a new age of scientific minds and materialistic tendencies. In this gigantic struggle between the secular and the spiritual, the religion of Jesus will eventually triumph.

After Pentecost 2075:3

Religion does need new leaders, spiritual men and women who will dare to depend solely on Jesus and his incomparable teachings. If Christianity persists in neglecting its spiritual mission while it continues to busy itself with social and material problems, the spiritual renaissance must await the coming of these new teachers of Jesus' religion who will be exclusively devoted to the spiritual regeneration of men. And then will these spirit-born souls quickly supply the leadership and inspiration requisite for the social, moral, economic, and political reorganization of the world.

Primitive man lived a life of superstitious bondage to religious fear. Modern, civilized men dread the thought of falling under the dominance of strong religious convictions. Thinking man has always feared to be *held* by a religion. When a strong and moving religion threatens to dominate him, he invariably tries to rationalize, traditionalize, and institutionalize it, thereby hoping to gain control of it. By such procedure, even a revealed religion becomes man-made and man-dominated. Modern men and women of intelligence evade the religion of Jesus because of their fears of what it will do *to* them—and *with* them. And all such fears are well founded. The religion of Jesus does, indeed, dominate and transform its believers, demanding that men dedicate their lives to seeking for a knowledge of the will of the Father in heaven and requiring that the energies of living be consecrated to the unselfish service of the brotherhood of man.

The world needs more firsthand religion. Even Christianity—the best of the religions of the twentieth century—is not only a religion about Jesus, but it is so largely one which men experience secondhand. They take their religion wholly as handed down by their accepted religious teachers. What an awakening the world would experience if it could only see Jesus as he really lived on earth and know, firsthand, his life-giving teachings!

After Pentecost 2082:9 & 2083:2,4

"The kingdom of God is within you" was probably the greatest pronouncement Jesus ever made, next to the declaration that his Father is a living and loving spirit.

In winning souls for the Master, it is not the first mile of compulsion, duty, or convention that will transform man and his world, but rather the second mile of free service and liberty-loving devotion that betokens the Jesusonian reaching forth to grasp his brother in love and sweep him on under spiritual guidance toward the higher and divine goal of mortal existence. Christianity even now willingly goes the first mile, but mankind languishes and stumbles along in moral darkness because there are so few genuine second-milers—so few professed followers of Jesus who really live and love as he taught his disciples to live and love and serve.

The call to the adventure of building a new and transformed human society by means of the spiritual rebirth of Jesus' brotherhood of the kingdom should thrill all who believe in him as men have not been stirred since the days when they walked about on earth as his companions in the flesh.

After Pentecost 2084:4-6

~ VI ~

Evolving Civilization

1. Society in Upheaval

By nature, humans are not peaceful creatures. The function of revealed religion is therefore to continually upgrade us to a more harmonious plane of existence. Today, as in the past, society is ready for another infusion of truth—this time to carry it through a materialistic age. The passages that follow can help prompt such an infusion, ushering in a new age of spiritual grace on our weathered planet.

Over the past century the velocity of civilization's progress has increased exponentially. Without the aid of superhuman sources, such a growth spurt is apt to revert us to a simple urge for living—pursuing the satisfaction of momentary desires in lieu of eternal values.

Occidental civilization of the twentieth century groans wearily under the tremendous overload of luxury and the inordinate multiplication of human desires and longings. Modern society is enduring the strain of one of its most dangerous phases of far-flung interassociation and highly complicated interdependence.   Dawn of Civilization 765:2

Hunger and love drove men together; vanity and ghost fear held them together. But these emotions alone, without the influence of peace-promoting revelations, are unable to endure the strain of the suspicions and irritations of human interassociations. Without help from superhuman sources the strain of society breaks down upon reaching certain limits, and these very influences of social mobilization—hunger, love, vanity, and fear—conspire to plunge mankind into war and bloodshed.

The peace tendency of the human race is not a natural endowment; it is derived from the teachings of revealed religion, from the accumulated

Paysage compose avec ruines antiques; Pierre Patel le pere (1605-1676)
© Louvre, Paris

experience of the progressive races, but more especially from the teachings of Jesus, the Prince of Peace.   Dawn of Civilization 766:5,6

The present social order is not necessarily right—not divine or sacred—but mankind will do well to move slowly in making changes. That which you have is vastly better than any system known to your ancestors. Make certain that when you change the social order you change for the better. Do not be persuaded to experiment with the discarded formulas of your forefathers. Go forward, not backward! Let evolution proceed! Do not take a backward step.
                                   Primitive Human Institutions 782:5

The greatest twentieth-century influences contributing to the furtherance of civilization and the advancement of culture are the marked increase in world travel and the unparalleled improvements in methods of communication. But the improvement in education has not kept pace with the expanding social structure; neither has the modern appreciation of ethics developed in correspondence with growth along more purely intellectual and scientific lines. And modern civilization is at a standstill in spiritual development and the safeguarding of the home institution.   Development of Modern Civilization 909:6

Modern man is confronted with the task of making more readjustments of human values in one generation than have been made in two thousand years. And this all influences the social attitude toward religion, for religion is a way of living as well as a technique of thinking.

True religion must ever be, at one and the same time, the eternal foundation and the guiding star of all enduring civilizations.
                                   Later Evolution of Religion 1013:9,10

Urantia society can never hope to settle down as in past ages. The social ship has steamed out of the sheltered bays of established tradition and has begun its cruise upon the high seas of evolutionary destiny; and the soul of man, as never before in the world's history, needs carefully to scrutinize its charts of morality and painstakingly to observe the compass of religious guidance. The paramount mission of religion as a social influence is to stabilize the ideals of mankind during these dangerous times of transition from one phase of civilization to another, from one level of culture to another.

Religion has no new duties to perform, but it is urgently called upon to function as a wise guide and experienced counselor in all of these new and rapidly changing human situations. Society is becoming more mechanical, more compact, more complex, and more critically interdependent. Religion must function to prevent these new and intimate interassociations from becoming mutually retrogressive or even destructive. Religion must act as the cosmic salt which prevents the ferments of progression from destroying the cultural savor of civilization. These new social relations and economic upheavals can result in lasting brotherhood only by the ministry of religion.

The Social Problems of Religion 1086:6 & 1087:1

The more complex civilization becomes, the more difficult will become the art of living. The more rapid the changes in social usage, the more complicated will become the task of character development. Every ten generations mankind must learn anew the art of living if progress is to continue. And if man becomes so ingenious that he more rapidly adds to the complexities of society, the art of living will need to be remastered in less time, perhaps every single generation. If the evolution of the art of living fails to keep pace with the technique of existence, humanity will quickly revert to the simple urge of living—the attainment of the satisfaction of present desires. Thus will humanity remain immature; society will fail in growing up to full maturity.   Rodan of Alexandria 1772:4

2. Justice

"Eye for eye and tooth for a tooth" governed the justice system of our ancestors. The passages below, however, suggest that justice is forever a group function, not an individual one.

For the maintenance of peace and harmony, says The Urantia Book, justice should be swiftly administered to any person deemed a wrongdoer by a group of peers; but individual revenge has no part in these realms of light and life.

Of the many reasons known to me as to why Lucifer and his confeder-
ates were not sooner interned or adjudicated, I am permitted to recite the
following:
1. Mercy requires that every wrongdoer have sufficient time in which to
formulate a deliberate and fully chosen attitude regarding his evil thoughts
and sinful acts.
2. Supreme justice is dominated by a Father's love; therefore will justice
never destroy that which mercy can save. Time to accept salvation is vouch-
safed every evildoer.   Problems of the Lucifer Rebellion 617:1-3

Natural justice is a man-made theory; it is not a reality. In nature, justice
is purely theoretic, wholly a fiction. Nature provides but one kind of justice—inevitable conformity of results to causes.
                                        Evolution of Human Government 794:13

But as time passed, it was learned that the severity of the punishment
was not so valuable a deterrent to crime as was its certainty and swiftness.
                                        Evolution of Human Government 796:5

These government funds have long been honestly administered. Next to
treason and murder, the heaviest penalties meted out by the courts are
attached to betrayal of public trust. Social and political disloyalty are now
looked upon as being the most heinous of all crimes.
                                        Government on a Neighboring Planet 814:11

The methods of this people in dealing with crime, insanity, and degen-
eracy, while in some ways pleasing, will, no doubt, in others prove shock-
ing to most Urantians. Ordinary criminals and the defectives are placed,
by sexes, in different agricultural colonies and are more than self-support-
ing. The more serious habitual criminals and the incurably insane are sen-
tenced to death in the lethal gas chambers by the courts. Numerous crimes
aside from murder, including betrayal of governmental trust, also carry
the death penalty, and the visitation of justice is sure and swift.
    These people are passing out of the negative into the positive era of
law. Recently they have gone so far as to attempt the prevention of crime
by sentencing those who are believed to be potential murderers and major
criminals to life service in the detention colonies. If such convicts subsequently demonstrate that they have become more normal, they may be

either paroled or pardoned. The homicide rate on this continent is only one per cent of that among the other nations.

Efforts to prevent the breeding of criminals and defectives were begun over one hundred years ago and have already yielded gratifying results. There are no prisons or hospitals for the insane. For one reason, there are only about ten per cent as many of these groups as are found on Urantia.   Government on a Neighboring Planet 818:4-6

The Master, when on earth, admonished his followers that justice is never a personal act; it is always a group function.
               Growth of the Trinity Concept 1146:1

As man shakes off the shackles of fear, as he bridges continents and oceans with his machines, generations and centuries with his records, he must substitute for each transcended restraint a new and voluntarily assumed restraint in accordance with the moral dictates of expanding human wisdom. These self-imposed restraints are at once the most powerful and the most tenuous of all the factors of human civilization—concepts of justice and ideals of brotherhood.
               Supreme and Ultimate - Time and Space 1302:7

Meeting a poor man who had been falsely accused, Jesus went with him before the magistrate and, having been granted special permission to appear in his behalf, made that superb address in the course of which he said: "Justice makes a nation great, and the greater a nation the more solicitous will it be to see that injustice shall not befall even its most humble citizen. Woe upon any nation when only those who possess money and influence can secure ready justice before its courts! It is the sacred duty of a magistrate to acquit the innocent as well as to punish the guilty. Upon the impartiality, fairness, and integrity of its courts the endurance of a nation depends. Civil government is founded on justice, even as true religion is founded on mercy." The judge reopened the case, and when the evidence had been sifted, he discharged the prisoner.   The Sojourn at Rome 1462:1

"Ganid, it is true, you do not understand. Mercy ministry is always the work of the individual, but justice punishment is the function of the social, governmental, or universe administrative groups. As an individual I am beholden to show mercy; I must go to the rescue of the assaulted lad, and

St. George and the Dragon; Rogier van der
Weyden (1432/1435) © National Gallery
of Art, Washington

in all consistency I may employ sufficient force to restrain the aggressor. And that is just what I did. I achieved the deliverance of the assaulted lad; that was the end of mercy ministry. Then I forcibly detained the aggressor a sufficient length of time to enable the weaker party to the dispute to make his escape, after which I withdrew from the affair. I did not proceed to sit in judgment on the aggressor, thus to pass upon his motive—to adjudicate all that entered into his attack upon his fellow—and then undertake to execute the punishment which my mind might dictate as just recompense for his wrongdoing. Ganid, mercy may be lavish, but justice is precise.   The Return From Rome 1469:1

Jesus had great difficulty in getting them to understand his personal practice of nonresistance. He absolutely refused to defend himself, and it appeared to the apostles that he would be pleased if they would pursue the same policy. He taught them not to resist evil, not to combat injustice or injury, but he did not teach passive tolerance of wrongdoing. And he made it plain on this afternoon that he approved of the social punishment of evildoers and criminals, and that the civil government must sometimes employ force for the maintenance of social order and in the execution of justice.

He never ceased to warn his disciples against the evil practice of *retaliation;* he made no allowance for revenge, the idea of getting even. He deplored the holding of grudges. He disallowed the idea of an eye for an eye and a tooth for a tooth. He discountenanced the whole concept of private and personal revenge, assigning these matters to civil government, on the one hand, and to the judgment of God, on the other. He made it clear to the three that his teachings applied to the *individual*, not the state.

Ordination of the Twelve 1579:6,7

"The Father in heaven loves his children, and therefore should you learn to love one another; the Father in heaven forgives you your sins; therefore should you learn to forgive one another. If your brother sins against you, go to him and with tact and patience show him his fault. And do all this between you and him alone. If he will listen to you, then have you won your brother. But if your brother will not hear you, if he persists in the error of his way, go again to him, taking with you one or two mutual friends that you may thus have two or even three witnesses to confirm your testimony and establish the fact that you have dealt justly and mercifully with your offending brother. Now if he refuses to hear your brethren, you may tell the whole story to the congregation, and then, if he refuses to hear the brotherhood, let them take such action as they deem wise; let such an unruly member become an outcast from the kingdom. While you cannot pretend to sit in judgment on the souls of your fellows, and while you may not forgive sins or otherwise presume to usurp the prerogatives of the supervisors of the heavenly hosts, at the same time, it has been committed to your hands that you should maintain temporal order in the kingdom on earth.   The Decapolis Tour 1762:5

Thus did Jesus teach the dangers and illustrate the unfairness of sitting in personal judgment upon one's fellows. Discipline must be maintained, justice must be administered, but in all these matters the wisdom of the brotherhood should prevail. Jesus invested legislative and judicial authority in the *group*, not in the *individual*. Even this investment of authority in the group must not be exercised as personal authority. There is always danger that the verdict of an individual may be warped by prejudice or distorted by passion. Group judgment is more likely to remove the dangers and eliminate the unfairness of personal bias. Jesus sought always to minimize the elements of unfairness, retaliation, and vengeance.

The Decapolis Tour 1764:1

3. Welfare

Nothing is more dangerous to a society than wholesale unemployment. Welfare for an extended period of time is demeaning to an able-bodied citizen. How can such situations be avoided? By encouraging teaching institutions to diversify student capabilities and enhancing skills in a variety of trades to fall back on in the event of future unemployment.

While the ideal of society is universal freedom, idleness should never be tolerated. All able-bodied persons should be compelled to do at least a self-sustaining amount of work.   Primitive Human Institutions 780:2

Place-finding devices. The next age of social development will be embodied in a better and more effective co-operation and co-ordination of ever-increasing and expanding specialization. And as labor more and more diversifies, some technique for directing individuals to suitable employment must be devised. Machinery is not the only cause for unemployment among the civilized peoples of Urantia. Economic complexity and the steady increase of industrial and professional specialism add to the problems of labor placement.

It is not enough to train men for work; in a complex society there must also be provided efficient methods of place finding. Before training citizens in the highly specialized techniques of earning a living, they should be trained in one or more methods of commonplace labor, trades or callings which could be utilized when they were transiently unemployed in their specialized work. No civilization can survive the long-time harboring of large classes of unemployed. In time, even the best of citizens will become distorted and demoralized by accepting support from the public treasury. Even private charity becomes pernicious when long extended to able-bodied citizens.   Development of Modern Civilization 910:4,5

Jesus listened to all they had to say, thanked them for their confidence, and, in declining to go to Alexandria, in substance said, "My hour has not yet come." They were nonplused by his apparent indifference to the honor they had sought to confer upon him. Before taking leave of Jesus, they presented him with a purse in token of the esteem of his Alexandrian friends and in compensation for the time and expense of coming over to Caesarea to confer with them. But he likewise refused the money, saying: "The house of Joseph has never received alms, and we cannot eat another's bread as long as I have strong arms and my brothers can labor."

Jesus' Early Manhood 1414:2

Doing the Father's will. Jesus' teaching to trust in the overcare of the heavenly Father was not a blind and passive fatalism. He quoted with approval, on this afternoon, an old Hebrew saying: "He who will not work shall not eat."   Ordination of the Twelve 1579:4

The Master did not say that men should never entertain their friends at meat, but he did say that his followers should make feasts for the poor and the unfortunate. Jesus had a firm sense of justice, but it was always tempered with mercy. He did not teach his apostles that they were to be imposed upon by social parasites or professional alms-seekers. The nearest he came to making sociological pronouncements was to say, "Judge not, that you be not judged."

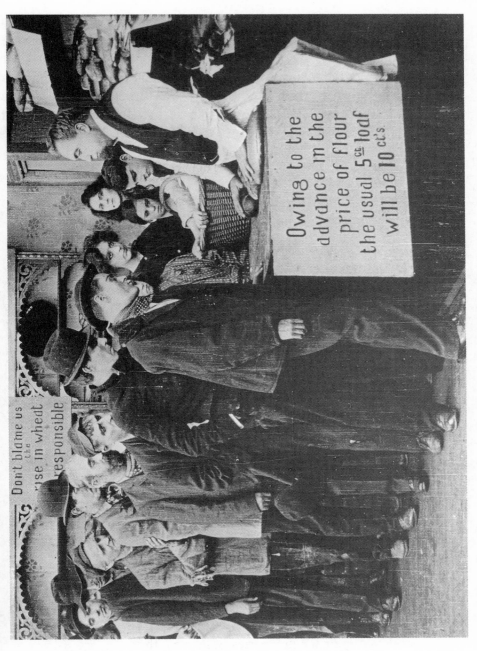

A Corner in Wheat; David Ward Griffith
(1909) © Museum of Modern Art Film
Stills Archive

He made it clear that indiscriminate kindness may be blamed for many social evils. The following day Jesus definitely instructed Judas that no apostolic funds were to be given out as alms except upon his request or upon the joint petition of two of the apostles. In all these matters it was the practice of Jesus always to say, "Be as wise as serpents but as harmless as doves." It seemed to be his purpose in all social situations to teach patience, tolerance, and forgiveness.   Ordination of the Twelve 1580:7,8

4. Materialism

The mother of modern secularism was the medieval Christian church, which accused of heresy all learned individuals who dared to challenge its authority. The father of materialism was the godless attitude of early scientists who, protesting the rigid policies of the church, brashly claimed everything would be discovered in time, even how life was created. To them God was a myth.

The worst of the materialistic age, noted for its harvest of wars, is nearly over and it has left intact the religion of Jesus. Hence we are able, at the tail end of the age, to access worthy values to live by.

Below is a 2,100 year old passage from the Old Testament, in which even a man of ancient times proclaimed the naiveté of materialism:

> For all men were by nature foolish who
>   were in ignorance of God,
> and who from the good things seen did
>   not succeed in knowing him who is,
> and from studying the works did not
>   discern the artisan;
> But either fire, or wind, or the swift air,
>   or the circuit of the stars, or the mighty
>   water,
> or the luminaries of heaven, the
>   governors of the world, they considered
>   gods.
> Now if out of joy in their beauty they
>   thought them gods,

> let them know how far more excellent is
>   the Lord than these;
> for the original source of beauty fashioned
>   them.
> Or if they were struck by the might and
>   energy,
>   let them from these things realize how
>   much more powerful is he who made
>   them.
> For from the greatness and the beauty of
>   created things
>   their original author, by analogy, is seen.
> But yet, for these the blame is less;
> For they indeed have gone astray perhaps,
>   though they seek God and wish to find
>   him.
> For they search busily among his works,
>   but are distracted by what they see,
>   because the things seen are fair.
> But again, not even these are pardonable.
> For they so far succeeded in knowledge
>   that they could speculate about the world,
>   how did they not more quickly find its
>   LORD?
>   The Book of Wisdom 13:1-9 (NAB)

The very fact that a mortal materialist can deny the existence of supermaterial realities in and of itself demonstrates the presence, and indicates the working, of spirit synthesis and cosmic consciousness in his human mind.   Personality Survival 1228:4

Science deals with *facts*; religion is concerned only with *values*. Through enlightened philosophy the mind endeavors to unite the meanings of both facts and values, thereby arriving at a concept of complete *reality*. Remember that science is the domain of knowledge, philosophy the realm of wisdom, and religion the sphere of the faith experience.
                    Real Nature of Religion 1110:5

Religion effectually cures man's sense of idealistic isolation or spiritual loneliness; it enfranchises the believer as a son of God, a citizen of a new and meaningful universe. Religion assures man that, in following the gleam of righteousness discernible in his soul, he is thereby identifying himself with the plan of the Infinite and the purpose of the Eternal. Such a liberated soul immediately begins to feel at home in this new universe, his universe.

When you experience such a transformation of faith, you are no longer a slavish part of the mathematical cosmos but rather a liberated volitional son of the Universal Father. No longer is such a liberated son fighting alone against the inexorable doom of the termination of temporal existence; no longer does he combat all nature, with the odds hopelessly against him; no longer is he staggered by the paralyzing fear that, perchance, he has put his trust in a hopeless phantasm or pinned his faith to a fanciful error.

Now, rather, are the sons of God enlisted together in fighting the battle of reality's triumph over the partial shadows of existence. At last all creatures become conscious of the fact that God and all the divine hosts of a well-nigh limitless universe are on their side in the supernal struggle to attain eternity of life and divinity of status. Such faith-liberated sons have certainly enlisted in the struggles of time on the side of the supreme forces and divine personalities of eternity; even the stars in their courses are now doing battle for them; at last they gaze upon the universe from within, from God's viewpoint, and all is transformed from the uncertainties of material isolation to the sureties of eternal spiritual progression. Even time itself becomes but the shadow of eternity cast by Paradise realities upon the moving panoply of space.   Real Nature of Religion 1117:1-3

Those who would invent a religion without God are like those who would gather fruit without trees, have children without parents. You cannot have effects without causes; only the I AM is causeless. The fact of religious experience implies God, and such a God of personal experience must be a personal Deity. You cannot pray to a chemical formula, supplicate a mathematical equation, worship a hypothesis, confide in a postulate, commune with a process, serve an abstraction, or hold loving fellowship with a law.   Foundations of Religious Faith 1126:3

New York Afternoon,
Jason Elstrott (1998)
New Orleans LA.

Ideas may take origin in the stimuli of the outer world, but ideals are born only in the creative realms of the inner world. Today the nations of the world are directed by men who have a superabundance of ideas, but they are poverty-stricken in ideals. That is the explanation of poverty, divorce, war, and racial hatreds.   The Adjuster and the Soul 1220:9

Jesus gives peace to his fellow doers of the will of God but not on the order of the joys and satisfactions of this material world. Unbelieving materialists and fatalists can hope to enjoy only two kinds of peace and soul comfort: Either they must be stoics, with steadfast resolution determined to face the inevitable and to endure the worst; or they must be optimists, ever indulging that hope which springs eternal in the human breast, vainly longing for a peace which never really comes.

Final Admonitions and Warnings 1954:4

A lasting social system without a morality predicated on spiritual realities can no more be maintained than could the solar system without gravity.   After Pentecost 2075:12

Scientists have unintentionally precipitated mankind into a materialistic panic; they have started an unthinking run on the moral bank of the ages, but this bank of human experience has vast spiritual resources; it can stand the demands being made upon it. Only unthinking men become panicky about the spiritual assets of the human race. When the materialistic-secular panic is over, the religion of Jesus will not be found bankrupt. The spiritual bank of the kingdom of heaven will be paying out faith, hope, and moral security to all who draw upon it "in His name."

At the time of this writing the worst of the materialistic age is over; the day of a better understanding is already beginning to dawn. The higher minds of the scientific world are no longer wholly materialistic in their philosophy, but the rank and file of the people still lean in that direction as a result of former teachings. But this age of physical realism is only a passing episode in man's life on earth. Modern science has left true religion—the teachings of Jesus as translated in the lives of his believers—untouched. All science has done is to destroy the childlike illusions of the misinterpretations of life.   After Pentecost 2076:7,9

Science is a quantitative experience, religion a qualitative experience, as regards man's life on earth. Science deals with phenomena; religion, with origins, values, and goals.

One of the great troubles with modern life is that man thinks he is too busy to find time for spiritual meditation and religious devotion.

Materialism reduces man to a soulless automaton and constitutes him merely an arithmetical symbol finding a helpless place in the mathematical formula of an unromantic and mechanistic universe. But whence comes all this vast universe of mathematics without a Master Mathematician? Science may expatiate on the conservation of matter, but religion validates the conservation of men's souls—it concerns their experience with spiritual realities and eternal values.   After Pentecost 2077:1,3,4

Any scientific interpretation of the material universe is valueless unless it provides due recognition for the *scientist*. No appreciation of art is genuine unless it accords recognition to the *artist*. No evaluation of morals is worth while unless it includes the *moralist*. No recognition of philosophy is edifying if it ignores the *philosopher*, and religion cannot exist without the real experience of the *religionist* who, in and through this very experience, is seeking to find God and to know him. Likewise is the universe of universes without significance apart from the I AM, the infinite God who made it and unceasingly manages it.

The universe is not like the laws, mechanisms, and the uniformities which the scientist discovers, and which he comes to regard as science, but rather like the curious, thinking, choosing, creative, combining, and discriminating *scientist* who thus observes universe phenomena and classifies the mathematical facts inherent in the mechanistic phases of the material side of creation. Neither is the universe like the art of the artist, but rather like the striving, dreaming, aspiring, and advancing *artist* who seeks to transcend the world of material things in an effort to achieve a spiritual goal.
                                  After Pentecost 2080:3,7

Modern secularism has been fostered by two world-wide influences. The father of secularism was the narrow-minded and godless attitude of nineteenth- and twentieth-century so-called science—atheistic science. The mother of modern secularism was the totalitarian medieval Christian church. Secularism had its inception as a rising protest against the almost complete domination of Western civilization by the institutionalized Christian church.

Materialism denies God, secularism simply ignores him; at least that was the earlier attitude. More recently, secularism has assumed a more militant attitude, assuming to take the place of the religion whose totalitarian bondage it onetime resisted. Twentieth-century secularism tends to affirm that man does not need God. But beware! this godless philosophy of human society will lead only to unrest, animosity, unhappiness, war, and world-wide disaster.

Secularism can never bring peace to mankind. Nothing can take the place of God in human society. But mark you well! do not be quick to surrender the beneficent gains of the secular revolt from ecclesiastical totalitarianism. Western civilization today enjoys many liberties and satisfactions as a result of the secular revolt. The great mistake of secularism was this: In revolting against the almost total control of life by religious authority, and after attaining the liberation from such ecclesiastical tyranny, the secularists went on to institute a revolt against God himself, sometimes tacitly and sometimes openly.

To the secularistic revolt you owe the amazing creativity of American industrialism and the unprecedented material progress of Western civilization. And because the secularistic revolt went too far and lost sight of God and *true* religion, there also followed the unlooked-for harvest of world wars and international unsettledness.   After Pentecost 2081:2,5-7

But paganized and socialized Christianity stands in need of new contact with the uncompromised teachings of Jesus; it languishes for lack of a new vision of the Master's life on earth. A new and fuller revelation of the religion of Jesus is destined to conquer an empire of materialistic secularism and to overthrow a world sway of mechanistic naturalism. Urantia is now quivering on the very brink of one of its most amazing and enthralling epochs of social readjustment, moral quickening, and spiritual enlightenment.   After Pentecost 2082:7

5. World Peace

The cross-fertilization of ideas has done more to promote world peace than all the efforts of the United Nations. Years ago, a college friend of mine facilitated an orientation class of exchange students, which I attended whenever I could. The students from—Iran, Malaysia, Ethiopia,

Pakistan, and South America—would circulate a Time magazine to get a conversation going. Then in broken English, accompanied by profuse hand gestures, they would describe their families, their home life, their religions, and the even how much they disliked their governments back home.

Suspicious strangers at the start of the term, they soon began helping one another with class work. Many of the students even became close friends demonstrating the vital role communication and personal contact plays in cultivating world peace.

The bestowal Son is the Prince of Peace. He arrives with the message, "Peace on earth and good will among men." On normal worlds this is a dispensation of world-wide peace; the nations no more learn war. But such salutary influences did not attend the coming of your bestowal Son, Christ Michael. Urantia is not proceeding in the normal order. Your world is out of step in the planetary procession. Your Master, when on earth, warned his disciples that his advent would not bring the usual reign of peace on Urantia. He distinctly told them that there would be "wars and rumors of wars," and that nation would rise against nation. At another time he said, "Think not that I have come to bring peace upon earth."

While Jesus has shown the way to the immediate attainment of spiritual brotherhood, the realization of social brotherhood on your world depends much on the achievement of the following personal transformations and planetary adjustments:

1. *Social fraternity.* Multiplication of international and interracial social contacts and fraternal associations through travel, commerce, and competitive play. Development of a common language and the multiplication of multilinguists. The racial and national interchange of students, teachers, industrialists, and religious philosophers.

2. *Intellectual cross-fertilization.* Brotherhood is impossible on a world whose inhabitants are so primitive that they fail to recognize the folly of unmitigated selfishness. There must occur an exchange of national and racial literature. Each race must become familiar with the thought of all races; each nation must know the feelings of all nations. Ignorance breeds suspicion, and suspicion is incompatible with the essential attitude of sympathy and love.

3. *Ethical awakening.* Only ethical consciousness can unmask the immorality of human intolerance and the sinfulness of fratricidal strife. Only

a moral conscience can condemn the evils of national envy and racial jealousy. Only moral beings will ever seek for that spiritual insight which is essential to living the golden rule.

4. *Political wisdom.* Emotional maturity is essential to self-control. Only emotional maturity will insure the substitution of international techniques of civilized adjudication for the barbarous arbitrament of war. Wise statesmen will sometime work for the welfare of humanity even while they strive to promote the interest of their national or racial groups.

5. *Spiritual insight.* The brotherhood of man is, after all, predicated on the recognition of the fatherhood of God. The quickest way to realize the brotherhood of man on Urantia is to effect the spiritual transformation of present-day humanity. The only technique for accelerating the natural trend of social evolution is that of applying spiritual pressure from above, thus augmenting moral insight while enhancing the soul capacity of every mortal to understand and love every other mortal. Mutual understanding and fraternal love are transcendent civilizers and mighty factors in the world-wide realization of the brotherhood of man.

Planetary Mortal Epochs 597:2 - 598:2

War is the natural state and heritage of evolving man; peace is the social yardstick measuring civilization's advancement.

The Evolution of Human Government 783:4

The nations of Urantia have already entered upon the gigantic struggle between nationalistic militarism and industrialism, and in many ways this conflict is analogous to the agelong struggle between the herder-hunter and the farmer. But if industrialism is to triumph over militarism, it must avoid the dangers which beset it. The perils of budding industry on Urantia are:

1. The strong drift toward materialism, spiritual blindness.
2. The worship of wealth-power, value distortion.
3. The vices of luxury, cultural immaturity.
4. The increasing dangers of indolence, service insensitivity.
5. The growth of undesirable racial softness, biologic deterioration.
6. The threat of standardized industrial slavery, personality stagnation. Labor is ennobling but drudgery is benumbing.

The Evolution of Human Government 786:2-8

Full Earth Apollo 17 (1972)

The peace of Urantia will be promoted far more by international trade organizations than by all the sentimental sophistry of visionary peace planning. Trade relations have been facilitated by development of language and by improved methods of communication as well as by better transportation.   The Evolution of Human Government 787:4

There can be no lasting religious peace on Urantia until all religious groups freely surrender all their notions of divine favor, chosen people, and religious sovereignty. Only when God the Father becomes supreme will men become religious brothers and live together in religious peace on earth.

War on Urantia will never end so long as nations cling to the illusive notions of unlimited national sovereignty.　The Transition Years 1487:7,9

Urantia nations have not possessed real sovereignty; they never have had a sovereignty which could protect them from the ravages and devastations of world wars. In the creation of the global government of mankind, the nations are not giving up sovereignty so much as they are actually creating a real, bona fide, and lasting world sovereignty which will henceforth be fully able to protect them from all war. Local affairs will be handled by local governments; national affairs, by national governments; international affairs will be administered by global government.

World peace cannot be maintained by treaties, diplomacy, foreign policies, alliances, balances of power, or any other type of makeshift juggling with the sovereignties of nationalism. World law must come into being and must be enforced by world government—the sovereignty of all mankind.

The individual will enjoy far more liberty under world government. Today, the citizens of the great powers are taxed, regulated, and controlled almost oppressively, and much of this present interference with individual liberties will vanish when the national governments are willing to trustee their sovereignty as regards international affairs into the hands of global government.

Under global government the national groups will be afforded a real opportunity to realize and enjoy the personal liberties of genuine democracy. The fallacy of self-determination will be ended. With global regulation of money and trade will come the new era of world-wide peace. Soon may a global language evolve, and there will be at least some hope of sometime having a global religion—or religions with a global viewpoint.

Collective security will never afford peace until the collectivity includes all mankind.

The political sovereignty of representative mankind government will bring lasting peace on earth, and the spiritual brotherhood of man will forever insure good will among all men. And there is no other way whereby peace on earth and good will among men can be realized.

The Transition Years 1491:2-7

~ VII ~

Divinity

1. The Nature of God

God, we learn in <u>The Urantia Book</u>, *is the upholder of the universe and the source of everything from the tiniest part of an atom to the awesome power of gravity that holds together the planets, the sun, and the galaxies. To comprehend God's might, picture the power released by the splitting of a miniscule atom.*

Yet God is far more than an impersonal force of cohesion, and even more than some distant inertia that once set life in motion. Not one to sit back dispassionately observing life on earth, he has a personality you can come to know: God is love. He loves us, he is aware of us, and his spirit lives within us.

Heaven, as we envision it—a realm portrayed by angels sitting blissfully on a cloud at the right hand of God—cannot be approached simply by dying. Rather we come to know God through progressive spiritual communion. Within each of us is a drive for perfection, to become more like our Creator. This determination is what will carry us through billions of years and from star system to star system, our souls becoming ever more spiritual and less material, until we are truly pure, strong, and worthy enough to stand in God's presence. At each step along the way, God will deliver a more expanded view of his personality.

For now, our task is to strive to align ourselves with the will of our Father in heaven. The more aligned we are, the closer we will come to knowing God.

On a planet of sex creatures, in a world where the impulses of parental emotion are inherent in the hearts of its intelligent beings, the term Father becomes a very expressive and appropriate name for the eternal God. He is best known, most universally acknowledged, on your planet, Urantia,

by the name *God*. The name he is given is of little importance; the significant thing is that you should know him and aspire to be like him. Your
prophets of old truly called him "the everlasting God" and referred to him
as the one who "inhabits eternity."   The Universal Father 23:3

"God is spirit." He is a universal spiritual presence. The Universal Father is an infinite spiritual reality; he is "the sovereign, eternal, immortal,
invisible, and only true God." Even though you are "the offspring of God,"
you ought not to think that the Father is like yourselves in form and physique because you are said to be created "in his image"—indwelt by Mystery Monitors dispatched from the central abode of his eternal presence.
Spirit beings are real, notwithstanding they are invisible to human eyes;
even though they have not flesh and blood.
    Said the seer of old: "Lo, he goes by me, and I see him not; he passes on
also, but I perceive him not." We may constantly observe the works of
God, we may be highly conscious of the material evidences of his majestic
conduct, but rarely may we gaze upon the visible manifestation of his
divinity, not even to behold the presence of his delegated spirit of human
indwelling.
    The Universal Father is not invisible because he is hiding himself away
from the lowly creatures of materialistic handicaps and limited spiritual
endowments. The situation rather is: "You cannot see my face, for no
mortal can see me and live." No material man could behold the spirit God
and preserve his mortal existence. The glory and the spiritual brilliance of
the divine personality presence is impossible of approach by the lower
groups of spirit beings or by any order of material personalities. The spiritual luminosity of the Father's personal presence is a "light which no mortal man can approach; which no material creature has seen or can see."
But it is not necessary to see God with the eyes of the flesh in order to
discern him by the faith-vision of the spiritualized mind.
                                                      The Universal Father 25:1-3

Do not permit the magnitude of God, his infinity, either to obscure or
eclipse his personality. "He who planned the ear, shall he not hear? He
who formed the eye, shall he not see?" The Universal Father is the acme of
divine personality; he is the origin and destiny of personality throughout
all creation. God is both infinite and personal; he is an infinite personality.
The Father is truly a personality, notwithstanding that the infinity of his

person places him forever beyond the full comprehension of material and finite beings.

God is not hiding from any of his creatures. He is unapproachable to so many orders of beings only because he "dwells in a light which no material creature can approach." The immensity and grandeur of the divine personality is beyond the grasp of the unperfected mind of evolutionary mortals. He "measures the waters in the hollow of his hand, measures a universe with the span of his hand. It is he who sits on the circle of the earth, who stretches out the heavens as a curtain and spreads them out as a universe to dwell in." "Lift up your eyes on high and behold who has created all these things, who brings out their worlds by number and calls them all by their names"; and so it is true that "the invisible things of God are partially understood by the things which are made."

The Universal Father 27:3,5

Without God and except for his great and central person, there would be no personality throughout all the vast universe of universes. *God is personality.*

Notwithstanding that God is an eternal power, a majestic presence, a transcendent ideal, and a glorious spirit, though he is all these and infinitely more, nonetheless, he is truly and everlastingly a perfect Creator personality, a person who can "know and be known," who can "love and be loved," and one who can befriend us; while you can be known, as other humans have been known, as the friend of God. He is a real spirit and a spiritual reality.

The Universal Father 28:4,5

God is to science a cause, to philosophy an idea, to religion a person, even the loving heavenly Father. God is to the scientist a primal force, to the philosopher a hypothesis of unity, to the religionist a living spiritual experience. Man's inadequate concept of the personality of the Universal Father can be improved only by man's spiritual progress in the universe and will become truly adequate only when the pilgrims of time and space finally attain the divine embrace of the living God on Paradise.

The Universal Father 30:1

Man does not achieve union with God as a drop of water might find unity with the ocean. Man attains divine union by progressive reciprocal spiritual communion, by personality intercourse with the personal God, by increasingly attaining the divine nature through wholehearted and intelligent conformity to the divine will. Such a sublime relationship can exist only between personalities.   The Universal Father 31:2

No thing is new to God, and no cosmic event ever comes as a surprise; he inhabits the circle of eternity. He is without beginning or end of days. To God there is no past, present, or future; all time is present at any given moment. He is the great and only I AM.   The Universal Father 34:4

The creature not only exists in God, but God also lives in the creature. "We know we dwell in him because he lives in us; he has given us his spirit. This gift from the Paradise Father is man's inseparable companion." "He is the ever-present and all-pervading God." "The spirit of the everlasting Father is concealed in the mind of every mortal child." "Man goes forth searching for a friend while that very friend lives within his own heart." "The true God is not afar off; he is a part of us; his spirit speaks from within us." "The Father lives in the child. God is always with us. He is the guiding spirit of eternal destiny."   Attributes of God 45:2

Mortal man cannot possibly know the infinitude of the heavenly Father. Finite mind cannot think through such an absolute truth or fact. But this same finite human being can actually feel—literally experience— the full and undiminished impact of such an infinite Father's LOVE. Such a love can be truly experienced, albeit while quality of experience is unlimited, quantity of such an experience is strictly limited by the human capacity for spiritual receptivity and by the associated capacity to love the Father in return.

Therefore man's nearest and dearest approach to God is by and through love, for God is love.   Attributes of God 50:4,5

The Father unceasingly pours forth energy, light, and life. The work of God is literal as well as spiritual. "He stretches out the north over the empty space and hangs the earth upon nothing."

God's Relation to the Universe 55:4

The consciousness of a victorious human life on earth is born of that creature faith which dares to challenge each recurring episode of existence when confronted with the awful spectacle of human limitations, by

Le Paradis; Jacopo Tintoretto (1518-1594) Louvre, Paris

the unfailing declaration: Even if I cannot do this, there lives in me one who can and will do it, a part of the Father-Absolute of the universe of universes. And that is "the victory which overcomes the world, even your faith."   God's Relation to the Universe 59:5

The Father desires all his creatures to be in personal communion with him. He has on Paradise a place to receive all those whose survival status and spiritual nature make possible such attainment. Therefore settle in your philosophy now and forever: To each of you and to all of us, God is approachable, the Father is attainable, the way is open; the forces of divine love and the ways and means of divine administration are all interlocked in an effort to facilitate the advancement of every worthy intelligence of every universe to the Paradise presence of the Universal Father.
                                   God's Relation to the Individual 63:6

God-consciousness, as it is experienced by an evolving mortal of the realms, must consist of three varying factors, three differential levels of reality realization. There is first the mind consciousness—the comprehension of the *idea* of God. Then follows the soul consciousness—the realization of the *ideal* of God. Last, dawns the spirit consciousness—the realization of the *spirit reality* of God. By the unification of these factors of the divine realization, no matter how incomplete, the mortal *personality* at all times overspreads all conscious levels with a realization of the personality of God.   God's Relation to the Individual 69:6

The love of the Father absolutely individualizes each personality as a unique child of the Universal Father, a child without duplicate in infinity, a will creature irreplaceable in all eternity. The Father's love glorifies each child of God, illuminating each member of the celestial family, sharply silhouetting the unique nature of each personal being against the impersonal levels that lie outside the fraternal circuit of the Father of all. The love of God strikingly portrays the transcendent value of each will creature, unmistakably reveals the high value which the Universal Father has placed upon each and every one of his children from the highest creator personality of Paradise status to the lowest personality of will dignity among the savage tribes of men in the dawn of the human species on some evolutionary world of time and space.   The Universe of Universe 138:4

It is a mystery that God is a highly personal self-conscious being with residential headquarters, and at the same time personally present in such a vast universe and personally in contact with such a well-nigh infinite number of beings. That such a phenomenon is a mystery beyond human comprehension should not in the least lessen your faith. Do not allow the magnitude of the infinity, the immensity of the eternity, and the grandeur and glory of the matchless character of God to overawe, stagger, or discourage you; for the Father is not very far from any one of you; he dwells within you, and in him do we all literally move, actually live, and veritably have our being.   The Universe of Universe 139:1

No matter how much you may grow in Father comprehension, your mind will always be staggered by the unrevealed infinity of the Father-I AM, the unexplored vastness of which will always remain unfathomable and incomprehensible throughout all the cycles of eternity. No matter how much of God you may attain, there will always remain much more of him, the existence of which you will not even suspect. And we believe that this is just as true on transcendental levels as it is in the domains of finite existence. The quest for God is endless!

                                    Universe Levels of Reality 1169:4

Although the Universal Father is personally resident on Paradise, at the very center of the universes, he is also actually present on the worlds of space in the minds of his countless children of time, for he indwells them as the Mystery Monitors. The eternal Father is at one and the same time farthest removed from, and most intimately associated with, his planetary mortal sons.   Origin and Nature of Thought Adjusters 1176:1

Said Jacob to Jesus: "But, Rabbi, Moses and the olden prophets tell us that Yahweh is a jealous God, a God of great wrath and fierce anger. The prophets say he hates evildoers and takes vengeance on those who obey not his law. You and your disciples teach us that God is a kind and compassionate Father who so loves all men that he would welcome them into this new kingdom of heaven, which you proclaim is so near at hand."

When Jacob finished speaking, Jesus replied: "Jacob, you have well stated the teachings of the olden prophets who taught the children of their generation in accordance with the light of their day. Our Father in Paradise is changeless. But the concept of his nature has enlarged and grown

from the days of Moses down through the times of Amos and even to the
generation of the prophet Isaiah. And now have I come in the flesh to
reveal the Father in new glory and to show forth his love and mercy to all
men on all worlds. As the gospel of this kingdom shall spread over the
world with its message of good cheer and good will to all men, there will
grow up improved and better relations among the families of all nations.
As time passes, fathers and their children will love each other more, and
thus will be brought about a better understanding of the love of the Father
in heaven for his children on earth. Remember, Jacob, that a good and true
father not only loves his family as a whole—as a family—but he also truly
loves and affectionately cares for each *individual* member."

Passover at Jerusalem 1597:1,2

The Master, during the course of this final prayer with his apostles,
alluded to the fact that he had manifested the Father's name to the world.
And that is truly what he did by the revelation of God through his perfected life in the flesh. The Father in heaven had sought to reveal himself
to Moses, but he could proceed no further than to cause it to be said, "I
AM." And when pressed for further revelation of himself, it was only
disclosed, "I AM that I AM." But when Jesus had finished his earth life,
this name of the Father had been so revealed that the Master, who was the
Father incarnate, could truly say:

I am the bread of life.
I am the living water.
I am the light of the world.
I am the desire of all ages.
I am the open door to eternal salvation.
I am the reality of endless life.
I am the good shepherd.
I am the pathway of infinite perfection.
I am the resurrection and the life.
I am the secret of eternal survival.
I am the way, the truth, and the life.
I am the infinite Father of my finite children.
I am the true vine; you are the branches.
I am the hope of all who know the living truth.
I am the living bridge from one world to another.
I am the living link between time and eternity.

Thus did Jesus enlarge the living revelation of the name of God to all generations. As divine love reveals the nature of God, eternal truth discloses his name in ever-enlarging proportions. In Gethsemane 1965:3-10

2.   Progressive Religion

The watchword of the universe is <u>progress</u>. Life evolved over millions of years from mold to man. Social systems advanced in fits and starts from tribal living to democracy. Religion, initially rooted in fear and superstition, took up the concept of a wrathful God who punished wrongdoers with eternal fire, and progressed to espouse service to humanity and devotion to our loving Father in heaven. Real religion is not static; it is an active living faith.

Can you not advance in your concept of God's dealing with man to that level where you recognize that the watchword of the universe is progress? Through long ages the human race has struggled to reach its present position. Throughout all these millenniums Providence has been working out the plan of progressive evolution. The two thoughts are not opposed in practice, only in man's mistaken concepts.

God's Relation to the Universe 54:5

It is not so much that man is conscious of God as that man yearns for God that results in universe ascension. What you are today is not so important as what you are becoming day by day and in eternity.

The Adjuster and the Soul 1216:6

My brother, good and evil are merely words symbolizing relative levels of human comprehension of the observable universe. If you are ethically lazy and socially indifferent, you can take as your standard of good the current social usages. If you are spiritually indolent and morally unprogressive, you may take as your standards of good the religious practices and traditions of your contemporaries. But the soul that survives time and emerges into eternity must make a living and personal choice between good and evil as they are determined by the true values of the spiritual standards established by the divine spirit which the Father in heaven has

Saint Apollonia Destroys a Pagan Idol; Antonio Vivarini (1450)
© National Gallery of Art, Washington

sent to dwell within the heart of man. This indwelling spirit is the standard
of personality survival. The Sojourn at Rome 1457:5

The spiritually blind individual who logically follows scientific dicta-
tion, social usage, and religious dogma stands in grave danger of sacrific-
ing his moral freedom and losing his spiritual liberty. Such a soul is destined to become an intellectual parrot, a social automaton, and a slave to
religious authority. The Sojourn at Rome 1458:1

Truth cannot be defined with words, only by living. Truth is always
more than knowledge. Knowledge pertains to things observed, but truth
transcends such purely material levels in that it consorts with wisdom and
embraces such imponderables as human experience, even spiritual and living realities. Knowledge originates in science; wisdom, in true philosophy;
truth, in the religious experience of spiritual living. Knowledge deals with
facts; wisdom, with relationships; truth, with reality values.

Man tends to crystallize science, formulate philosophy, and dogmatize
truth because he is mentally lazy in adjusting to the progressive struggles
of living, while he is also terribly afraid of the unknown. Natural man is
slow to initiate changes in his habits of thinking and in his techniques of
living. The Sojourn at Rome 1459:2,3

Then Jesus went on to say: "When your children are very young and
immature, and when you must chastise them, they may reflect that their
father is angry and filled with resentful wrath. Their immaturity cannot
penetrate beyond the punishment to discern the father's farseeing and corrective affection. But when these same children become grown-up men
and women, would it not be folly for them to cling to these earlier and
misconceived notions regarding their father? As men and women they
should now discern their father's love in all these early disciplines. And
should not mankind, as the centuries pass, come the better to understand
the true nature and loving character of the Father in heaven?

What profit have you from successive generations of spiritual illumination
if you persist in viewing God as Moses and the prophets saw him? I say to
you, Jacob, under the bright light of this hour you should see the Father as
none of those who have gone before ever beheld him.

Passover at Jerusalem 1597:4

The apostles learned that the Jews were spiritually stagnant and dying because they had crystallized truth into a creed; that when truth becomes formulated as a boundary line of self-righteous exclusiveness instead of serving as signposts of spiritual guidance and progress, such teachings lose their creative and life-giving power and ultimately become merely preservative and fossilizing.

Increasingly they learned from Jesus to look upon human personalities in terms of their possibilities in time and in eternity. They learned that many souls can best be led to love the unseen God by being first taught to love their brethren whom they can see. And it was in this connection that new meaning became attached to the Master's pronouncement concerning unselfish service for one's fellows: "Inasmuch as you did it to one of the least of my brethren, you did it to me."

Fleeing Through Northern Galilee 1727:3,4

The religion of the spirit means effort, struggle, conflict, faith, determination, love, loyalty, and progress. The religion of the mind—the theology of authority—requires little or none of these exertions from its formal believers. Tradition is a safe refuge and an easy path for those fearful and halfhearted souls who instinctively shun the spirit struggles and mental uncertainties associated with those faith voyages of daring adventure out upon the high seas of unexplored truth in search for the farther shores of spiritual realities as they may be discovered by the progressive human mind and experienced by the evolving human soul.

Fleeing Through Northern Galilee 1729:6

I have called upon you to be born again, to be born of the spirit. I have called you out of the darkness of authority and the lethargy of tradition into the transcendent light of the realization of the possibility of making for yourselves the greatest discovery possible for the human soul to make— the supernal experience of finding God for yourself, in yourself, and of yourself, and of doing all this as a fact in your own personal experience. And so may you pass from death to life, from the authority of tradition to the experience of knowing God; thus will you pass from darkness to light, from a racial faith inherited to a personal faith achieved by actual experience; and thereby will you progress from a theology of mind handed down by your ancestors to a true religion of spirit which shall be built up in your souls as an eternal endowment.

Fleeing Through Northern Galilee 1731:1

At last, true religion is delivered from the custody of priests and all sacred classes and finds its real manifestation in the individual souls of men.   Bestowal of the Spirit of Truth 2063:4

3. Prayer

Prayer is not the repetition of prescribed phrases. Nor is it a request for God to solve our problems. Rather, it is a means of seeking needed sustenance while resolving the problems ourselves. Even as a child, Jesus insisted on having "just a little talk with my Father in heaven" after he completed his formal prayers.

Pray outdoors—let nature envelop you and soothe your tensions. When you have finished praying, remain in quiet receptivity as the spirit within you speaks to your soul.

In all your praying be fair; do not expect God to show partiality, to love you more than his other children, your friends, neighbors, even enemies....When the prayer seeks nothing for the one who prays nor anything for his fellows, then such attitudes of the soul tend to the levels of true worship. Egoistic prayers involve confessions and petitions and often consist in requests for material favors. Prayer is somewhat more ethical when it deals with forgiveness and seeks wisdom for enhanced self-control.

But prayer need not always be individual. Group or congregational praying is very effective in that it is highly socializing in its repercussions. When a group engages in community prayer for moral enhancement and spiritual uplift, such devotions are reactive upon the individuals composing the group; they are all made better because of participation. Even a whole city or an entire nation can be helped by such prayer devotions. Confession, repentance, and prayer have led individuals, cities, nations, and whole races to mighty efforts of reform and courageous deeds of valorous achievement.

If you truly desire to overcome the habit of criticizing some friend, the quickest and surest way of achieving such a change of attitude is to establish the habit of praying for that person every day of your life. But the social repercussions of such prayers are dependent largely on two conditions:

1. The person who is prayed for should know that he is being prayed for.

2. The person who prays should come into intimate social contact with the person for whom he is praying.   Evolution of Prayer 998:1,5,6,7

Prayer is not a technique for curing real and organic diseases, but it has contributed enormously to the enjoyment of abundant health and to the cure of numerous mental, emotional, and nervous ailments. And even in actual bacterial disease, prayer has many times added to the efficacy of other remedial procedures. Prayer has turned many an irritable and complaining invalid into a paragon of patience and made him an inspiration to all other human sufferers.

Do not be so slothful as to ask God to solve your difficulties, but never hesitate to ask him for wisdom and spiritual strength to guide and sustain you while you yourself resolutely and courageously attack the problems at hand.

Pray as Jesus taught his disciples—honestly, unselfishly, with fairness, and without doubting.   Evolution of Prayer 999:5,8,9

The great religious teachers and the prophets of past ages were not extreme mystics. They were God-knowing men and women who best served their God by unselfish ministry to their fellow mortals. Jesus often took his apostles away by themselves for short periods to engage in meditation and prayer, but for the most part he kept them in service-contact with the multitudes. The soul of man requires spiritual exercise as well as spiritual nourishment.

Religious persons must not regard every vivid psychologic presentiment and every intense emotional experience as a divine revelation or a spiritual communication. Genuine spiritual ecstasy is usually associated with great outward calmness and almost perfect emotional control.

Evolution of Prayer 1000:3,4

Modern man is perplexed by the thought of talking things over with God in a purely personal way. Many have abandoned regular praying; they only pray when under unusual pressure—in emergencies. Man should be unafraid to talk to God, but only a spiritual child would undertake to persuade, or presume to change, God.

But real praying does attain reality. Even when the air currents are ascending, no bird can soar except by outstretched wings. Prayer elevates man because it is a technique of progressing by the utilization of the ascending spiritual currents of the universe.

Genuine prayer adds to spiritual growth, modifies attitudes, and yields that satisfaction which comes from communion with divinity. It is a spontaneous outburst of God-consciousness.

God answers man's prayer by giving him an increased revelation of truth, an enhanced appreciation of beauty, and an augmented concept of goodness. Prayer is a subjective gesture, but it contacts with mighty objective realities on the spiritual levels of human experience; it is a meaningful reach by the human for superhuman values. It is the most potent spiritual-growth stimulus.

Words are irrelevant to prayer; they are merely the intellectual channel in which the river of spiritual supplication may chance to flow. God answers the soul's attitude, not the words.

Prayer is not a technique of escape from conflict but rather a stimulus to growth in the very face of conflict. Pray only for values, not things; for growth, not for gratification.

If you would engage in effective praying, you should bear in mind the laws of prevailing petitions:

1. You must qualify as a potent prayer by sincerely and courageously facing the problems of universe reality. You must possess cosmic stamina.

2. You must have honestly exhausted the human capacity for human adjustment. You must have been industrious.

3. You must surrender every wish of mind and every craving of soul to the transforming embrace of spiritual growth. You must have experienced an enhancement of meanings and an elevation of values.

4. You must make a wholehearted choice of the divine will. You must obliterate the dead center of indecision.

5. You not only recognize the Father's will and choose to do it, but you have effected an unqualified consecration, and a dynamic dedication, to the actual doing of the Father's will.

6. Your prayer will be directed exclusively for divine wisdom to solve

the specific human problems encountered in the Paradise ascension—the attainment of divine perfection.

7. And you must have faith—living faith.

Evolution of Prayer 1002:1-11

During this year Joseph and Mary had trouble with Jesus about his prayers. He insisted on talking to his heavenly Father much as he would talk to Joseph, his earthly father. This departure from the more solemn and reverent modes of communication with Deity was a bit disconcerting to his parents, especially to his mother, but there was no persuading him to change; he would say his prayers just as he had been taught, after which he insisted on having "just a little talk with my Father in heaven."

Early Childhood of Jesus 1360:1

"Be willing, then, to take up your responsibilities and follow me. Do your good deeds in secret; when you give alms, let not the left hand know what the right hand does. And when you pray, go apart by yourselves and use not vain repetitions and meaningless phrases. Always remember that the Father knows what you need even before you ask him. And be not given to fasting with a sad countenance to be seen by men."

Ordination of the Twelve 1577:5

"Prayer is entirely a personal and spontaneous expression of the attitude of the soul toward the spirit; prayer should be the communion of sonship and the expression of fellowship. Prayer, when indited by the spirit, leads to co-operative spiritual progress. The ideal prayer is a form of spiritual communion which leads to intelligent worship. True praying is the sincere attitude of reaching heavenward for the attainment of your ideals.

"Prayer is the breath of the soul and should lead you to be persistent in your attempt to ascertain the Father's will.... Again I say to you: Ask and it shall be given you; seek and you shall find; knock and it shall be opened to you. For every one who asks receives; he who seeks finds; and to him who knocks the door of salvation will be opened.

"Your persistence, however, is not to win favor with God but to change your earth attitude and to enlarge your soul's capacity for spirit receptivity.

Christina's World; Andrew Wyeth (1948)
© The Museum of Modern Art, New York

"But when you pray, you exercise so little faith. Genuine faith will remove mountains of material difficulty which may chance to lie in the path of soul expansion and spiritual progress."

                    Gilboa and the Decapolis 1618:6,1619:1,3,4

But the apostles were not yet satisfied; they desired Jesus to give them a model prayer which they could teach the new disciples. After listening to this discourse on prayer, James Zebedee said: "Very good, Master, but we do not desire a form of prayer for ourselves so much as for the newer believers who so frequently beseech us, `Teach us how acceptably to pray to the Father in heaven.'"

When James had finished speaking, Jesus said: "If, then, you still desire such a prayer, I would present the one which I taught my brothers and sisters in Nazareth":

> Our Father who is in heaven,
>   Hallowed be your name.
> Your kingdom come; your will be done
>   On earth as it is in heaven.
> Give us this day our bread for tomorrow;
>   Refresh our souls with the water of life.
> And forgive us every one our debts
>   As we also have forgiven our debtors.
> Save us in temptation, deliver us from evil,
>   And increasingly make us perfect like yourself.

Jesus taught the twelve always to pray in secret; to go off by themselves amidst the quiet surroundings of nature or to go in their rooms and shut the doors when they engaged in prayer.

Jesus gave the apostles the prayer in collective form as they had prayed it in the Nazareth home. He never taught a formal personal prayer, only group, family, or social petitions. And he never volunteered to do that.

Jesus taught that effective prayer must be:

1. Unselfish—not alone for oneself.
2. Believing—according to faith.
3. Sincere—honest of heart.
4. Intelligent—according to light.

5. Trustful—in submission to the Father's all-wise will.
Gilboa and the Decapolis 1619:5,6, 1620:1-10,12,14-20

Prayer is an antidote for harmful introspection. At least, prayer as the Master taught it is such a beneficent ministry to the soul. Jesus consistently employed the beneficial influence of praying for one's fellows. The Master usually prayed in the plural, not in the singular. Only in the great crises of his earth life did Jesus ever pray for himself.

Prayer is the breath of the spirit life in the midst of the material civilization of the races of mankind. Worship is salvation for the pleasure-seeking generations of mortals.

As prayer may be likened to recharging the spiritual batteries of the soul, so worship may be compared to the act of tuning in the soul to catch the universe broadcasts of the infinite spirit of the Universal Father.

Prayer is the sincere and longing look of the child to its spirit Father; it is a psychologic process of exchanging the human will for the divine will. Prayer is a part of the divine plan for making over that which is into that which ought to be. Gilboa and the Decapolis 1621:5-8

Let your real petitions always be in secret. Do not let men hear your personal prayers. Prayers of thanksgiving are appropriate for groups of worshipers, but the prayer of the soul is a personal matter. There is but one form of prayer which is appropriate for all God's children, and that is: "Nevertheless, your will be done."

Jesus warned his followers against thinking that their prayers would be rendered more efficacious by ornate repetitions, eloquent phraseology, fasting, penance, or sacrifices. But he did exhort his believers to employ prayer as a means of leading up through thanksgiving to true worship. Jesus deplored that so little of the spirit of thanksgiving was to be found in the prayers and worship of his followers. He quoted from the Scriptures on this occasion, saying: "It is a good thing to give thanks to the Lord and to sing praises to the name of the Most High, to acknowledge his loving-kindness every morning and his faithfulness every night, for God has made me glad through his work. In everything I will give thanks according to the will of God." First Preaching Tour 1640:1,4

Jesus taught his followers that, when they had made their prayers to the Father, they should remain for a time in silent receptivity to afford the

indwelling spirit the better opportunity to speak to the listening soul. The
spirit of the Father speaks best to man when the human mind is in an
attitude of true worship. We worship God by the aid of the Father's indwelling spirit and by the illumination of the human mind through the ministry of truth. Worship, taught Jesus, makes one increasingly like the being
who is worshiped. Worship is a transforming experience whereby the finite gradually approaches and ultimately attains the presence of the Infinite.   First Preaching Tour 1641:1

How long will it take the world of believers to understand that prayer is
not a process of getting your way but rather a program of taking God's
way, an experience of learning how to recognize and execute the Father's
will? It is entirely true that, when your will has been truly aligned with his,
you can ask anything conceived by that will-union, and it will be granted.
And such a will-union is effected by and through Jesus even as the life of
the vine flows into and through the living branches.
                                      The Farewell Discourse 1946:2

Jesus brought to God, as a man of the realm, the greatest of all offerings: the consecration and dedication of his own will to the majestic service of doing the divine will. Jesus always and consistently interpreted
religion wholly in terms of the Father's will. When you study the career of
the Master, as concerns prayer or any other feature of the religious life,
look not so much for what he taught as for what he did. Jesus never prayed
as a religious duty. To him prayer was a sincere expression of spiritual
attitude, a declaration of soul loyalty, a recital of personal devotion, an
expression of thanksgiving, an avoidance of emotional tension, a prevention of conflict, an exaltation of intellection, an ennoblement of desire, a
vindication of moral decision, an enrichment of thought, an invigoration
of higher inclinations, a consecration of impulse, a clarification of viewpoint, a declaration of faith, a transcendental surrender of will, a sublime
assertion of confidence, a revelation of courage, the proclamation of discovery, a confession of supreme devotion, the validation of consecration,
a technique for the adjustment of difficulties, and the mighty mobilization
of the combined soul powers to withstand all human tendencies toward
selfishness, evil, and sin.   The Faith of Jesus 2088:5

4. Thought Adjuster: Formation of the Soul

According to The Urantia Book, when you were about five years old, God sent a fragment of his infinite self to dwell within you. If you went on to live a good life, then when you die, that piece of God and your surviving soul will eventually fuse into one, and you will become an eternal being.

The piece of God that now resides within you is called the "Thought Adjuster." This spirit is not an "alien" being following you around, watching your every move, and reporting on your behavior; nor is it "adjusting" your thoughts and telling you what to think, like some "big brother" mind-control operation. To the contrary, the Adjuster is a translator that "fine-tunes" the thoughts of the animal mind so they can be better comprehended by the ministering angels. The Adjuster also translates incoming messages—answers to your prayers—in simple terms you can comprehend.

The Thought Adjuster creates within us a thirst for righteousness and a craving for divine perfection. If we choose to devote our lives to performing the will of the Father, the Thought Adjuster will relay information that leads not to a life of ease, but rather to ever-increasing challenges on a voyage of discovery through the universe. In this sense the Adjuster is our companion on the eternal quest.

If the finite mind of man is unable to comprehend how so great and so majestic a God as the Universal Father can descend from his eternal abode in infinite perfection to fraternize with the individual human creature, then must such a finite intellect rest assurance of divine fellowship upon the truth of the fact that an actual fragment of the living God resides within the intellect of every normal-minded and morally conscious Urantia mortal. The indwelling Thought Adjusters are a part of the eternal Deity of the Paradise Father. Man does not have to go farther than his own inner experience of the soul's contemplation of this spiritual-reality presence to find God and attempt communion with him.

God's Relation to the Individual 62:1

Your deepest nature—the divine Adjuster—creates within you a hunger and thirst for righteousness, certain craving for divine perfection.

Religion is the faith act of the recognition of this inner urge to divine attainment; and thus is brought about that soul trust and assurance of which you become conscious as the way of salvation, the technique of the survival of personality and all those values which you have come to look upon as being true and good.   Real Nature of Religion 1107:4

I wish it were possible for me to help evolving mortals to achieve a better understanding and attain a fuller appreciation of the unselfish and superb work of the Adjusters living within them, who are so devoutly faithful to the task of fostering man's spiritual welfare. These Monitors are efficient ministers to the higher phases of men's minds; they are wise and experienced manipulators of the spiritual potential of the human intellect. These heavenly helpers are dedicated to the stupendous task of guiding you safely inward and upward to the celestial haven of happiness. These tireless toilers are consecrated to the future personification of the triumph of divine truth in your life everlasting. They are the watchful workers who pilot the God-conscious human mind away from the shoals of evil while expertly guiding the evolving soul of man toward the divine harbors of perfection on far-distant and eternal shores. The Adjusters are loving leaders, your safe and sure guides through the dark and uncertain mazes of your short earthly career; they are the patient teachers who so constantly urge their subjects forward in the paths of progressive perfection. They are the careful custodians of the sublime values of creature character. I wish you could love them more, co-operate with them more fully, and cherish them more affectionately.   Relation of Adjusters to Individuals 1203:4

I cannot but observe that so many of you spend so much time and thought on mere trifles of living, while you almost wholly overlook the more essential realities of everlasting import, those very accomplishments which are concerned with the development of a more harmonious working agreement between you and your Adjusters. The great goal of human existence is to attune to the divinity of the indwelling Adjuster; the great achievement of mortal life is the attainment of a true and understanding consecration to the eternal aims of the divine spirit who waits and works within your mind. But a devoted and determined effort to realize eternal destiny is wholly compatible with a light-hearted and joyous life and with a successful and honorable career on earth. Co-operation with the Thought Adjuster does not entail self-torture, mock piety, or hypocritical and ostentatious self-abasement; the ideal life is one of loving service rather than an existence of fearful apprehension.

You can consciously augment Adjuster harmony by:

1. Choosing to respond to divine leading; sincerely basing the human life on the highest consciousness of truth, beauty, and goodness, and then co-ordinating these qualities of divinity through wisdom, worship, faith, and love.

2. Loving God and desiring to be like him—genuine recognition of the divine fatherhood and loving worship of the heavenly Parent.

3. Loving man and sincerely desiring to serve him—wholehearted recognition of the brotherhood of man coupled with an intelligent and wise affection for each of your fellow mortals.

4. Joyful acceptance of cosmic citizenship—honest recognition of your progressive obligations to the Supreme Being, awareness of the interdependence of evolutionary man and evolving Deity. This is the birth of cosmic morality and the dawning realization of universal duty.

Relation of Adjusters to Individuals 1206:2,5-8

Certain abrupt presentations of thoughts, conclusions, and other pictures of mind are sometimes the direct or indirect work of the Adjuster; but far more often they are the sudden emergence into consciousness of ideas which have been grouping themselves together in the submerged mental levels, natural and everyday occurrences of normal and ordinary psychic function inherent in the circuits of the evolving animal mind.

There exists a vast gulf between the human and the divine, between man and God. The Urantia races are so largely electrically and chemically controlled, so highly animallike in their common behavior, so emotional in their ordinary reactions, that it becomes exceedingly difficult for the Monitors to guide and direct them. You are so devoid of courageous decisions and consecrated co-operation that your indwelling Adjusters find it next to impossible to communicate directly with the human mind. Even when they do find it possible to flash a gleam of new truth to the evolving mortal soul, this spiritual revelation often so blinds the creature as to precipitate a convulsion of fanaticism or to initiate some other intellectual upheaval which results disastrously. Many a new religion and strange "ism" has arisen from the aborted, imperfect, misunderstood, and garbled communications of the Thought Adjusters.

Self-Portrait; Joan Miro (1937)
© Museum of Modern Art, New York

Do not confuse and confound the mission and influence of the Adjuster with what is commonly called conscience; they are not directly related. Conscience is a human and purely psychic reaction. It is not to be despised, but it is hardly the voice of God to the soul, which indeed the Adjuster's would be if such a voice could be heard. Conscience, rightly, admonishes you to do right; but the Adjuster, in addition, endeavors to tell you what truly is right; that is, when and as you are able to perceive the Monitor's leading.   Relation of Adjusters to Individuals 1207:3,5,7

When the development of the intellectual nature proceeds faster than that of the spiritual, such a situation renders communication with the Thought Adjuster both difficult and dangerous. Likewise, overspiritual development tends to produce a fanatical and perverted interpretation of the spirit leadings of the divine indweller. Lack of spiritual capacity makes it very difficult to transmit to such a material intellect the spiritual truths resident in the higher superconsciousness. It is to the mind of perfect poise, housed in a body of clean habits, stabilized neural energies, and balanced chemical function—when the physical, mental, and spiritual powers are in triune harmony of development—that a maximum of light and truth can be imparted with a minimum of temporal danger or risk to the real welfare of such a being.   Relation of Adjusters to Individuals 1209:4

The chief difficulty you experience in contacting with your Adjusters consists in this very inherent material nature. So few mortals are real thinkers; you do not spiritually develop and discipline your minds to the point of favorable liaison with the divine Adjusters. The ear of the human mind is almost deaf to the spiritual pleas which the Adjuster translates from the manifold messages of the universal broadcasts of love proceeding from the Father of mercies. The Adjuster finds it almost impossible to register these inspiring spirit leadings in an animal mind so completely dominated by the chemical and electrical forces inherent in your physical natures.
Relation of Adjusters to Individuals 1213:1

"The soul is the self-reflective, truth-discerning, and spirit-perceiving part of man which forever elevates the human being above the level of the animal world. Self-consciousness, in and of itself, is not the soul. Moral self-consciousness is true human self-realization and constitutes the foundation of the human soul, and the soul is that part of man which represents the potential survival value of human experience. Moral choice and spiritual attainment, the ability to know God and the urge to be like him, are the characteristics of the soul. The soul of man cannot exist apart from moral thinking and spiritual activity. A stagnant soul is a dying soul. But the soul of man is distinct from the divine spirit which dwells within the mind. The divine spirit arrives simultaneously with the first moral activity of the human mind, and that is the occasion of the birth of the soul.

The Return from Rome 1478:3

5. Dreams

Do you remember your nighttime dreams? If so, you may be happy to know that the rapid graphic idea processions seen in your dreams can give you a glimpse of what language in heaven will be like.

Also while you sleep, the Thought Adjuster may be effecting deep spiritual transformations in your superconscious. As a rule, it is better to err on the side of caution than to assume you can interpret the often time garbled message of your spirit.

But in the language of Nebadon we could, in a half hour's address, cover the subject matter of the entire lifetime of a Urantia mortal. Your only hope of comprehending these transactions is to pause and consider the technique of your disordered and garbled dream life—how you can in a few seconds traverse years of experience in these fantasies of the night season.   The Celestial Artisans 503:7

All down through the ages men have stood in awe of the apparitions of the night season, and the Hebrews were no exception. They truly believed that God spoke to them in dreams, despite the injunctions of Moses against this idea. And Moses was right, for ordinary dreams are not the methods employed by the personalities of the spiritual world when they seek to communicate with material beings.   Early Evolution of Religion 954:9

Supreme and self-acting Adjusters are often able to contribute factors of spiritual import to the human mind when it flows freely in the liberated

Maiden's Dream; Lorenzo Lotto (1480-1556)
© National Gallery of Art, Washington

but controlled channels of creative imagination. At such times, and sometimes during sleep, the Adjuster is able to arrest the mental currents, to stay the flow, and then to divert the idea procession; and all this is done in order to effect deep spiritual transformations in the higher recesses of the superconsciousness.

It is sometimes possible to have the mind illuminated, to hear the divine voice that continually speaks within you, so that you may become partially conscious of the wisdom, truth, goodness, and beauty of the potential personality constantly indwelling you.

But your unsteady and rapidly shifting mental attitudes often result in thwarting the plans and interrupting the work of the Adjusters. Their work is not only interfered with by the innate natures of the mortal races, but this ministry is also greatly retarded by your own preconceived opinions, settled ideas, and long-standing prejudices. Because of these handicaps, many times only their unfinished creations emerge into consciousness, and confusion of concept is inevitable. Therefore, in scrutinizing mental situations, safety lies only in the prompt recognition of each and every thought and experience for just what it actually and fundamentally is, disregarding entirely what it might have been.

Relation of Adjusters to Universe Creatures 1199:2-4

Man's dream experiences, that disordered and disconnected parade of the un-co-ordinated sleeping mind, present adequate proof of the failure of the Adjusters to harmonize and associate the divergent factors of the mind of man. The Adjusters simply cannot, in a single lifetime, arbitrarily co-ordinate and synchronize two such unlike and diverse types of thinking as the human and the divine.

During the slumber season the Adjuster attempts to achieve only that which the will of the indwelt personality has previously fully approved by the decisions and choosings which were made during times of fully wakeful consciousness, and which have thereby become lodged in the realms of the supermind, the liaison domain of human and divine interrelationship.

While their mortal hosts are asleep, the Adjusters try to register their creations in the higher levels of the material mind, and some of your grotesque dreams indicate their failure to make efficient contact. The absurdities of dream life not only testify to pressure of unexpressed emotions but also bear witness to the horrible distortion of the representations of the spiritual concepts presented by the Adjusters. Your own passions, urges, and other innate tendencies translate themselves into the picture and substitute their unexpressed desires for the divine messages which the indwellers are endeavoring to put into the psychic records during unconscious sleep.

It is extremely dangerous to postulate as to the Adjuster content of the dream life. The Adjusters do work during sleep, but your ordinary dream experiences are purely physiologic and psychologic phenomena. Likewise, it is hazardous to attempt the differentiation of the Adjusters' concept registry from the more or less continuous and conscious reception of the dictations of mortal conscience. These are problems which will have to be solved through individual discrimination and personal decision. But a human being would do better to err in rejecting an Adjuster's expression through believing it to be a purely human experience than to blunder into exalting a reaction of the mortal mind to the sphere of divine dignity. Remember, the influence of a Thought Adjuster is for the most part, though not wholly, a superconscious experience.

Relation of Adjusters to Individuals 1208:1-4

6. Trinity

God as Trinity serves as a lens enabling us to unravel the meaning of our lives. This Trinity is made up of the Thought God (spirit), the Word God (Jesus, or the philosophy of living), and the God of Action (the Holy Spirit, the physical world, or very simply, Mother Nature).

To understand this concept, imagine the spectrum of life in the universe. Then envision pure spirit at one end of this continuum and the physical world at the other end. How do you, a mortal of animal origin, reach the heights of spirituality? By following the philosophy of living, as revealed by the successive revelations of God. In this way, your animal mind, through righteous living, will build your soul, and after death you will become spirit.

To assist you in visualizing the Trinity, consider the following diagram:

Universal Father	Eternal Son	Infinite Spirit
Thought God	Word God	God of Action
Religion	Philosophy	Science
Faith	Wisdom	Knowledge
Values	Meanings	Things
Spirit	Soul	Mind

God the Father loves men; God the Son serves men; God the Spirit inspires the children of the universe to the ever-ascending adventure of finding God the Father by the ways ordained by God the Sons through the ministry of the grace of God the Spirit.   Attributes of God 53:6

And so it is: You worship God; pray to, and commune with, the Son; and work out the details of your earthly sojourn in connection with the intelligences of the Infinite Spirit operating on your world and throughout your universe.   God's Relation to the Individual 66:1

Back in eternity, when the Universal Father's "first" infinite and absolute thought finds in the Eternal Son such a perfect and adequate word for its divine expression, there ensues the supreme desire of both the Thought-God and the Word-God for a universal and infinite agent of mutual expression and combined action.

In the dawn of eternity both the Father and the Son become infinitely cognizant of their mutual interdependence, their eternal and absolute oneness; and therefore do they enter into an infinite and everlasting covenant of divine partnership. This never-ending compact is made for the execution of their united concepts throughout all of the circle of eternity; and ever since this eternity event the Father and the Son continue in this divine union.

We are now face to face with the eternity origin of the Infinite Spirit, the Third Person of Deity. The very instant that God the Father and God the Son conjointly conceive an identical and infinite action—the execution of an absolute thought-plan—that very moment, the Infinite Spirit springs full-fledgedly into existence.

In thus reciting the order of the origin of the Deities, I do so merely to enable you to think of their relationship. In reality they are all three existent from eternity; they are existential. They are without beginning or ending of days; they are co-ordinate, supreme, ultimate, absolute, and infinite. They are and always have been and ever shall be. And they are three distinctly individualized but eternally associated persons, God the Father, God the Son, and God the Spirit.

In the eternity of the past, upon the personalization of the Infinite Spirit the divine personality cycle becomes perfect and complete. The God of Action is existent, and the vast stage of space is set for the stupendous drama of creation—the universal adventure—the divine panorama of the eternal ages.

A Vision of the Trinity to Pope St Clement; Giovanni Tiepolo (1696-1770)
© National Gallery of London

The first act of the Infinite Spirit is the inspection and recognition of his divine parents, the Father-Father and the Mother-Son. He, the Spirit, unqualifiedly identifies both of them. He is fully cognizant of their separate personalities and infinite attributes as well as of their combined nature and united function. Next, voluntarily, with transcendent willingness and inspiring spontaneity, the Third Person of Deity, notwithstanding his equality with the First and Second Persons, pledges eternal loyalty to God the Father and acknowledges everlasting dependence upon God the Son.

The Infinite Spirit 90:1-6

The First, Second, and Third Persons of Deity are equal to each other, and they are one. "The Lord our God is one God." There is perfection of purpose and oneness of execution in the divine Trinity of eternal Deities. The Father, the Son, and the Conjoint Actor are truly and divinely one. Of a truth it is written: "I am the first, and I am the last, and beside me there is no God."

The Paradise Trinity 115:3

Through the recognition of the Trinity concept the mind of man can hope to grasp something of the interrelationship of love and law in the time-space creations. Through spiritual faith man gains insight into the love of God but soon discovers that this spiritual faith has no influence on the ordained laws of the material universe.

Growth of the Trinity Concept 1145:4

7. How God Guides Earth's Progress

From the limited view of this lifetime—an era filled with war, hatred, hunger, poverty, and autocracy—God's efforts to guide earth's progress may seem less than admirable. But when we stretch our vision to encompass a million-year span, we can see that humanity has emerged from a dark cave of superstition and come into the light as beings with an eternal future. God's steady hand is indeed guiding earth's progress.

Revelation is evolutionary but always progressive. Down through the ages of a world's history, the revelations of religion are ever-expanding and successively more enlightening. It is the mission of revelation to sort and censor the successive religions of evolution. But if revelation is to exalt and upstep the religions of evolution, then must such divine visitations portray teachings which are not too far removed from the thought and reactions of the age in which they are presented. Thus must and does revelation always keep in touch with evolution. Always must the religion of revelation be limited by man's capacity of receptivity.

There have been many events of religious revelation but only five of epochal significance. These were as follows:

1. *The Dalamatian teachings.* The true concept of the First Source and Center was first promulgated on Urantia by the one hundred corporeal members of Prince Caligastia's staff. This expanding revelation of Deity went on for more than three hundred thousand years until it was suddenly terminated by the planetary secession and the disruption of the teaching regime. Except for the work of Van, the influence of the Dalamatian revelation was practically lost to the whole world. Even the Nodites had forgotten this truth by the time of Adam's arrival. Of all who received the teachings of the one hundred, the red men held them longest, but the idea of the Great Spirit was but a hazy concept in Amerindian religion when contact with Christianity greatly clarified and strengthened it.

2. *The Edenic teachings.* Adam and Eve again portrayed the concept of the Father of all to the evolutionary peoples. The disruption of the first Eden halted the course of the Adamic revelation before it had ever fully started. But the aborted teachings of Adam were carried on by the Sethite priests, and some of these truths have never been entirely lost to the world. The entire trend of Levantine religious evolution was modified by the teachings of the Sethites. But by 2500 B.C. mankind had largely lost sight of the revelation sponsored in the days of Eden.

3. *Melchizedek of Salem.* This emergency Son of Nebadon inaugurated the third revelation of truth on Urantia. The cardinal precepts of his teachings were trust and faith. He taught trust in the omnipotent beneficence of God and proclaimed that faith was the act by which men earned God's favor. His teachings gradually commingled with the beliefs and practices of various evolutionary religions and finally developed into those theologic systems present on Urantia at the opening of the first millennium after Christ.

4. *Jesus of Nazareth.* Christ Michael presented for the fourth time to Urantia the concept of God as the Universal Father, and this teaching has generally persisted ever since. The essence of his teaching was love and service, the loving worship which a creature son voluntarily gives in recognition of, and response to, the loving ministry of God his Father; the freewill service which such creature sons bestow upon their brethren in the joyous realization that in this service they are likewise serving God the Father.

5. *The Urantia Papers.* The papers, of which this is one, constitute the most recent presentation of truth to the mortals of Urantia. These papers differ from all previous revelations, for they are not the work of a single universe personality but a composite presentation by many beings. But no revelation short of the attainment of the Universal Father can ever be complete. All other celestial ministrations are no more than partial, transient, and practically adapted to local conditions in time and space. While such admissions as this may possibly detract from the immediate force and authority of all revelations, the time has arrived on Urantia when it is advisable to make such frank statements, even at the risk of weakening the future influence and authority of this, the most recent of the revelations of truth to the mortal races of Urantia.

Later Evolution of Religion 1007:1,4-7, 1008:1,2

~ VIII ~

The Universe

To begin to comprehend the infinite nature of the universe, look up at the stars on a clear night. What you will see is the velvety splendor of the Milky Way spilling across the sky. Yet the Milky Way, with its hundreds of millions of stars, is only one of many huge galaxies.

How many large galaxies do you suppose astronomers have identified in the sky? A doctor I've asked replied, "Hundreds." An engineer told me, "Thousands." A recently published astronomy book reported hundreds of millions of such galaxies. More recent discoveries by the Hubble space telescope place the count at more than a billion!

1. Angels

Whereas human beings are evolutionary creatures capable of reproducing, angels are a direct creation of God and are incapable of procreating. Our mission is not to worship these beings, but rather to feel their presence. Angels and humans are fellow servants of God. As his ministers, angels aid and comfort us. They are faithful companions who will work alongside us for ages to come.

Angels do not have material bodies, but they are definite and discrete beings; they are of spirit nature and origin. Though invisible to mortals, they perceive you as you are in the flesh without the aid of transformers or translators; they intellectually understand the mode of mortal life, and they share all of man's nonsensuous emotions and sentiments. They appreciate and greatly enjoy your efforts in music, art, and real humor. They are fully cognizant of your moral struggles and spiritual difficulties. They love human beings, and only good can result from your efforts to understand and love them.

Though seraphim are very affectionate and sympathetic beings, they are not sex-emotion creatures. They are much as you will be on the mansion worlds, where you will "neither marry nor be given in marriage but will be as the angels of heaven." For all who "shall be accounted worthy to attain the mansion worlds neither marry nor are given in marriage; neither do they die any more, for they are equal to the angels."

Angels are superior to you in spiritual status, but they are not your judges or accusers. No matter what your faults, "the angels, although greater in power and might, bring no accusation against you." Angels do not sit in judgment on mankind, neither should individual mortals prejudge their fellow creatures.

You do well to love them, but you should not adore them; angels are not objects of worship. The great seraphim, Loyalatia, when your seer "fell down to worship before the feet of the angel," said: "See that you do it not; I am a fellow servant with you and with your races, who are all enjoined to worship God."

Ministering Spirits of the Local Universe 419:1,2,4,5

Your conventional idea of angels has been derived in the following way: During moments just prior to physical death a reflective phenomenon sometimes occurs in the human mind, and this dimming consciousness seems to visualize something of the form of the attending angel, and this is immediately translated into terms of the habitual concept of angels held in that individual's mind.

The erroneous idea that angels possess wings is not wholly due to olden notions that they must have wings to fly through the air. Human beings have sometimes been permitted to observe seraphim that were being prepared for transport service, and the traditions of these experiences have largely determined the Urantian concept of angels. In observing a transport seraphim being made ready to receive a passenger for interplanetary transit, there may be seen what are apparently double sets of wings extending from the head to the foot of the angel. In reality these wings are energy insulators—friction shields.

When celestial beings are to be enseraphimed for transfer from one world to another, they are brought to the headquarters of the sphere and, after due registry, are inducted into the transit sleep. Meantime, the transport seraphim moves into a horizontal position immediately above the universe energy pole of the planet. While the energy shields are wide open,

Psyche ranimee par le basier de l'Amour; Antonio
Canova (1757-1822) © Louvre, Paris

the sleeping personality is skillfully deposited, by the officiating seraphic assistants, directly on top of the transport angel. Then both the upper and lower pairs of shields are carefully closed and adjusted.

And now, under the influence of the transformers and the transmitters, a strange metamorphosis begins as the seraphim is made ready to swing into the energy currents of the universe circuits. To outward appearance the seraphim grows pointed at both extremities and becomes so enshrouded in a queer light of amber hue that very soon it is impossible to distinguish the enseraphimed personality. When all is in readiness for departure, the chief of transport makes the proper inspection of the carriage of life, carries out the routine tests to ascertain whether or not the angel is properly encircuited, and then announces that the traveler is properly enseraphimed, that the energies are adjusted, that the angel is insulated, and that everything is in readiness for the departing flash. The mechanical controllers, two of them, next take their positions. By this time the transport seraphim has become an almost transparent, vibrating, torpedo-shaped outline of glistening luminosity. Now the transport dispatcher of the realm summons the auxiliary batteries of the living energy transmitters, usually one thousand in number; as he announces the destination of the transport, he reaches out and touches the near point of the seraphic carriage, which shoots forward with lightninglike speed, leaving a trail of celestial luminosity as far as the planetary atmospheric investment extends. In less than ten minutes the marvelous spectacle will be lost even to reinforced seraphic vision.

The Seraphic Hosts 438:4-7

The angels really find it hard to understand why you will so persistently allow your higher intellectual powers, even your religious faith, to be so dominated by fear, so thoroughly demoralized by the thoughtless panic of dread and anxiety. Seraphic Guardians of Destiny 1243:2

Seraphim function as teachers of men by guiding the footsteps of the human personality into paths of new and progressive experiences. To accept the guidance of a seraphim rarely means attaining a life of ease. In following this leading you are sure to encounter, and if you have the courage, to traverse, the rugged hills of moral choosing and spiritual progress.

Seraphic Guardians of Destiny 1245:3

Angels are so near you and care so feelingly for you that they figuratively "weep because of your willful intolerance and stubbornness." Seraphim do not shed physical tears; they do not have physical bodies; neither do they possess wings. But they do have spiritual emotions, and they do experience feelings and sentiments of a spiritual nature which are in certain ways comparable to human emotions.

The seraphim act in your behalf quite independent of your direct appeals; they are executing the mandates of their superiors, and thus they function regardless of your passing whims or changing moods. This does not imply that you may not make their tasks either easier or more difficult, but rather that angels are not directly concerned with your appeals or with your prayers.

In the life of the flesh the intelligence of angels is not directly available to mortal men. They are not overlords or directors; they are simply guardians. The seraphim *guard* you; they do not seek directly to influence you; you must chart your own course, but these angels then act to make the best possible use of the course you have chosen. They do not (ordinarily) arbitrarily intervene in the routine affairs of human life. But when they receive instructions from their superiors to perform some unusual exploit, you may rest assured that these guardians will find some means of carrying out these mandates. They do not, therefore, intrude into the picture of human drama except in emergencies and then usually on the direct orders of their superiors. They are the beings who are going to follow you for many an age, and they are thus receiving an introduction to their future work and personality association.

Seraphic Guardians of Destiny 1246:1-3

As they journeyed up the hills from Jericho to Bethany, Nathaniel walked most of the way by the side of Jesus, and their discussion of children in relation to the kingdom of heaven led indirectly to the consideration of the ministry of angels. Nathaniel finally asked the Master this question: "Seeing that the high priest is a Sadducee, and since the Sadducees do not believe in angels, what shall we teach the people regarding the heavenly ministers?" Then, among other things, Jesus said:

"The angelic hosts are a separate order of created beings; they are entirely different from the material order of mortal creatures, and they function as a distinct group of universe intelligences. Angels are not of that group of creatures called 'the Sons of God' in the Scriptures; neither are they the glorified spirits of mortal men who have gone on to progress through the mansions on high. Angels are a direct creation, and they do not reproduce themselves. The angelic hosts have only a spiritual kinship with the human race. As man progresses in the journey to the Father in Paradise, he does traverse a state of being at one time analogous to the state of the angels, but mortal man never becomes an angel.

"The angels never die, as man does. The angels are immortal unless, perchance, they become involved in sin as did some of them with the deceptions of Lucifer. The angels are the spirit servants in heaven, and they are neither all-wise nor all-powerful. But all of the loyal angels are truly pure and holy.

"And do you not remember that I said to you once before that, if you had your spiritual eyes anointed, you would then see the heavens opened and behold the angels of God ascending and descending? It is by the ministry of the angels that one world may be kept in touch with other worlds, for have I not repeatedly told you that I have other sheep not of this fold? And these angels are not the spies of the spirit world who watch upon you and then go forth to tell the Father the thoughts of your heart and to report on the deeds of the flesh. The Father has no need of such service inasmuch as his own spirit lives within you. But these angelic spirits do function to keep one part of the heavenly creation informed concerning the doings of other and remote parts of the universe. And many of the angels, while functioning in the government of the Father and the universes of the Sons, are assigned to the service of the human races. When I taught you that many of these seraphim are ministering spirits, I spoke not in figurative language nor in poetic strains. And all this is true, regardless of your difficulty in comprehending such matters.

"Many of these angels are engaged in the work of saving men, for have I not told you of the seraphic joy when one soul elects to forsake sin and begin the search for God? I did even tell you of the joy in the presence of the angels of heaven over one sinner who repents, thereby indicating the existence of other and higher orders of celestial beings who are likewise concerned in the spiritual welfare and with the divine progress of mortal man.

"Also are these angels very much concerned with the means whereby man's spirit is released from the tabernacles of the flesh and his soul escorted to the mansions in heaven. Angels are the sure and heavenly guides of the soul of man during that uncharted and indefinite period of time which intervenes between the death of the flesh and the new life in the spirit abodes."   Visit to Philadelphia 1840:6 - 1841:5

2. Death and Resurrection

The Urantia Book speaks of three kinds of death: physical death, mind death, and spiritual death. In the first two instances we have nothing to fear; the body simply quits, or the brain dies. When confronted with spiritual death, on the other hand, we risk losing our eternal future.

As for life after death, two great myths permeate our civilization:

- **Bad people die and go to hell and burn for eternity.**

We are presented with many paths to choose in life. A person who repeatedly walks a path to evil will eventually reach a place of no return. No slow-turning barbecue spit will be awaiting his arrival, however, for the Creator of the universe does not recognize evil. Instead, this individual, having embraced a reality that is not part of God, will annihilate himself through his iniquity.

Then will you look for their places, but they shall not be found. "And they who know you among the worlds will be astonished at you; you have been a terror, but never shall you be any more."

The Lucifer Rebellion 611:6

- **Good people go to heaven where everything is perfect and their troubles are over.**

Although heaven is resplendent in its perfection, human beings will not be able to experience the full splendor of it for millions of years. After death, a person who has lived in alignment with God's will takes on a "morontia" body—a form similar to the body Jesus bore as he tarried on earth for a season after his death. As the individual progresses from world to world, working his way toward Paradise, this morontia body will increasingly dematerialize until nearly all that is left is spirit. At that point, he will be ready to see perfection, as well as God himself.

The foundation of the universe is material, but the essence of life is spirit.

Energy - Mind and Matter 67:3

"He shall send his angels, and they shall gather together his elect from the four winds."

The Inhabited Worlds 568:8

Love of adventure, curiosity, and dread of monotony—these traits inherent in evolving human nature—were not put there just to aggravate and annoy you during your short sojourn on earth, but rather to suggest to you that death is only the beginning of an endless career of adventure, an everlasting life of anticipation, an eternal voyage of discovery.

Central and Divine Universe 159:6

Even the infinite love of God cannot force the salvation of eternal survival upon any mortal creature who does not choose to survive. Mercy has great latitude of bestowal, but, after all, there are mandates of justice which even love combined with mercy cannot effectively abrogate. Again Jesus quoted from the Hebrew scriptures: "I have called and you refused to hear; I stretched out my hand, but no man regarded. You have set at naught all my counsel, and you have rejected my reproof, and because of this rebellious attitude it becomes inevitable that you shall call upon me and fail to receive an answer. Having rejected the way of life, you may seek me diligently in your times of suffering, but you will not find me."

First Preaching Tour 1638:5

When material life has run its course, if no choice has been made for the ascendant life, or if these children of time definitely decide against the Havona adventure, death automatically terminates their probationary careers. There is no adjudication of such cases; there is no resurrection from such a second death. They simply become as though they had not been.

Seven Mansion Worlds 532:5

The Jewish traditions of heaven and hell and the doctrine of devils as recorded in the Hebrew scriptures, while founded on the lingering traditions of Lucifer and Caligastia, were principally derived from the Zoroastrians during the times when the Jews were under the political and cultural dominance of the Persians. Zoroaster, like the Egyptians, taught the "day of judgment," but he connected this event with the end of the world.

Melchizedek Teachings in the Levant 1050:2

How futile to make puerile appeals to such a God to modify his changeless decrees so that we can avoid the just consequences of the operation of his wise natural laws and righteous spiritual mandates! "Be not deceived; God is not mocked, for whatsoever a man sows that shall he also reap."

Graveyard; © Harriet Blum (1996) Santa Fe , New Mexico

True, even in the justice of reaping the harvest of wrongdoing, this divine justice is always tempered with mercy. Infinite wisdom is the eternal arbiter which determines the proportions of justice and mercy which shall be meted out in any given circumstance. The greatest punishment (in reality an inevitable consequence) for wrongdoing and deliberate rebellion against the government of God is loss of existence as an individual subject of that government. The final result of wholehearted sin is annihilation. In the last analysis, such sin-identified individuals have destroyed themselves by becoming wholly unreal through their embrace of iniquity.

Nature of God 36:7

Planetary Mortals. Mortals are all animal-origin evolutionary beings of ascendant potential. In origin, nature, and destiny these various groups and types of human beings are not wholly unlike the Urantia peoples. The human races of each world receive the same ministry of the Sons of God and enjoy the presence of the ministering spirits of time. After natural death all types of ascenders fraternize as one morontia family on the mansion worlds.

Personalities of the Grand Universe 340:12

The passing of time is of no moment to sleeping mortals; they are wholly unconscious and oblivious to the length of their rest. On reassembly of personality at the end of an age, those who have slept five thousand years will react no differently than those who have rested five days. Aside from this time delay these survivors pass on through the ascension regime identically with those who avoid the longer or shorter sleep of death.

Such a reassociation of soul and Adjuster is quite properly called a resurrection, a reassembly of personality factors; but even this does not entirely explain the reappearance of the surviving *personality*. Though you will probably never understand the fact of such an inexplicable transaction, you will sometime experientially know the truth of it if you do not reject the plan of mortal survival.

Personalities of the Grand Universe 341:2,5

From the Temple of New Life there extend seven radial wings, the resurrection halls of the mortal races. Each of these structures is devoted to the assembly of one of the seven races of time. There are one hundred thousand personal resurrection chambers in each of these seven wings terminating in the circular class assembly halls, which serve as the awak-

Awakened Responses; Patty West Elstrott (1996) New Orleans

ening chambers for as many as one million individuals. These halls are surrounded by the personality assembly chambers of the blended races of the normal post-Adamic worlds. Regardless of the technique which may be employed on the individual worlds of time in connection with special or dispensational resurrections, the real and conscious reassembly of actual and complete personality takes place in the resurrection halls of mansonia number one. Throughout all eternity you will recall the profound memory impressions of your first witnessing of these resurrection mornings.

From the resurrection halls you proceed to the Melchizedek sector, where you are assigned permanent residence. Then you enter upon ten days of personal liberty. You are free to explore the immediate vicinity of your new home and to familiarize yourself with the program which lies immediately ahead. You also have time to gratify your desire to consult the registry and call upon your loved ones and other earth friends who may have preceded you to these worlds. At the end of your ten-day period of leisure you begin the second step in the Paradise journey, for the mansion worlds are actual training spheres, not merely detention planets.

Seven Mansion Worlds 533:4,5

If you are not to be detained on mansion world number one, at the end of ten days you will enter the translation sleep and proceed to world number two, and every ten days thereafter you will thus advance until you arrive on the world of your assignment.   Seven Mansion Worlds 534:2

Your Adjuster memory remains fully intact as you ascend the morontia life. Those mental associations that were purely animalistic and wholly material naturally perished with the physical brain, but everything in your mental life which was worth while, and which had survival value, was counterparted by the Adjuster and is retained as a part of personal memory all the way through the ascendant career. You will be conscious of all your worth-while experiences as you advance from one mansion world to another and from one section of the universe to another—even to Paradise.

Though you have morontia bodies, you continue, through all seven of these worlds, to eat, drink, and rest. You partake of the morontia order of food, a kingdom of living energy unknown on the material worlds. Both food and water are fully utilized in the morontia body; there is no residual waste. Pause to consider: Mansonia number one is a very material sphere, presenting the early beginnings of the morontia regime. You are still a near human and not far removed from the limited viewpoints of mortal life, but each world discloses definite progress. From sphere to sphere you grow less material, more intellectual, and slightly more spiritual. The spiritual progress is greatest on the last three of these seven progressive worlds.

Seven Mansion Worlds 535:1,2

A real birth of cosmic consciousness takes place on mansonia number five. You are becoming universe minded. This is indeed a time of expanding horizons. It is beginning to dawn upon the enlarging minds of the ascending mortals that some stupendous and magnificent, some supernal and divine, destiny awaits all who complete the progressive Paradise ascension, which has been so laboriously but so joyfully and auspiciously begun. At about this point the average mortal ascender begins to manifest bona fide experiential enthusiasm for the Havona ascent. Study is becoming voluntary, unselfish service natural, and worship spontaneous. A real morontia character is budding; a real morontia creature is evolving.

Seven Mansion Worlds 537:5

The Gods cannot—at least they do not—transform a creature of gross animal nature into a perfected spirit by some mysterious act of creative magic. When the Creators desire to produce perfect beings, they do so by direct and original creation, but they never undertake to convert animal-origin and material creatures into beings of perfection in a single step.

The morontia life, extending as it does over the various stages of the local universe career, is the only possible approach whereby material mortals could attain the threshold of the spirit world. What magic could death, the natural dissolution of the material body, hold that such a simple step should instantly transform the mortal and material mind into an immortal and perfected spirit? Such beliefs are but ignorant superstitions and pleasing fables.

The Morontia Life 541:1,2

Paul learned of the existence of the morontia worlds and of the reality of morontia materials, for he wrote, "They have in heaven a better and more enduring substance." And these morontia materials are real, literal, even as in "the city which has foundations, whose builder and maker is God." And each of these marvelous spheres is "a better country, that is, a heavenly one."

The Morontia Life 542:4

Area and Building Custodians. Even the material and morontia structures increase in perfection and grandeur as you advance in the mansonia career. As individuals and as groups you are permitted to make certain changes in the abodes assigned as headquarters for your sojourn on the different mansion worlds. Many of the activities of these spheres take place in the open enclosures of the variously designated circles, squares, and triangles. The majority of the mansion world structures are roofless, being enclosures of magnificent construction and exquisite embellishment. The climatic and other physical conditions prevailing on the architectural worlds make roofs wholly unnecessary.   The Morontia Life 546:8

One of the purposes of the morontia career is to effect the permanent eradication from the mortal survivors of such animal vestigial traits as procrastination, equivocation, insincerity, problem avoidance, unfairness, and ease seeking. The mansonia life early teaches the young morontia pupils that postponement is in no sense avoidance. After the life in the flesh, time is no longer available as a technique of dodging situations or of circumventing disagreeable obligations.   The Morontia Life 551:3

Urantians generally recognize only one kind of death, the physical cessation of life energies; but concerning personality survival there are really three kinds:

1. *Spiritual (soul) death.* If and when mortal man has finally rejected survival, when he has been pronounced spiritually insolvent..... This kind of death is final in its significance irrespective of the temporary continuation of the living energies of the physical and mind mechanisms. From the cosmic standpoint the mortal is already dead; the continuing life merely indicates the persistence of the material momentum of cosmic energies.

2. *Intellectual (mind) death.* When the vital circuits of higher adjutant ministry are disrupted through the aberrations of intellect or because of the partial destruction of the mechanism of the brain, and if these conditions pass a certain critical point of irreparability, the indwelling Adjuster is immediately released to depart for Divinington. On the universe records a mortal personality is considered to have met with death whenever the essential mind circuits of human will-action have been destroyed. And again, this is death, irrespective of the continuing function of the living mechanism of the physical body. The body minus the volitional mind is no longer human, but according to the prior choosing of the human will, the soul of such an individual may survive.

3. *Physical (body and mind) death.* When death overtakes a human being, the Adjuster remains in the citadel of the mind until it ceases to function as an intelligent mechanism, about the time that the measurable brain energies cease their rhythmic vital pulsations. Following this dissolution the Adjuster takes leave of the vanishing mind, just as unceremoniously as

Rosette; © Tony and Daphne Hallas Astro Photo
Oakview CA.

entry was made years before, and proceeds to Divinington by way of Uversa.

There can be no exhibition of any sort of personality or ability to engage in communications with other personalities until after completion of survival. Those who go to the mansion worlds are not permitted to send messages back to their loved ones. It is the policy throughout the universes to forbid such communication during the period of a current dispensation.

Personality Survival 1229:8,8 & 1230:1,2,5

There is something real, something of human evolution, something additional to the Mystery Monitor, which survives death. This newly appearing entity is the soul, and it survives the death of both your physical body and your material mind. This entity is the conjoint child of the combined life and efforts of the human you in liaison with the divine you, the Adjuster. This child of human and divine parentage constitutes the surviving element of terrestrial origin; it is the morontia self, the immortal soul.

Personality Survival 1234:1

But much of your past life and its memories, having neither spiritual meaning nor morontia value, will perish with the material brain; much of material experience will pass away as onetime scaffolding which, having bridged you over to the morontia level, no longer serves a purpose in the universe. But personality and the relationships between personalities are never scaffolding; mortal memory of personality relationships has cosmic value and will persist. On the mansion worlds you will know and be known, and more, you will remember, and be remembered by, your onetime associates in the short but intriguing life on Urantia.

Personality Survival 1235:4

To a certain extent, the appearance of the material body-form is responsive to the character of the personality identity; the physical body does, to a limited degree, reflect something of the inherent nature of the personality. Still more so does the morontia form. In the physical life, mortals may be outwardly beautiful though inwardly unlovely; in the morontia life, and increasingly on its higher levels, the personality form will vary directly in accordance with the nature of the inner person. On the spiritual level, outward form and inner nature begin to approximate complete identification, which grows more and more perfect on higher and higher spirit levels.

Personality Survival 1236:1

You have been instructed to a certain extent about the organization and personnel of the central universe, the superuniverses, and the local universes; you have been told something about the character and origin of some of the various personalities who now rule these far-flung creations. You have also been informed that there are in process of organization vast galaxies of universes far out beyond the periphery of the grand universe, in the first outer space level. It has also been intimated in the course of these narratives that the Supreme Being is to disclose his unrevealed tertiary function in these now uncharted regions of outer space; and you have also been told that the finaliters of the Paradise corps are the experiential children of the Supreme.

We believe that the mortals of Adjuster fusion, together with their finaliter associates, are destined to function in some manner in the administration of the universes of the first outer space level. We have not the slightest doubt that in due time these enormous galaxies will become inhabited universes. And we are equally convinced that among the administrators thereof will be found the Paradise finaliters whose natures are the cosmic consequence of the blending of creature and Creator.

What an adventure! What a romance! A gigantic creation to be administered by the children of the Supreme, these personalized and humanized Adjusters, these Adjusterized and eternalized mortals, these mysterious combinations and eternal associations of the highest known manifestation of the essence of the First Source and Center and the lowest form of intelligent life capable of comprehending and attaining the Universal Father. We conceive that such amalgamated beings, such partnerships of Creator and creature, will become superb rulers, matchless administrators, and understanding and sympathetic directors of any and all forms of intelligent life which may come into existence throughout these future universes of the first outer space level.   Personality Survival 1239:5-7

It is indeed an epoch in the career of an ascending mortal, this first awakening on the shores of the mansion world; there, for the first time, actually to see your long-loved and ever-present angelic companions of earth days; there also to become truly conscious of the identity and presence of the divine Monitor who so long indwelt your mind on earth. Such an experience constitutes a glorious awakening, a real resurrection.
                        Seraphic Guardians of Destiny 1248:1

The last rest of time has been enjoyed; the last transition sleep has been experienced; now you awake to life everlasting on the shores of the eternal abode. "And there shall be no more sleep. The presence of God and his Son are before you, and you are eternally his servants; you have seen his face, and his name is your spirit. There shall be no night there; and they need no light of the sun, for the Great Source and Center gives them light; they shall live forever and ever. And God shall wipe away all tears from their eyes; there shall be no more death, neither sorrow nor crying, neither shall there be any more pain, for the former things have passed away."

Ministry of Primary Supernaphim 299:5

3. Universe Inhabitants

Here you will encounter the great variety of evolutionary creatures who inhabit the universe. Evolutionary creatures adapt to all types of planets—those with heavy atmospheres, like Venus, light atmospheres, like Mars, or no atmosphere, such as the moon.

I like to imagine that after I die I will move on to a more diversely populated world. There I will become fast friends with a former inhabitant of a gas giant planet like Jupiter, who in his mortal life resembled a glowing green gas bag. Then I would know that I had died and awakened in heaven. Together, we would begin the long climb inward, in search of Paradise.

There is a standard and basic pattern of vegetable and animal life in each system. But the Life Carriers are oftentimes confronted with the necessity of modifying these basic patterns to conform to the varying physical conditions which confront them on numerous worlds of space. They foster a generalized system type of mortal creature, but there are seven distinct physical types as well as thousands upo
n thousands of minor variants of these seven outstanding differentiations:

1. Atmospheric types.
2. Elemental types.
3. Gravity types.
4. Temperature types.
5. Electric types.
6. Energizing types.

The Satania system contains all of these types and numerous intermediate groups, although some are very sparingly represented.

1. *The atmospheric types.* The physical differences of the worlds of mortal habitation are chiefly determined by the nature of the atmosphere; other influences which contribute to the planetary differentiation of life are relatively minor.

The present atmospheric status of Urantia is almost ideal for the support of the breathing type of man, but the human type can be so modified that it can live on both the superatmospheric and the subatmospheric planets. Such modifications also extend to the animal life, which differs greatly on the various inhabited spheres. There is a very great modification of animal orders on both the sub- and the superatmospheric worlds.

Of the atmospheric types in Satania, about two and one-half per cent are subbreathers, about five per cent superbreathers, and over ninety-one per cent are mid-breathers, altogether accounting for ninety-eight and one-half per cent of the Satania worlds.

Beings such as the Urantia races are classified as mid-breathers; you represent the average or typical breathing order of mortal existence. If intelligent creatures should exist on a planet with an atmosphere similar to that of your near neighbor, Venus, they would belong to the superbreather group, while those inhabiting a planet with an atmosphere as thin as that of your outer neighbor, Mars, would be denominated subbreathers.

If mortals should inhabit a planet devoid of air, like your moon, they would belong to the separate order of nonbreathers. This type represents a radical or extreme adjustment to the planetary environment and is separately considered. Nonbreathers account for the remaining one and one-half per cent of Satania worlds.

2. *The elemental types.* These differentiations have to do with the relation of mortals to water, air, and land, and there are four distinct species of intelligent life as they are related to these habitats. The Urantia races are of the land order.

In Satania, of the elemental types, seven per cent are water, ten per cent air, seventy per cent land, and thirteen per cent combined land-and-air types. But these modifications of early intelligent creatures are neither human fishes nor human birds. They are of the human and prehuman types, neither superfishes nor glorified birds but distinctly mortal.

3. *The gravity types.* By modification of creative design, intelligent beings are so constructed that they can freely function on spheres both smaller

Ascent to the Threefold Mansion of Light
Vincent Ventola, Private Collection
Chicago, Illinois

and larger than Urantia, thus being, in measure, accommodated to the gravity of those planets which are not of ideal size and density.

The various planetary types of mortals vary in height, the average in Nebadon being a trifle under seven feet. Some of the larger worlds are peopled with beings who are only about two and one-half feet in height.

4. *The temperature types.* It is possible to create living beings who can withstand temperatures both much higher and much lower than the life range of the Urantia races.

5. *The electric types.* The electric, magnetic, and electronic behavior of the worlds varies greatly. There are ten designs of mortal life variously fashioned to withstand the differential energy of the spheres.

6. *The energizing types.* Not all worlds are alike in the manner of taking in energy. Not all inhabited worlds have an atmospheric ocean suited to respiratory exchange of gases, such as is present on Urantia.

The Inhabited Planets 560:7 & 561:1-14 & 562:2-6 & 563:1

The majority of inhabited planets are peopled with the breathing type of intelligent beings. But there are also orders of mortals who are able to live on worlds with little or no air. Of the Orvonton inhabited worlds this type amounts to less than seven per cent. In Nebadon this percentage is less than three. In all Satania there are only nine such worlds.

There are so very few of the nonbreather type of inhabited worlds in Satania because this more recently organized section of Norlatiadek still abounds in meteoric space bodies; and worlds without a protective friction atmosphere are subject to incessant bombardment by these wanderers. Even some of the comets consist of meteor swarms, but as a rule they are disrupted smaller bodies of matter.

Millions upon millions of meteorites enter the atmosphere of Urantia daily, coming in at the rate of almost two hundred miles a second. On the nonbreathing worlds the advanced races must do much to protect themselves from meteor damage by making electrical installations which operate to consume or shunt the meteors. Great danger confronts them when they venture beyond these protected zones. These worlds are also subject to disastrous electrical storms of a nature unknown on Urantia. During such times of tremendous energy fluctuation the inhabitants must take refuge in their special structures of protective insulation.

Life on the worlds of the nonbreathers is radically different from what it is on Urantia. The nonbreathers do not eat food or drink water as do the

Urantia races. The reactions of the nervous system, the heat-regulating mechanism, and the metabolism of these specialized peoples are radically different from such functions of Urantia mortals. Almost every act of living, aside from reproduction, differs, and even the methods of procreation are somewhat different.

You would be more than interested in the planetary conduct of this type of mortal because such a race of beings inhabits a sphere in close proximity to Urantia. The Inhabited Worlds 563:4-1 & 562:4

There are great differences between the mortals of the different worlds, even among those belonging to the same intellectual and physical types, but all mortals of will dignity are erect animals, bipeds.

The average special physical-sense endowment of human beings is twelve, though the special senses of the three-brained mortals are extended slightly beyond those of the one- and two-brained types; they can see and hear considerably more than the Urantia races.

Young are usually born singly, multiple births being the exception, and the family life is fairly uniform on all types of planets. Sex equality prevails on all advanced worlds; male and female are equal in mind endowment and spiritual status. We do not regard a planet as having emerged from barbarism so long as one sex seeks to tyrannize over the other.

Seasons and temperature variations occur on all sunlighted and sun-heated planets. Agriculture is universal on all atmospheric worlds; tilling the soil is the one pursuit that is common to the advancing races of all such planets.

Mortals all have the same general struggles with microscopic foes in their early days, such as you now experience on Urantia, though perhaps not so extensive. The length of life varies on the different planets from twenty-five years on the primitive worlds to near five hundred on the more advanced and older spheres. The Inhabited Planets 564:3,5-8

Brain-type series. The one physical uniformity of mortals is the brain and nervous system; nevertheless, there are three basic organizations of the brain mechanism: the one-, the two-, and the three-brained types. Urantians are of the two-brained type, somewhat more imaginative, adventurous, and philosophical than the one-brained mortals but somewhat less spiritual, ethical, and worshipful than the three-brained orders. These brain differences characterize even the prehuman animal existences.

From the two-hemisphere type of the Urantian cerebral cortex you can, by analogy, grasp something of the one-brained type. The third brain of the three-brained orders is best conceived as an evolvement of your lower or rudimentary form of brain, which is developed to the point where it functions chiefly in control of physical activities, leaving the two superior brains free for higher engagements: one for intellectual functions and the other for the spiritual-counterparting activities of the Thought Adjuster.

Spirit-reception series. There are three groups of mind design as related to contact with spirit affairs. This classification does not refer to the one-, two-, and three-brained orders of mortals; it refers primarily to gland chemistry, more particularly to the organization of certain glands comparable to the pituitary bodies. The races on some worlds have one gland, on others two, as do Urantians, while on still other spheres the races have three of these unique bodies. The inherent imagination and spiritual receptivity is definitely influenced by this differential chemical endowment.

Of the spirit-reception types, sixty-five per cent are of the second group, like the Urantia races. Twelve per cent are of the first type, naturally less receptive, while twenty-three per cent are more spiritually inclined during terrestrial life. But such distinctions do not survive natural death; all of these racial differences pertain only to the life in the flesh.

The Inhabited Planets 566:1,2,7,8

4. Universe Geography

This section is riddled with unfamiliar place-names and extraordinarily large numbers. You will read about Havona, the worlds that surround Paradise; Uversa, our superuniverse; and Orvonton, the capital of Uversa. You will also come upon earth's register number on the universe rolls of inhabited planets: 5,342,482,337,666.

The most important point to remember as you pore over these passages is that only a tiny fraction of the universe is now inhabited. As you achieve increasing degrees of perfection in various worlds, you will arrive at Paradise. And once you've come to know God, guess who is going to help develop all the real estate he keeps creating? That's right—welcome to your eternal future.

Butterfly Nebula (IC 1318); Chuck Vaughn (1997)

The God of Action functions and the dead vaults of space are astir. One billion perfect spheres flash into existence.   The Infinite Spirit 91:1

Paradise is the eternal center of the universe of universes and the abiding place of the Universal Father, the Eternal Son, the Infinite Spirit, and their divine co-ordinates and associates. This central Isle is the most gigantic organized body of cosmic reality in all the master universe. Paradise is a material sphere as well as a spiritual abode. All of the intelligent creation of the Universal Father is domiciled on material abodes; hence must the absolute controlling center also be material, literal. And again it should be reiterated that spirit things and spiritual beings are *real*.

We all know the direct course to pursue to find the Universal Father. You are not able to comprehend much about the divine residence because of its remoteness from you and the immensity of the intervening space, but those who are able to comprehend the meaning of these enormous distances know God's location and residence just as certainly and literally as you know the location of New York, London, Rome, or Singapore, cities definitely and geographically located on Urantia. If you were an intelligent navigator, equipped with ship, maps, and compass, you could readily find these cities. Likewise, if you had the time and means of passage, were spiritually qualified, and had the necessary guidance, you could be piloted through universe upon universe and from circuit to circuit, ever journeying inward through the starry realms, until at last you would stand before the central shining of the spiritual glory of the Universal Father. Provided with all the necessities for the journey, it is just as possible to find the personal presence of God at the center of all things as to find distant cities on your own planet. That you have not visited these places in no way disproves their reality or actual existence. That so few of the universe creatures have found God on Paradise in no way disproves either the reality of his existence or the actuality of his spiritual person at the center of all things.   Eternal Isle of Paradise 118:1,5

The vertical cross section of total space would slightly resemble a maltese cross, with the horizontal arms representing pervaded (universe) space and the vertical arms representing unpervaded (reservoir) space.
                                            Eternal Isle of Paradise 124:4

The relatively quiet zones between the space levels, such as the one separating the seven superuniverses from the first outer space level, are enormous elliptical regions of quiescent space activities. These zones separate the vast galaxies which race around Paradise in orderly procession. You may visualize the first outer space level, where untold universes are now in process of formation, as a vast procession of galaxies swinging around Paradise, bounded above and below by the midspace zones of quiescence and bounded on the inner and outer margins by relatively quiet space zones.

This alternate zoning of the master universe, in association with the alternate clockwise and counterclockwise flow of the galaxies, is a factor in the stabilization of physical gravity designed to prevent the accentuation of gravity pressure to the point of disruptive and dispersive activities. Such an arrangement exerts antigravity influence and acts as a brake upon otherwise dangerous velocities.   Eternal Isle of Paradise 125:1,3

The universe of universes is not an infinite plane, a boundless cube, nor a limitless circle; it certainly has dimensions. The laws of physical organization and administration prove conclusively that the whole vast aggregation of force-energy and matter-power functions ultimately as a space unit, as an organized and co-ordinated whole. The observable behavior of the material creation constitutes evidence of a physical universe of definite limits. The final proof of both a circular and delimited universe is afforded by the, to us, well-known fact that all forms of basic energy ever swing around the curved path of the space levels of the master universe in obedience to the incessant and absolute pull of Paradise gravity.
                                The Universe of Universe 128:4

Proceeding outward from Paradise through the horizontal extension of pervaded space, the master universe is existent in six concentric ellipses, the space levels encircling the central Isle:
1. The Central Universe—Havona.
2. The Seven Superuniverses.
3. The First Outer Space Level.
4. The Second Outer Space Level.
5. The Third Outer Space Level.
6. The Fourth and Outermost Space Level.

The Origin of the Milky Way ; Jacopo Tintoretto (1570)
© National Gallery , London

(Jupiter, wishing to immortalize the infant Hercules, whose mother
was the mortal Alcmene, fed him at the breast of the sleeping goddess
Juno. According to the legend, lilies sprouted where Juno's milk fell to
earth, and the stars of the Milky Way appeared where the milk spilled
heavenward.)

Havona, the central universe, is not a time creation; it is an eternal existence. This never-beginning, never-ending universe consists of one billion spheres of sublime perfection and is surrounded by the enormous dark gravity bodies. At the center of Havona is the stationary and absolutely stabilized Isle of Paradise, surrounded by its twenty-one satellites. Owing to the enormous encircling masses of the dark gravity bodies about the fringe of the central universe, the mass content of this central creation is far in excess of the total known mass of all seven sectors of the grand universe.

The Paradise-Havona System, the eternal universe encircling the eternal Isle, constitutes the perfect and eternal nucleus of the master universe; all seven of the superuniverses and all regions of outer space revolve in established orbits around the gigantic central aggregation of the Paradise satellites and the Havona spheres.

The Seven Superuniverses are not primary physical organizations; nowhere do their boundaries divide a nebular family, neither do they cross a local universe, a prime creative unit. Each superuniverse is simply a geographic space clustering of approximately one seventh of the organized and partially inhabited post-Havona creation, and each is about equal in the number of local universes embraced and in the space encompassed. *Nebadon*, your local universe, is one of the newer creations in *Orvonton*, the seventh superuniverse.

The Grand Universe is the present organized and inhabited creation. It consists of the seven superuniverses, with an aggregate evolutionary potential of around seven trillion inhabited planets, not to mention the eternal spheres of the central creation. But this tentative estimate takes no account of architectural administrative spheres, neither does it include the outlying groups of unorganized universes. The present ragged edge of the grand universe, its uneven and unfinished periphery, together with the tremendously unsettled condition of the whole astronomical plot, suggests to our star students that even the seven superuniverses are, as yet, uncompleted. As we move from within, from the divine center outward in any one direction, we do, eventually, come to the outer limits of the organized and inhabited creation; we come to the outer limits of the grand universe. And it is near this outer border, in a far-off corner of such a magnificent creation, that your local universe has its eventful existence.

The Outer Space Levels. Far out in space, at an enormous distance from the seven inhabited superuniverses, there are assembling vast and unbelievably stupendous circuits of force and materializing energies. Between the energy circuits of the seven superuniverses and this gigantic outer belt of force activity, there is a space zone of comparative quiet, which varies in width but averages about four hundred thousand light-years. These space zones are free from star dust—cosmic fog. Our students of these phenomena are in doubt as to the exact status of the space-forces existing in this zone of relative quiet which encircles the seven superuniverses. But about one-half million light-years beyond the periphery of the present grand universe we observe the beginnings of a zone of an unbelievable energy action which increases in volume and intensity for over twenty-five million light-years. These tremendous wheels of energizing forces are situated in the first outer space level, a continuous belt of cosmic activity encircling the whole of the known, organized, and inhabited creation.

Still greater activities are taking place beyond these regions, for the Uversa physicists have detected early evidence of force manifestations more than fifty million light-years beyond the outermost ranges of the phenomena in the first outer space level. These activities undoubtedly presage the organization of the material creations of the second outer space level of the master universe.

The Universe of Universes 129:1 - 130:1

We know very little of the significance of these tremendous phenomena of outer space. A greater creation of the future is in process of formation. We can observe its immensity, we can discern its extent and sense its majestic dimensions, but otherwise we know little more about these realms than do the astronomers of Urantia. As far as we know, no material beings on the order of humans, no angels or other spirit creatures, exist in this outer ring of nebulae, suns, and planets. This distant domain is beyond the jurisdiction and administration of the superuniverse governments.

The Universe of Universes 131:2

Excluding the Paradise-Havona spheres, the plan of universe organization provides for the following units:

Superuniverses 7
Major sectors 70
Minor sectors 7,000
Local universes 700,000
Constellations 70,000,000
Local systems 7,000,000,000
Inhabitable planets 7,000,000,000,000

All such estimates are approximations at best, for new systems are constantly evolving while other organizations are temporarily passing out of material existence.

Practically all of the starry realms visible to the naked eye on Urantia belong to the seventh section of the grand universe, the superuniverse of Orvonton. The vast Milky Way starry system represents the central nucleus of Orvonton, being largely beyond the borders of your local universe. This great aggregation of suns, dark islands of space, double stars, globular clusters, star clouds, spiral and other nebulae, together with myriads of individual planets, forms a watchlike, elongated-circular grouping of about one seventh of the inhabited evolutionary universes.

The Seven Superuniverse 167:1-17

The Sagittarius sector and all other sectors and divisions of Orvonton are in rotation around Uversa, and some of the confusion of Urantian star observers arises out of the illusions and relative distortions produced by the following multiple revolutionary movements:

1. The revolution of Urantia around its sun.

2. The circuit of your solar system about the nucleus of the former Andronover nebula.

3. The rotation of the Andronover stellar family and the associated clusters about the composite rotation-gravity center of the star cloud of Nebadon.

4. The swing of the local star cloud of Nebadon and its associated creations around the Sagittarius center of their minor sector.

5. The rotation of the one hundred minor sectors, including Sagittarius, about their major sector.

6. The whirl of the ten major sectors, the so-called star drifts, about the Uversa headquarters of Orvonton.

The Andromeda Galaxy, M31 Carl and Christopher Weber (1997)
Tierra del Sol, CA

7. The movement of Orvonton and six associated superuniverses around
Paradise and Havona, the counterclockwise processional of the
superuniverse space level.   The Seven Superuniverses 168:3-10

Paradise force organizers are nebulae originators; they are able to initiate about their space presence the tremendous cyclones of force which, when once started, can never be stopped or limited until the all-pervading forces are mobilized for the eventual appearance of the ultimatonic units of universe matter. Thus are brought into being the spiral and other nebulae, the mother wheels of the direct-origin suns and their varied systems. In outer space there may be seen ten different forms of nebulae, phases of primary universe evolution, and these vast energy wheels had the same origin as did those in the seven superuniverses.

Nebulae vary greatly in size and in the resulting number and aggregate mass of their stellar and planetary offspring. A sun-forming nebula just north of the borders of Orvonton, but within the superuniverse space level, has already given origin to approximately forty thousand suns, and the mother wheel is still throwing off suns, the majority of which are many times the size of yours. Some of the larger nebulae of outer space are giving origin to as many as one hundred million suns.

The Seven Superuniverse 169:4,5

There are not many sun-forming nebulae active in Orvonton at the present time, though Andromeda, which is outside the inhabited superuniverse, is very active. This far-distant nebula is visible to the naked eye, and when you view it, pause to consider that the light you behold left those distant suns almost one million years ago.   The Seven Superuniverse 170:1

Irrespective of origin, the various spheres of space are classifiable into the following major divisions:
1. The suns—the stars of space.
2. The dark islands of space.
3. Minor space bodies—comets, meteors, and planetesimals.
4. The planets, including the inhabited worlds.
5. Architectural spheres—worlds made to order.

With the exception of the architectural spheres, all space bodies have had an evolutionary origin, evolutionary in the sense that they have not been brought into being by fiat of Deity, evolutionary in the sense that the creative acts of God have unfolded by a time-space technique through the operation of many of the created and eventuated intelligences of Deity.

The Seven Superuniverses 172:3-9

But in the master universe there are as many suns as there are glasses of water in the oceans of your world.

In your superuniverse not one cool planet in forty is habitable by beings of your order. And, of course, the superheated suns and the frigid outlying worlds are unfit to harbor higher life. In your solar system only three planets are at present suited to harbor life. Urantia, in size, density, and location, is in many respects ideal for human habitation.

An almost endless variety of creature life and other living manifestations characterizes the countless worlds of space. There are, however, certain points of similarity in a group of worlds associated in a given system, while there also is a universe pattern of intelligent life. There are physical relationships among those planetary systems which belong to the same physical circuit, and which closely follow each other in the endless swing around the circle of universes.

The Seven Superuniverses 173:0,5,6

When mass becomes overaggregated and threatens to unbalance energy, to deplete the physical power circuits, the physical controllers intervene unless gravity's own further tendency to overmaterialize energy is defeated by the occurrence of a collision among the dead giants of space, thus in an instant completely dissipating the cumulative collections of gravity.

Nebulae may disperse, suns burn out, systems vanish, and planets perish, but the universes do not run down.

The Seven Superuniverses 176:1,5

When there develops such a spiritual harmony in a local universe that its individual and combined circuits become indistinguishable from those of the superuniverse, when such identity of function and oneness of ministry actually prevail, then does the local universe immediately swing into the settled circuits of light and life, becoming at once eligible for admission into the spiritual confederation of the perfected union of the supercreation. The requisites for admission to the councils of the Ancients of Days, membership in the superuniverse confederation, are:

1. *Physical Stability.* The stars and planets of a local universe must be in equilibrium; the periods of immediate stellar metamorphosis must be over. The universe must be proceeding on a clear track; its orbit must be safely and finally settled.

2. *Spiritual Loyalty.* There must exist a state of universal recognition of, and loyalty to, the Sovereign Son of God who presides over the affairs of such a local universe. There must have come into being a state of harmonious co-operation between the individual planets, systems, and constellations of the entire local universe.

Your local universe is not even reckoned as belonging to the settled physical order of the superuniverse, much less as holding membership in the recognized spiritual family of the supergovernment.

The Seven Superuniverses 177:14-17

Orvonton, the seventh superuniverse, the one to which your local universe belongs, is known chiefly because of its tremendous and lavish bestowal of merciful ministry to the mortals of the realms. It is renowned for the manner in which justice prevails as tempered by mercy and power rules as conditioned by patience, while the sacrifices of time are freely made to secure the stabilization of eternity. Orvonton is a universe demonstration of love and mercy

Your world is called Urantia, and it is number 606 in the planetary group, or system, of Satania. This system has at present 619 inhabited worlds, and more than two hundred additional planets are evolving favorably toward becoming inhabited worlds at some future time.

The grand universe number of your world, Urantia, is 5,342,482,337,666. That is the registry number on Uversa and on Paradise, your number in the catalogue of the inhabited worlds. I know the physical-sphere registry number, but it is of such an extraordinary size that it is of little practical significance to the mortal mind.   The Seven Superuniverses 182:1,4,7

Your planet is a member of an enormous cosmos; you belong to a well-nigh infinite family of worlds, but your sphere is just as precisely administered and just as lovingly fostered as if it were the only inhabited world in all existence.   The Seven Superuniverses,183:1

Satania is not a uniform physical system, a single astronomic unit or organization. Its 619 inhabited worlds are located in over five hundred different physical systems. Only five have more than two inhabited worlds, and of these only one has four peopled planets, while there are forty-six having two inhabited worlds.

The Satania system of inhabited worlds is far removed from Uversa and that great sun cluster which functions as the physical or astronomic center of the seventh superuniverse. From Jerusem, the headquarters of Satania, it is over two hundred thousand light-years to the physical center of the superuniverse of Orvonton, far, far away in the dense diameter of the Milky Way. Satania is on the periphery of the local universe, and Nebadon is now well out towards the edge of Orvonton. From the outermost system of inhabited worlds to the center of the superuniverse is a trifle less than two hundred and fifty thousand light-years.

Evolution of the Local Universes 359:7,8

Urantia is comparatively isolated on the outskirts of Satania, your solar system, with one exception, being the farthest removed from Jerusem, while Satania itself is next to the outermost system of Norlatiadek, and this constellation is now traversing the outer fringe of Nebadon. You were truly among the least of all creation until Michael's bestowal elevated your planet to a position of honor and great universe interest. Sometimes the last is first, while truly the least becomes greatest.

Physical Aspects of the Local Universe 466:4,5

The foundation of the universe is material, but the essence of life is spirit. The Father of spirits is also the ancestor of universes; the eternal Father of the Original Son is also the eternity-source of the original pattern, the Isle of Paradise.

Matter—energy—for they are but diverse manifestations of the same cosmic reality, as a universe phenomenon is inherent in the Universal Father. "In him all things consist." Matter may appear to manifest inherent energy and to exhibit self-contained powers, but the lines of gravity involved in the energies concerned in all these physical phenomena are derived from, and are dependent on, Paradise. The ultimaton, the first measurable form of energy, has Paradise as its nucleus.

Energy-Mind and Matter 467:3,4

But energy, though springing from the Infinite, is not infinitely manifest; there are outer limits to the presently conceived master universe.

Energy is eternal but not infinite; it ever responds to the all-embracing grasp of Infinity. Forever force and energy go on; having gone out from Paradise, they must return thereto, even if age upon age be required for the completion of the ordained circuit. That which is of Paradise Deity origin can have only a Paradise destination or a Deity destiny.

Energy-Mind and Matter 468:4,5

5. Universe Travel

Following is a simple travelogue for your future life in heaven. Included are a few interesting stops you may want to make when you get there, as well as an indication of the speeds you will be traveling. Bon voyage!

To me, these executive worlds are the most interesting and intriguing spots outside of Paradise. In no other place in the wide universe can one observe such varied activities, involving so many different orders of living beings, having to do with operations on so many diverse levels, occupations at once material, intellectual, and spiritual. When I am accorded a period of release from assignment, if I chance to be on Paradise or in Havona, I usually proceed to one of these busy worlds of the Seven Master Spirits, there to inspire my mind with such spectacles of enterprise, devotion, loyalty, wisdom, and effectiveness. Nowhere else can I observe such an amazing interassociation of personality performances on all seven levels of universe reality. And I am always stimulated by the activities of those who well know how to do their work, and who so thoroughly enjoy doing it.   Sacred Spheres of Paradise 151:1

Trinity-origin beings possess prerogatives of transit which make them independent of transport personalities, such as seraphim. We all possess the power of moving about freely and quickly in the universe of universes. Excepting the Inspired Trinity Spirits, we cannot attain the almost unbelievable velocity of the Solitary Messengers, but we are able so to utilize the sum total of the transport facilities in space that we can reach any point in a superuniverse, from its headquarters, in less than one year of Urantia time. It required 109 days of your time for me to journey from Uversa to Urantia.

Through these same avenues we are enabled to intercommunicate instantaneously. Our entire order of creation finds itself in touch with every individual embraced within every division of the children of the Paradise Trinity save only the Inspired Spirits.

Co-ordinate Trinity-Origin Beings 222:8-222:9

Ambassadors and Emissaries of Special Assignment. Local universes situated within the same superuniverse customarily exchange ambassadors selected from their native orders of sonship. But to avoid delay, Solitary Messengers are frequently asked to go as ambassadors from one local creation to another, to represent and interpret one realm to another. For example: When a newly inhabited realm is discovered, it may prove to be so remote in space that a long time will pass before an enseraphimed ambassador can reach this far-distant universe. An enseraphimed being cannot possibly exceed the velocity of 558,840 Urantia miles in one second of your time. Massive stars, crosscurrents, and detours, as well as attraction tangents, will all tend to retard such speed so that on a long journey the velocity will average about 550,000 miles per second.

The universe is well supplied with spirits who utilize gravity for purposes of transit; they can go anywhere any time—instanter—but they are not persons. Certain other gravity traversers are personal beings, such as Gravity Messengers and Transcendental Recorders, but they are not available to the super- and the local universe administrators. The worlds teem with angels and men and other highly personal beings, but they are handicapped by time and space: The limit of velocity for most nonenseraphimed beings is 186,280 miles of your world per second of your time; the midway creatures and certain others can, often do, attain double velocity—372,560 miles per second—while the seraphim and others can traverse space at triple velocity, about 558,840 miles per second. There are, however, no transit or messenger personalities who function between the instantaneous velocities of the gravity traversers and the comparatively slow speeds of the seraphim, except the Solitary Messengers.

Solitary Messengers are, therefore, generally used for dispatch and service in those situations where personality is essential to the achievement of the assignment, and where it is desired to avoid the loss of time which would be occasioned by the sending of any other readily available type of personal messenger. They are the only definitely personalized beings who can synchronize with the combined universal currents of the grand universe. Their velocity in traversing space is variable, depending on a great variety of interfering influences, but the record shows that on the journey to fulfill this mission my associate messenger proceeded at the rate of 841,621,642,000 of your miles per second of your time.

It is wholly beyond my ability to explain to the material type of mind how a spirit can be a real person and at the same time traverse space at

The Assumption of the Virgin; Nicholas Poussin
(1626) © National Gallery of Art, Washington

such tremendous velocities. But these very Solitary Messengers actually come to, and go from, Urantia at these incomprehensible speeds; indeed, the whole economy of universal administration would be largely deprived of its personal element were this not a fact.

The Solitary Messengers are able to function as emergency lines of communication throughout remote space regions, realms not embraced within the established circuits of the grand universe. It develops that one messenger, when so functioning, can transmit a message or send an impulse through space to a fellow messenger about one hundred light-years away as Urantia astronomers estimate stellar distances.

Of the myriads of beings who co-operate with us in the conduct of the affairs of the superuniverse, none are more important in practical helpfulness and timesaving assistance. In the universes of space we must reckon with the handicaps of time; hence the great service of the Solitary Messengers, who, by means of their personal prerogatives of communication, are somewhat independent of space and, by virtue of their tremendous transit velocities, are so nearly independent of time.

The Solitary Messenger 260:2,6-261:4

Morontia mortals are student visitors only within the confines of the local universe of their origin. They may visit in a superuniverse capacity only after they have attained spirit status. Fully one half of our visitor colony consists of "stopovers," beings enroute elsewhere who pause to visit the Orvonton capital. These personalities may be executing a universe assignment, or they may be enjoying a period of leisure—freedom from assignment. The privilege of intrauniverse travel and observation is a part of the career of all ascending beings. The human desire to travel and observe new peoples and worlds will be fully gratified during the long and eventful climb to Paradise through the local, super-, and central universes.

Personalities of the Grand Universe 340:1

The "energy range" of seraphim is wholly adequate for local universe and even for superuniverse requirements, but they could never withstand the energy demands entailed by such a long journey as that from Uversa to Havona. Such an exhaustive journey requires the special powers of a primary seconaphim of transport endowments. Transporters take on energy for flight while in transit and recuperate personal power at the end of the journey.

The Seraphic Hosts 430:5

Mount Seraph is the highest elevation on Jerusem, almost fifteen thousand feet, and is the point of departure for all transport seraphim. Numerous mechanical developments are used in providing initial energy for escaping the planetary gravity and overcoming the air resistance. A seraphic transport departs every three seconds of Urantia time throughout the light period and, sometimes, far into the recession. The transporters take off at about twenty-five standard miles per second of Urantia time and do not attain standard velocity until they are over two thousand miles away from Jerusem.

Transports arrive on the crystal field, the so-called sea of glass. Around this area are the receiving stations for the various orders of beings who traverse space by seraphic transport. Near the polar crystal receiving station for student visitors you may ascend the pearly observatory and view the immense relief map of the entire headquarters planet.

Local System Headquarters 521:5,6

6. Eternity

Because we humans are creatures of time, we cannot comprehend eternity. But that does not mean we can't have fun trying.

I first glimpsed what might be thought of as infinity one day in elementary school when I realized there can always be a "bigger number." Since then I have had other intimations of eternity, especially while driving through open landscapes with ample time to ponder such immeasurable concepts. As I drive across the empty plains of Colorado, I watch the Front Range of the Rocky Mountains loom up before me, extending endlessly into the distance to the left and right. I know there are more mountains in the Continental Divide far south in Peru and up north in Alaska. Although I can't see them, I believe they exist, and I believe eternity does, too. God can see it all—the entire mountain range, every moment of reality, the past, the present, and the future.

An awareness of eternity can also accompany the wisdom acquired as we get older. A retrospective view of the past often sheds light on hard lessons we have grappled with. At the same time, our experiences in the past and present provide us with an image of what the future may be like depending on which of life's paths we choose.

In brief, the Infinite Spirit testifies that, since he is eternal, so also is the central universe eternal. And this is the traditional starting point of the history of the universe of universes. Absolutely nothing is known, and no records are in existence, regarding any event or transaction prior to this stupendous eruption of creative energy and administrative wisdom that crystallized the vast universe which exists, and so exquisitely functions, at the center of all things. Beyond this event lie the unsearchable transactions of eternity and the depths of infinity—absolute mystery.

The Infinite Spirit 91:6

Roughly: space seemingly originates just below nether Paradise; time just above upper Paradise. Time, as you understand it, is not a feature of Paradise existence, though the citizens of the central Isle are fully conscious of nontime sequence of events. Motion is not inherent on Paradise; it is volitional. But the concept of distance, even absolute distance, has very much meaning as it may be applied to relative locations on Paradise.

Eternal Isle of Paradise 120:3

Time is not reckoned on Paradise; the sequence of successive events is inherent in the concept of those who are indigenous to the central Isle. But time is germane to the Havona circuits and to numerous beings of both celestial and terrestrial origin sojourning thereon. Each Havona world has its own local time, determined by its circuit. All worlds in a given circuit have the same length of year since they uniformly swing around Paradise, and the length of these planetary years decreases from the outermost to the innermost circuit.

You have unwittingly read the truth when your eyes rested on the statement "A day is as a thousand years with God, as but a watch in the night." One Paradise-Havona day is just seven minutes, three and one-eighth seconds less than one thousand years of the present Urantia leap-year calendar.

Central and Divine Universe 153:2,3

Not until you traverse the last of the Havona circuits and visit the last of the Havona worlds, will the tonic of adventure and the stimulus of curiosity disappear from your career. And then will the urge, the forward impulse of eternity, replace its forerunner, the adventure lure of time.

Monotony is indicative of immaturity of the creative imagination and inactivity of intellectual co-ordination with the spiritual endowment. By

An Allegory with Venus and Time; Giovanni Tiepolo   (1740)
© National Gallery, London

the time an ascendant mortal begins the exploration of these heavenly worlds, he has already attained emotional, intellectual, and social, if not spiritual, maturity.   Central and Divine Universe 159:3,4

The sectors of time are like the flashes of personality in temporal form; they appear for a season, and then they are lost to human sight, only to reappear as new actors and continuing factors in the higher life of the endless swing around the eternal circle. Eternity can hardly be conceived as a straightaway drive, in view of our belief in a delimited universe moving over a vast, elongated circle around the central dwelling place of the Universal Father.

Frankly, eternity is incomprehensible to the finite mind of time. You simply cannot grasp it; you cannot comprehend it. I do not completely visualize it, and even if I did, it would be impossible for me to convey my concept to the human mind. Nevertheless, I have done my best to portray something of our viewpoint, to tell you somewhat of our understanding of things eternal. I am endeavoring to aid you in the crystallization of your thoughts about these values which are of infinite nature and eternal import.

There is in the mind of God a plan which embraces every creature of all his vast domains, and this plan is an eternal purpose of boundless opportunity, unlimited progress, and endless life. And the infinite treasures of such a matchless career are yours for the striving!

The goal of eternity is ahead! The adventure of divinity attainment lies before you! The race for perfection is on! whosoever will may enter, and certain victory will crown the efforts of every human being who will run the race of faith and trust, depending every step of the way on the leading of the indwelling Adjuster and on the guidance of that good spirit of the Universe Son, which so freely has been poured out upon all flesh.

Evolution of Local Universes 365:1-5

The individual's yardstick for time measurement is the length of his life. All creatures are thus time conditioned, and therefore do they regard evolution as being a long-drawn-out process. To those of us whose life span is not limited by a temporal existence, evolution does not seem to be such a protracted transaction. On Paradise, where time is nonexistent, these things are all *present* in the mind of Infinity and the acts of Eternity.

Overcontrol of Evolution 739:7

The human mind, as it seeks to penetrate the eternity-mystery of the origin and destiny of all that is called real, may helpfully approach the problem by conceiving eternity-infinity as an almost limitless ellipse which is produced by one absolute cause, and which functions throughout this universal circle of endless diversification, ever seeking some absolute and infinite potential of destiny.   Deity and Reality 1152:1

In the maturity of the developing self, the past and future are brought together to illuminate the true meaning of the present. As the self matures, it reaches further and further back into the past for experience, while its wisdom forecasts seek to penetrate deeper and deeper into the unknown future. And as the conceiving self extends this reach ever further into both past and future, so does judgment become less and less dependent on the momentary present. In this way does decision-action begin to escape from the fetters of the moving present, while it begins to take on the aspects of past-future significance.

Patience is exercised by those mortals whose time units are short; true maturity transcends patience by a forbearance born of real understanding.

To become mature is to live more intensely in the present, at the same time escaping from the limitations of the present. The plans of maturity, founded on past experience, are coming into being in the present in such manner as to enhance the values of the future.

Supreme and Ultimate-Time and Space 1295:5-7

On the levels of the infinite and the absolute the moment of the present contains all of the past as well as all of the future. I AM signifies also I WAS and I WILL BE. And this represents our best concept of eternity and the eternal.   Supreme and Ultimate-Time and Space 1296:1

"Because my Father is a God of love and delights in the practice of mercy, do not imbibe the idea that the service of the kingdom is to be one of monotonous ease. The Paradise ascent is the supreme adventure of all time, the rugged achievement of eternity."

Going Through Samaria 1608:3

Worship is the act of a part identifying itself with the Whole; the finite with the Infinite; the son with the Father; time in the act of striking step with eternity.   Going Through Samaria 1616:10

Said your Master, "Happy are they who mourn"—if a friend is at hand to comfort. There is positive strength in the knowledge that you live for the welfare of others, and that these others likewise live for your welfare and advancement. Man languishes in isolation. Human beings unfailingly become discouraged when they view only the transitory transactions of time. The present, when divorced from the past and the future, becomes exasperatingly trivial. Only a glimpse of the circle of eternity can inspire man to do his best and can challenge the best in him to do its utmost. And when man is thus at his best, he lives most unselfishly for the good of others, his fellow sojourners in time and eternity.

Rodan of Alexandria 1776:3

Mankind is slow to perceive that, in all that is personal, matter is the skeleton of morontia, and that both are the reflected shadow of enduring spirit reality. How long before you will regard time as the moving image of eternity and space as the fleeting shadow of Paradise realities?

The Resurrection 2021:2

Conclusion

And God-consciousness is equivalent to the integration of the self with the universe, and on its highest levels of spiritual reality. Only the spirit content of any value is imperishable. Even that which is true, beautiful, and good may not perish in human experience. If man does not choose to survive, then does the surviving Adjuster conserve those realities born of love and nurtured in service. And all these things are a part of the Universal Father. The Father is living love, and this life of the Father is in his Sons. And the spirit of the Father is in his Sons' sons—mortal men. When all is said and done, the Father idea is still the highest human concept of God.   The Faith of Jesus 2097:3

Postscript

This volume merely introduces the 2,097-page revelation known as The Urantia Book. To truly comprehend our place in the universe, and to appreciate the earthly struggle of existence, be sure to plunge into the original anthology, taking it from start to finish. When you do, realize that the material is easier to comprehend the farther in you go. Yet, there is an important reason the most difficult section comes first: - note the passage below;

The human mind would ordinarily crave to approach the cosmic philosophy portrayed in these revelations by proceeding from the simple and the finite to the complex and the infinite, from human origins to divine destinies. But that path does not lead to *spiritual wisdom*. Such a procedure is the easiest path to a certain form of *genetic knowledge,* but at best it can only reveal man's origin; it reveals little or nothing about his divine destiny.

Even in the study of man's biologic evolution on Urantia, there are grave objections to the exclusive historic approach to his present-day status and his current problems. The true perspective of any reality problem—human or divine, terrestrial or cosmic—can be had only by the full and unprejudiced study and correlation of three phases of universe reality: origin, history, and destiny.   Co-ordinate Trinity-origin Beings 215:2-3

If you taste truth in the words, "By the fruits you will know them," pour yourself a tall glass of water, settle in to your favorite reading spot, and dive in The Urantia Book. If you read ten pages a day, you will finish the book in seven months. You may not understand a word of this document for sentences on end, especially in the Foreword. But then you will discover a real nugget of a paragraph, and in time, the entire universe will open up and a vision of your eternal life will come into view.

Glossary

Adam & Eve Material Son and Daughter, a reproducing form of Sonship created by the Creator Son, to uplift the evolutionary races. Dispatched from Jerusem to earth 37,800 years ago.

Adamson The first-born son of Adam and Eve on Urantia born in approximately 35,900 B.C.

Adjuster See Thought Adjuster.

Amenemope an Egyptian teacher and seer who, in the post-Melchizedek period (see Machiventa), taught among other things that God-consciousness is the main factor which determines conduct.

Ancient of Days In power, scope of authority, and extent of jurisdiction, they are the most powerful and mighty of any of the direct rulers of the time- space creations. In all the vast universe of universes they alone are invested with the high powers of final judgment concerning the eternal extinction of will creatures.

Andon The first male human being, whose initial expression of human will choice occurred when he was ten years old, in 991,474 B.C. Was killed during an earthquake 32 years later at the age of 42 (see Fonta).

Andonite The first primitive human beings descended from and including Andon and Fonta.

Angels Angelic hosts are a separate order of created beings. They are not glorified spirits of mortal men. Seraphim function mainly as teachers of men.

Bestowal Sons The purpose of these creature incarnations is to enable such Creators to become wise, sympathetic, just, and understanding sovereigns. These bestowals are the last steps in their education and training for the sublime tasks of ruling the local universes in divine righteousness and by just judgment.

Caligastia served as Planetary Prince of Urantia he betrayed his trust and joined the Lucifer rebellion approximately 200,000 years ago.

Cano A brilliant leader of a Nodite colony near the Garden of Eden with whom Eve was encouraged by Serapatatia to mate, thereby causing the Adamic default approximately 37,800 years ago.

Central universe is a creation of eternity. At the center is the Isle of Paradise.

Conjoint Actor see Infinite Spirit

Creator Son The Creator Sons are the makers and rulers of the local universes of time and space.

Dalamatia The headquarters city of the Planetary Prince, once situated on the Persian Gulf in Mesopotamia, approximately 500,000 years ago.

Divinington One of seven sacred satellite spheres of the Father in circuit around Paradise. This world is the Paradise rendezvous of Thought Adjusters.

Edentia The headquarters world of Norlatiadek, the constellation to which our system belongs.

El Elyon Melchizedek term denoting Most High God.

Eternal Son is the perfect and final expression of the "first" personal and absolute concept of the Universal Father. Accordingly, whenever and however the Father personally and absolutely expresses himself, he does so through his Eternal Son, who ever has been, now is, and ever will be, the living and divine Word.

Eve Material Daughter who arrived on earth from Jerusem 37,800 years ago, see Adam

Finaliters Members of the Mortal Finaliter Corps. Ascendant mortals become a part of this corps when they have ascended to the sixth stage of spirit being, have become residents of Paradise, and have completed the progressive course in divinity.

Fonta The first female human being, whose initial expression of human will choice occurred when she was ten years old, in 991,474 B.C. Was killed during an earthquake 32 years later at the age of 42 (see Andon).

Force Organizers are the manipulators of the primordial or basic space-forces - the are the nebulae creators.

Grand Universe Seven superuniverse make up the present
organized grand universe, consisting of approximately
seven trillion inhabitable worlds plus the architectural
spheres and the one billion inhabited spheres of
Havona.

God the Supreme is the indispensable focalizer, summarizer, and
encompasser of evolutionary experience, effectively
unifying the results of this mode of reality perception
in his Deity nature.

Holy Spirit see Spirit of Truth

Havona The central and divine universe, and eternal, wholly
created, and perfect planetary family containing one
billion worlds arranged in seven concentric circuits
contiguous to and surrounding Paradise.

Immanuel Jesus' brother. The ambassador of Paradise Trinity on
Salvington

Infinite Spirit The third person of the Trinity. The Infinite Spirit is
the effective agent of the all-loving Father and the all-
merciful Son for the execution of their conjoint project
of drawing to themselves all truth- loving souls on all
worlds of time and space.

Ikhnaton The Egyptian pharaoh having clear concept of the revealed
religion of One God

Jerusem The headquarters world of Satania, our local system.

Jesus The Creator Son of our local universe, Nebadon

Laotta A Nodite woman, head of the western Garden of Eden
school, with whom Adam chose to mate after Eve had
defaulted in their planetary mission (see Serapatatia).

Life Carriers They are intrusted with designing and carrying
creature life to the planetary spheres. And after
planting this life on such new worlds, they remain
there for long periods to foster its development.

Local Universe is the handiwork of a Creator Son of the Paradise
order of Michael. It comprises one hundred
constellations, each embracing one hundred systems
of inhabited worlds. Each system will eventually
contain approximately one thousand inhabited
spheres.

Lucifer   The former System Sovereign who led Satania rebellion. Currently in custody awaiting judgment.

Machiventa The first name of the Melchizedek son who incarnated on Urantia during the times of Abraham in approximately 2,000 B.C. Also referred to as the "Sage of Salem." (see Melchizedek).

Mansion worlds The Creator Son, when on earth, spoke of the "many mansions in the Father's universe. In a certain sense, all fifty-six of the encicling worlds of Jerusem are devoted to the transitional culture of ascending mortals, but the seven satellites of world number one are more specifically known as the mansion worlds. On the mansion worlds the resurrected mortal survivors resume their lives just where they left off when overtaken by death.

Master universe includes the central universe, the inhabited seven superuniverse and the outer space levels.

Melchizedek The first of the four orders of descending sonship designated as local universe Sons of God, created by the Creator Son and Creative Spirit in collaboration with the Father Melchizedek in the early days of populating the local universe of Nebadon. The Father Melchizedek was created by the union of the Creator Son and the Creative Spirit. These Sons, who number more than ten million in the local universe, are self-governing and are primarily devoted to education and experiential training.

Michael   The Creator Son of Nebadon (Jesus).

Morontia   The morontia life, extending as it does over the various stages of the local universe career, is the only possible approach whereby mortals could attain the threshold of the spirit world. Always this morontia transition intervenes between the mortal estate and the subsequent spirit status of surviving human beings. Latin, mor or mora; to temporarily dwell, linger.

Mystery Monitor see Thought Adjuster.

Nebadon   The name of our local universe, which is governed by our Creator Son, Michael, together with his Creative Mother Spirit consort. Salvington is its headquarters sphere.

Nod   One of the 100 corporeal members of Caligastia's staff; headed the commission on industry and trade, and became the leader of those 60 staff members who joined the rebellion.

Nodites   Descendants of the rebel members of Caligastia's corporeal staff who derived their name from their leader, Nod.

Norlatiadek The constellation to which Urantia belongs. Constellations represent the 100 primary divisions of local universes and link the systems to local universe administration.

Orvonton   The seventh of the seven superuniverses which, in conjunction with the Paradise/Havona system, comprise the grand universe of time and space. Orvonton is divided into 10 major sectors, each of which is divided into 100 minor sectors. Each minor sector contains 1,000 local universes, each of which is comprised of 100 constellations. Each constellation is comprised of 100 local systems, each of which is comprised of a potential of 1,000 inhabited worlds.

Paradise   The eternal center of the universe of universe and the abiding place of the Universal Father, the Eternal Son, the Infinite Spirit, and their divine co-ordinates and associates. This central Isle is the most gigantic organized body of cosmic reality in all the master universe. Paradise is a material sphere as well as a spiritual abode.

Paradise Father The nature of God can best be understood by the revelation of the Father which Michael of Nebadon unfolded in his manifold teachings and in his superb mortal life in the flesh. The divine nature can also be better understood by man if he regards himself as a child of God.

Physical controllers are chiefly occupied in the adjustment of basic energies undiscovered on Urantia. These unknown energies are very essential to the interplanetary system of transport and to certain techniques of communication.

Planetary Prince the administrative head of an inhabited world.

Salvington The headquarters sphere of the local universe of Nebadon, personal home of the Creator Son, Michael, and the Creative Spirit (see Nebadon; Orvonton).

Sangik The Badonite family, descended from Andon and Fonta, in which the ancestors of the six colored races of Urantia were born in approximately 498,000 B.C.

Satan The fallen associate of Lucifer. In custody awaiting judgment.

Satania The administrative system of approximately 1,000 inhabitable planets to which Urantia belongs; one of the 10,000 such systems in Nebadon. Jerusem is the capital sphere of the Satania (see Orvonton).

Serapatatia The Nodite leader (descended from Caligastia's defaulted corporeal staff) manipulated by Caligastia to entrap Eve into the default of the Adamic mission by mating with Cano (see Cano; Laotta).

Seraphim See angels.

Seven Master Spirits are the primary personalities of the Infinite Spirit.

Son of Man At age fifteen Jesus found a passage in the Book of Enoch which influenced him in the later adoption of the term "Son of Man" as a designation for his bestowal mission on Urantia. He had thoroughly considered the idea of the Jewish Messiah and was firmly convinced that he was not to be that Messiah. He longed to help his Father's people, but he never expected to lead Jewish armies in overthrowing the foreign domination of Palestine.

Spirit of Truth comes to lead all believers into all truth, into the expanding knowledge of the experience of the living and growing spiritual consciousness of the reality of eternal and ascending sonship with God.

Supreme Being see God the Supreme.

Thought Adjuster It is the Adjuster who creates within man that unquenchable yearning and incessant longing to be like God, to attain Paradise, and there before the actual person of Deity to worship the infinite source of the divine gift. The Adjuster is the living presence which actually links the mortal son with his Paradise Father and draws him nearer and near to the Father.

Universal Father see Paradise Father.

Urantia Earth, the name by which our world (planet) is known in the universes.

Uversa The architectural and headquarters world of the seventh superuniverse, Orvonton, of which our local universe, Nebadon, is a part.

Van One of the 100 corporeal members of the staff of Caligastia; headed the supreme court of tribal coordination and racial cooperation. He was one of the 40 members of the 100 who did not join in the Lucifer rebellion, remaining loyal to Michael's government.

Index

What is *The Urantia Book*?

1. The Basics

We are not alone. The Universe is literally teeming with inhabited planets, evolving life, civilizations in various stages of development, celestial spheres, and spirit personalities.

We are not here by accident. The evolution of human beings on earth was planned. A glorious destiny of adventure, discovery and participation in the further evolution of the cosmos awaits each one of us.

A loving heavenly Father rules the universe by the power of his love. Our closeness and fellowship with God is limited only by our willingness and ability to open our inner life to his guidance and unconditional love. Anyone may choose to enjoy his presence in their lives.

Our little planet, Urantia, is poised on the brink of an enthralling epoch of social readjustment, moral quickening, and spiritual enlightenment — the threshold of true civilization.

2. Contents

Foreword – Deity, Divinity, God, personality and the foundational relationships of the cosmos is discussed.

Part I: The Universe of Universes — The nature of ultimate reality and the astronomical-cosmological organization of the universe is described. The relationship of the Paradise Trinity to universe personalities and realities is presented as the key to all events and phenomena. The Trinity, along with the Isle of Paradise — the material and gravitational center of the universe — is referred to as the source of all energy, matter, life and personality. An organized hierarchical universe is described which includes millions of inhabited planets in all stages of physical, mental, and spiritual evolution.

Part II: The Local Universe — The divine plan for creating, developing, and governing local universes is detailed. The presence and ministry of Jesus is the central universe reality through which everything else finds meaning and purpose. Personality survival is determined by our free will decisions about our relationship with God, by our loyalty to truth, beauty, and goodness as these values are sincerely understood. In spite of this, error, evil, and sin remain difficult realities challenging each of us. Growth toward perfection is seen as the fundamental orientation to life. This growth is evolutionary, cumulative, and virtually endless. It is achieved through loyalty to God and unselfish service to our fellow creatures.

Part III: The History of Urantia — A brief geophysical history of our planet sets the stage for an overview of our biological evolution. In addition, the development of civilization, culture, government, religion, the family, and other social institutions are described from the viewpoint of superhuman observers. The story is told in such a manner that the underlying archetypes of human religious civilization are revitalized, strengthening the foundations upon which further cultural development may take place. A description of human destiny is provided including a description of the worlds we will inhabit immediately following mortal death.

Part IV: The Life and Teachings of Jesus — Seven hundred pages devoted to the life of Jesus make up the most spiritually compelling biography of Jesus anywhere in print.

The Urantia Book relates over 16 times as much information about Jesus' life and teachings than does the Bible. The literary depth of *The Urantia Book* clearly reveals and touchingly portrays his combined humanity and divinity.

3. The Source

The Urantia Book is an anthology of 196 "papers" indited in the 1930's by superhuman personalities whose names are given with their respective papers in the book. The humans into whose hands the papers were delivered are now deceased. The means by which the papers were materialized was unique and is unknown to any living person.

Like all other sacred texts, the contents should not be evaluated by relying on claims of authorship or authority, but rather upon the "fruits of the spirit" which they produce. The new reader might explore the book as a fascinating piece of religious literature until such time as its spiritual quality authenticates its message and its source.

Although the Urantia Papers have been in print for nearly fifty years, no formal religion has sprung from their teachings. The spiritual insights of the book are used by teachers, ministers, and lay persons of many faiths to enrich the highest values in their own traditions. Many individuals outside established religious institutions have developed rich, personal spiritual lives as a result of reading *The Urantia Book.* An international network of independent study groups continues to develop. Several translations exist and more are currently in progress. *

* What is *The Urantia Book?* furnished courtesy of the The Fellowship of the Readers of *The Urantia Book.*

List of Illustrations

The Urantia Book Information

1. Urantia Foundation - Publisher
   533 Diversey Parkway
   Chicago, Illinois 60614
   ph# 773-525-3319 / fax#773-525-7739
   Internet http://www.urantia.org
   The Urantia Book in English, French, Spanish, Finnish, Dutch, and Russian.
   International Urantia Association - Study groups worldwide.

2. The Fellowship for Readers of *The Urantia Book*.
   529 Wrightwood Avenue
   Chicago, Illinois 60614
   ph# 773-327-0424 / fax# 773-327-6159
   Internet http://www.ubfellowship.org
   Study groups in 49 states and 9 countries.

3. The Jesusonian Foundation
   Box 18764
   Boulder, Colorado 80308
   ph# 1-800-767-5683 / fax 303-581-0454
   Order *The Good Cheer Catalog* - Derivative works, art, and books.

4. Mighty Messenger Press
   PO Box 23398
   Harahan, LA 70183
   Email: kelstrot@bellsouth.net
   (*The Fifth Revelation* book order form on following page)

5. Family Relations Foundation
   P.O. Box. 462
   Sebastopol, CA 95473
   Tales of Joshua. A great story and coloring book about Jesus for children.

Book Order Form

To order additional copies of *The Fifth Revelation* please
check your local friendly bookstore
Or contact;

Mighty Messenger Press
PO Box 23398
New Orleans, LA 70183
Fax# 504-739-2484
email: kelstrot@bellsouth.net

Name_____

Street Address or PO Box_____

City, State, ZIP_____

Cost is $15.95 + shipping $2.05 = $18 Please send Check or Credit Card

Mastercard or VISA #_____ Expiration Date_____

Signature_____

Comments, suggestions, or questions are welcome.

_____
_____
_____
_____
_____
_____
_____